# THE CHRISTIAN MIND OF C. S. LEWIS

# The Christian Mind
## *of* C. S. Lewis

Essays in Honor of Michael Travers

EDITED BY
ANDREW J. SPENCER

WIPF & STOCK · Eugene, Oregon

THE CHRISTIAN MIND OF C. S. LEWIS
Essays in Honor of Michael Travers

Copyright © 2019 Wipf and Stock Publishers. All rights reserved. Except for brief quotations in critical publications or reviews, no part of this book may be reproduced in any manner without prior written permission from the publisher. Write: Permissions, Wipf and Stock Publishers, 199 W. 8th Ave., Suite 3, Eugene, OR 97401.

Wipf & Stock
An Imprint of Wipf and Stock Publishers
199 W. 8th Ave., Suite 3
Eugene, OR 97401

www.wipfandstock.com

PAPERBACK ISBN: 978-1-5326-6164-8
HARDCOVER ISBN: 978-1-5326-6165-5
EBOOK ISBN: 978-1-5326-6166-2

Manufactured in the U.S.A.     DECEMBER 3, 2019

Scripture quotations marked ESV are from the ESV® Bible (The Holy Bible, English Standard Version®), copyright © 2001 by Crossway, a publishing ministry of Good News Publishers. Used by permission. All rights reserved.

Scripture texts marked NABRE are taken from the New American Bible, revised edition © 2010, 1991, 1986, 1970 Confraternity of Christian Doctrine, Washington, D.C. and are used by permission of the copyright owner. All Rights Reserved. No part of the New American Bible may be reproduced in any form without permission in writing from the copyright owner.

Scripture quotations marked NJB are from The New Jerusalem Bible, copyright © 1985 by Darton, Longman & Todd, Ltd. and Doubleday, a division of Random House, Inc. Reprinted by Permission. All rights reserved.

Scripture quotations marked NIV are taken from the Holy Bible, New International Version®, NIV®. Copyright © 1973, 1978, 1984, 2011 by Biblica, Inc.™ Used by permission of Zondervan. All rights reserved worldwide. www.zondervan.com The "NIV" and "New International Version" are trademarks registered in the United States Patent and Trademark Office by Biblica, Inc.™

Scripture quotations marked NASB are taken from the New American Standard Bible®. Copyright © 1960, 1962, 1963, 1968, 1971, 1972, 1973, 1975, 1977, 1995 by The Lockman Foundation Used by permission. www.Lockman.org

# Contents

*List of Contributors* | vii
*Acknowledgements* | ix

1. The Christian Mind of C. S. Lewis | 1
   —Andrew J. Spencer

2. Invitation to Glory: C. S. Lewis's Apologetic of Hope | 11
   —Michael E. Travers

3. "The Intolerable Compliment": Desire and Love in *The Chronicles of Narnia* | 29
   —Elizabeth Travers Parker

4. C. S. Lewis, *Architecton:* Revisiting the Rhetorical Man | 56
   —James Como

5. Psalm 19, Revelation, and the Integration of Faith, Learning, and Life | 72
   —Daniel J. Estes

6   The Fox and the Fool: "Wisdom of the Greeks" and the Godly Fool in *Till We Have Faces* | 91
    —Gene C. Fant, Jr.

7   Reality and Pre-Evangelism in the Christian Minds of C. S. Lewis and Francis Schaeffer | 109
    —Bruce Little

8   Disinterested Love in *The Screwtape Letters* and *The Great Divorce* | 131
    —C. Keith Callis

9   An "Inner Ring" or an Open Fellowship? An Evaluation of the Company of St. Anne's in *That Hideous Strength* | 151
    —Lindsey Panxhi

10  Ethics among Men without Chests | 168
    —Andrew J. Spencer

11  Lewis on Lament | 187
    —Heath A. Thomas

12  "As Ever in My Great Task-Master's Eye": Milton's Sonnet 7 and Productivity in the Christian Mind | 203
    —Leland Ryken

13  The Christian Mind of Michael Travers | 223
    —Andrew J. Spencer

*Subject Index* | 239

*Index of Works by C. S. Lewis* | 243

# List of Contributors

**C. Keith Callis**, Professor of English at Charleston Southern University.

**James Como**, Professor Emeritus of Rhetoric and Public Communication at York College (CUNY).

**Daniel Estes**, Distinguished Professor of Old Testament at Cedarville University.

**Gene C. Fant, Jr.**, President and Professor of English at North Greenville University

**Bruce Little**, Emeritus Professor of Philosophy and Director of the Francis A. Schaeffer Collection at Southeastern Baptist Theological Seminary.

**Lindsey Panxhi**, Assistant Professor of English and Director of the Honors Program at Oklahoma Baptist University.

**Elizabeth Travers Parker**, PhD candidate in Literature and Religion at Baylor University.

**Leland Ryken**, Professor of English Emeritus at Wheaton College.

**Andrew J. Spencer**, Senior Research Fellow at the Institute for Faith, Work, and Economics.

**Heath A. Thomas**, President and Professor of Old Testament at Oklahoma Baptist University.

**Michael E. Travers**, Professor of English at Oklahoma Baptist University and Southeastern Baptist Theological Seminary.

# Acknowledgements

I AM THANKFUL FOR the authors that contributed to this volume, which began as a wild idea as I grappled with sorrow in the days after Michael Travers's untimely death. The authors have been exceedingly patient with delays in the production in the book due to my workload and the competing demands of life. It would also not have been possible without the support of Michael's wife, Barbara, and their daughter, Elizabeth, who both helped to craft the theme of the book. Barbara has been exceedingly gracious in allowing me access to Michael's manuscripts as I crafted the final chapter of this volume, as well as providing much of the biographical material for that chapter and proofreading it to ensure it is factually accurate. Many former colleagues of Michael were also very responsive when I inquired about particular periods of his work history. They are too many to be named, but their help was important.

My longsuffering wife, Jennifer, also read every chapter several times. Dawn Jones was instrumental in proofreading a draft of the text. Many thanks, as well, to Aliel Cunningham, Jay Anderson, and James Wagner for their time in reading the volume and providing feedback. The book has benefited greatly from their keen eyes, though any mistakes that remain belong to me.

Most significantly, I am grateful for the patience of my family. In addition to her proofreading efforts, Jennifer has graciously allowed me to spend many evenings in my office writing and editing. And, of course, my children have borne with my frequent hermitages on weekend mornings, as I have tried to edit my first volume while holding down a full-time job entirely unrelated to my academic endeavors. I hope that my children will one day read this volume with fond memories of Michael Travers, an abiding interest in C. S. Lewis, a hope firmly grounded in Christ, and a recognition of the work that was going on behind my office door. That work, I hope, will be deemed worthy of the invested time, especially if it has helped me to more consistently embody the Christian mind as I seek to point them toward Christ.

# 1

# The Christian Mind of C. S. Lewis

*Andrew J. Spencer*

THERE IS SOMETHING ABOUT the character of C. S. Lewis that encourages happiness in fellowship and renewal of spirit. Some people read trendy novels for their popularity, but many of those who read Lewis do so in order to read other books better. Lewis's books provide a more compelling attraction than mere popularity. Lewis is read widely for many reasons, but those who read him deeply and frequently do so to meet with a mind that has encountered Christ.

It would be difficult to quantify Lewis's popularity. In some circles he is more popular than he ought to be, especially when his books are perceived as the final destination for studying literature. Though Lewis's work is excellent, there is little question he would be surprised at the focus he receives in some Christian circles. Lewis's work certainly deserves high praise, but those who have read him well recognize he is helpful in teaching readers how to think so they can read other literature better. He is pointing toward something beyond himself.

It is the Christian mind of C. S. Lewis that should be so very interesting. That mind is revealed on the pages of his various works. The books, essays, and poems that he wrote have profound interest to many because they direct the reader's attention to something deeper, richer, and truer than anything seen or heard in this life.

Lewis is a less polarizing figure than many other Christian writers of enduring popularity, though Lewis did hold many strong opinions. John Calvin, Martin Luther, Origen, Augustine of Hippo, and others are more doctrinally significant to the history of the church because of their theological contributions, but their work tends to be much more divisive. For example, some groups love John Calvin, while others despise him. He is enduringly popular in some circles and was highly prolific, but his appeal is much narrower than Lewis's. In fact, one of the intriguing aspects of Lewis's enduring popularity is that he seems to appeal to Christians of nearly all theological traditions. It is not unheard of for even secularists to find Lewis's work attractive, though I am not certain how long one can resist the siren call of the gospel in Lewis's imaginative and expository works. Nevertheless, Lewis is read by a broad coalition of scholars, clergy, and laypeople.

Many recent treatments of the life and work of C. S. Lewis begin with speculation about his enduring popularity. Alister McGrath begins his book, *The Intellectual World of C. S. Lewis*, by offering three reasons why Lewis remains popular: (1) the continued value of his apologetic work; (2) his religious appeal; and (3) his use of imagination in defense of the faith.[1] Michael Travers agreed with McGrath, but added his own considerations, writing:

> In addition to these reasons, there is an underlying reason for Lewis's ongoing importance: he wrote about things of first importance, timeless truths that he thought we needed to hear. In his writings, Lewis taps into the essential human condition in such a way that we catch glimpses of truths we had forgotten or perhaps suppressed, especially in our modern, Post-Enlightenment culture. One of these truths is that everyone is on a journey, hoping for heaven, even when we do not know it or refuse to admit it.[2]

Travers reflects on something most people interested in Lewis sense, but have a difficult time expressing: our interest in C. S. Lewis is partially driven by the mind of the person who wrote so beautifully about such important things. Many of us are interested in Lewis because he exemplified the Christian mind in what he wrote.

It is highly likely that Lewis would have winced at this reason for ongoing interest in his work. After all, this is the man who repeatedly rejected the notion that literature should be interpreted through the biography of the author, especially in his dialogue with E. M. Tillyard in *The Personal*

---

1. McGrath, *Intellectual World of C. S. Lewis*, 1–2.
2. Travers, "Myth Became Fact," 1.

*Heresy*.[3] And yet, it is unquestionable that the ongoing interest in Lewis is driven nearly as much by the world's fascination with something about the man as by enjoyment of his writing. The perpetual stream of biographies about Lewis is evidence of the world's interest in Lewis's personal history.[4] But the Christian mind is both personal and super-personal. It is embodied by individuals, like C. S. Lewis, but it is also transcendently super-personal because it relies on a common relationship to the great mind of the creator God.

Lewis embodies the Christian mind because he brings the world together into a cohesive unity. He was one of several people who seemed to embody the Christian mind in his time. Others on this list include T. S. Eliot, Dorothy L. Sayers, and other Christian humanists from the early twentieth century.[5] We might also include luminaries like Augustine of Hippo, Thomas Aquinas, and Abraham Kuyper on this list. These are people who, despite diverse theological backgrounds, seem to have seen the unity in the universe and meaningfully engaged with the Mind that first imagined the created order. This comes through in the pages of their books, which seem to be alive in such a way that enlivens the mind of the reader. The common thread running through all of their work is the vibrant life of the Christian mind.

This volume of essays, written in honor of Michael Travers, centers on the theme of the Christian mind of C. S. Lewis. The essays collected here explore some of the contours of Lewis's own intellectual history. More significantly, they try to show where Lewis is pointing and how he directs readers' attention to the things toward which he points.

It is impossible to write about Lewis without dealing with his biography, since his life and work were so inextricably linked. However, the biographical content in this volume is used to show where Lewis stood. As Christian authors seeking to point others to the same truths Lewis saw, we are attempting to see how he got to the place from which he pointed. The essays in this volume consider both topics, often simultaneously, in an effort to explore the Christian mind of C. S. Lewis and help others come closer to approximating the Christian mind in their own lives.

---

3. Lewis and Tillyard, *Personal Heresy*.

4. Notably, in a recent volume, historian Stephanie Derrick proposes ignorance—particularly among Lewis's American audience—as the primary reason for his continued popularity. Her thesis seems to both belie the ongoing contextualized study of Lewis and be generally uncharitable. Derrick, *Fame of C. S. Lewis*.

5. See the work of Alan Jacobs on the unique group of Christian humanists in Britain. Jacobs, *Year of Our Lord 1943*.

## THE CHRISTIAN MIND

In his 1963 book, Harry Blamires flatly states, "There is no longer a Christian mind."[6] Such a grim diagnosis might seem to undermine the premise of this volume and raise contentious questions about the future of the church. However, Blamires went on to qualify his statement, writing, "There is still, of course, a Christian ethic, a Christian practice, and a Christian spirituality."[7] In context, Blamires is offering two specific criticisms of Christianity writ large. First, most Christians fail to integrate their faith with all areas of knowledge. Due to this failure, many do not think primarily as citizens of the kingdom of God, but instead function mainly as citizens of their nation, their time, and their cultural context. They may claim their identity is primarily in Christ, but that is not always visible in the way they live their lives, speak to others, spend their money, and engage in political activism. To see that his diagnosis is largely correct, one need only observe the drift of self-identified Christians toward blind acceptance of sexual revisionism, of reductionistic materialism in science and economics, and of the prevalence of autonomous individualism in Western societies. Second, Blamires's criticism is that there are too few people who think about things Christianly to form a critical mass and sufficiently demonstrate the integrity of a Christian perspective on reality. Again, here the evidence is indisputable, as media coverage of religion repeatedly reveals the failure of journalists to understand even the rudimentary doctrines at the heart of Christianity. There is insufficient weight of Christian thinkers engaged in culture to provide a robust and distinct Christian perspective on the issues of the day.

In *The Christian Mind*, Blamires, a friend and student of C. S. Lewis, identifies six attributes of the Christian mind: (1) belief in the supernatural, (2) recognition of the difference between good and evil, (3) acceptance that there is an objective truth (even if we cannot know it perfectly), (4) the acceptance of authority, for example of Scripture, over our beliefs, (5) concern for people as individuals, and (6) belief in the goodness of creation, which leads to a positive valuation of this present life. There is solid evidence that C. S. Lewis demonstrated each one of the attributes on Blamires's list. This is part of what makes Lewis so enduringly influential among Christians.

Blamires's list of attributes is helpful, but it might be considered something of a concession to the checklist approach of modernity if applied too rigidly, apart from the context of his explanations. The bare list gives the idea that one might master some of the attributes and thus approximate the Christian mind. But to have the Christian mind is an all or nothing

---

6. Blamires, *Christian Mind*, 3.
7. Blamires, *Christian Mind*, 3.

condition. The Christian mind is more than the sum of its parts. Although Blamires's definition is helpful for getting a vision of the Christian mind, a more holistic discussion of the Christian mind is in order. Therefore, as a working definition for this volume, we will consider the Christian mind more organically.

At a most basic level, the Christian mind is one that recognizes the enduring truth and beauty of God. It is therefore drawn perpetually to asking questions about the true, the good, and the beautiful. This is a vision of reality that sees integrity in the universe because God himself, the eternal Three-in-One, is perfectly simple and without division. Comprehending this reality, even to the limited degree possible, entails looking at the wonder of reality outside of our own minds. Truth is discovered by observation, not introspection. The Christian mind is, therefore, one that is more interested in the world around than in itself.

Perhaps the best way to consider the nature of the Christian mind is to consider the mind of Christ. The apostle Paul, likely quoting some of the earliest Christian hymnody, describes the mind of Christ in his letter to the Philippians, saying, "Have this mind among yourselves" (2:5).[8] He goes on to describe Christ's selfless humiliation in the incarnation. But what precedes this phrase in verse 5 is critical to understanding the Christian mind, for there Paul lists virtuous actions that Christians can perform: "Do nothing from selfish ambition or conceit, but in humility count others more significant than yourselves. Let each of you look not only to his own interests, but also to the interests of others" (2:3–4). Christians cannot fully be like Christ, as he is described in verses 6–8, but having a Christian mind primarily entails embodying the selflessness and other-focus described in verses 3–4. For a person to have the mind of Christ, and for a critical mass of thinkers to have a Christian mind in society, those things outside ourselves must be more captivating to our imaginations than our personal interest. Such a vision of the world begins with God at the center and seeks to love others effectively as neighbors.

The beginning of wisdom is the fear of God (Prov 9:10), which should lead to devotion to God and service to neighbor. These, after all, are the two great commandments by which Jesus summarized the Old Testament Law (Matt 22:37–40). We see both in Lewis, though we see a movement toward neighbor-love perhaps more voluminously elaborated, since Lewis often self-consciously left theological explanations of the particulars of God's character and work to professional theologians. Those who knew him well did not question his fulfillment of the greatest commandment even as he

---

8. All references to Scripture in this essay will be to the English Standard Version.

tried to fulfill the second greatest.[9] The Christian mind of C. S. Lewis had a holy reverence of God and pointed others toward him.

In a culture that tends toward myopic self-interest, Lewis cries for others to see the world around. The Christian mind is one that sees the waterfall as sublime, recognizing that the sense of wonder at a gloriously powerful spectacle is more than an internal feeling; it is a response to something greater.[10] Lewis recognizes that it is our selfishness that blinds us and keeps us on the path to hell, even if the splendors of heaven are before us. He warns his readers that if we hold onto our pet sins we cannot enter the kingdom of God.[11] We must be able, at least in part, to see beyond ourselves.

Lewis stood against the corrosive elements of modernity explicitly, since it was the great challenge of his day. As Alan Jacobs argues, Lewis was one of a cluster of Christians seeking to recapture a common sense of humanity in the early twentieth century.[12] Contemporary readers that move beyond Lewis's most popular works will find helpful material even in a world saturated by post-modernism, post-post-modernism, or however the current vogue stream of philosophical critique is described. This is because Lewis's critique of his age was not founded by an attempt to create a different, novel vision of reality, but to point others toward a timeless understanding of the true, the good, and the beautiful.

The most essential element of the Christian mind is, quite logically, being in Christ—that is to say, having an identity firmly rooted in the Christian faith. For evangelical Christians, this is typically described as having a conversion experience, where one passes from unbelief to belief in the truths of Christianity.[13] For Roman Catholics and high church Protestants, a specific conversion experience is often less central, but Christian identity tends to be tied to devotional practice and faithful participation in the activities of the faith community. Lewis provides evidence of both of these forms of Christian identity. In all Christian streams, the purpose of conversion, devotional practices, and participation in the faith community are aimed at transformation of the individual's mind into the patterns affirmed by Scripture as understood through the particular stream of Christianity. Lewis's Christian identity is most clearly demonstrated by his oft-quoted

---

9. Como, *Branches to Heaven*, 100–108.
10. Lewis, *Abolition of Man*, 14–19.
11. Lewis, *Great Divorce*.
12. Jacobs, *Year of Our Lord 1943*.
13. Lewis's own dramatic conversion and his emphasis on decision (particularly in *The Great Divorce*) help explain Lewis's popularity among American evangelicals.

comment, "I believe in Christianity as I believe that the Sun has risen, not only because I see it, but because by it I see everything else."[14]

The Christian mind is one that self-consciously sees the whole world from within Christianity. The Christian mind understands that the Christian myth is the truest and most satisfying explanation of reality. In Lewis's essay "Meditations in a Toolshed," he describes the difference between looking at and looking along an experience. Though his argument states that people should be open to analysis from both inside and outside the experience, it seems he leans toward the higher value of descriptions about the nature of an experience from within it.[15] Such a position is not, of course, universally accepted. Each year, members of the American Academy of Religion have a hot debate prior to the conference whether believing Christians (particularly those pesky evangelicals) can rightly study Christianity. In their social media fora, the loudest voices argue that to believe a religion to be true disqualifies one from actually understanding it.[16] The Christian mind denies the truthfulness of that assertion and, in fact, proposes exactly the opposite: one cannot rightly understand the world outside of Christ. After all, Jesus unambiguously stated, "I am the way, the truth, and the life" (John 14:6). The Christian mind recognizes Jesus's words have implications for all reality, not merely salvation. Reality cannot make sense without the illuminating truth of Christianity.

Lewis embodied the Christian mind. His work remains significant and popular because he showed the implications of the Christian mind in his nonfiction work, often writing journalistic essays that applied Christianity to thorny questions of his day. Arguably more significantly, Lewis also offers an imaginative window into the Christian mind, showing through his fantasies what such a mind would look like. For those who find joy in the diverse genres in which Lewis wrote, a common element that continues to draw us in is the Christian mind that points us to the one who made the world.

## THE CHRISTIAN MIND OF C. S. LEWIS

This book traces out the Christian mind of C. S. Lewis through multiple genres of his writing. The authors are from various disciplines, with Bible scholars, English professors, a rhetorician, a philosopher, and an ethicist contributing chapters. The range of contributors is as wide as those who

---

14. Lewis, "Is Theology Poetry?," 21. This was one of Michael Travers's favorite and most frequently cited quotes from C. S. Lewis.

15. Lewis, "Meditations on a Toolshed," 607–610.

16. Inexplicably, those scholars engaged in identity studies often get a pass on this requirement for supposed disinterest.

knew Michael Travers well and shared his interests in Lewis and the Christian mind. There is unity within the essays because they are all dealing with the Christian mind of C. S. Lewis. Within the volume, there is a general thematic arc, which begins with more general discussion of Lewis's work and the Christian mind, later coming to more focused essays. However, as with any multi-authored volume, some essays may be more helpful to readers than others or may be closer to a given area of interest. Permission is granted for the reader to step in and out of the volume as interest and utility direct.

The second chapter of this volume contains a previously unpublished essay by Michael Travers, which outlines some of the major themes that tie the work of C. S. Lewis together. Travers shows how Lewis's works, especially his fiction, build on the major themes from Christian Scripture: creation, fall, redemption, and re-creation. This essay is followed by a contribution from Elizabeth Travers Parker, Michael's daughter, that incorporates some of Michael's unpublished research. She emphasizes the central role of the incarnation of Christ and its power to ignite our desire and love for the Trinity as seen in all of Lewis's fiction, but especially *The Chronicles of Narnia*.

The fourth chapter helps explain why the work of C. S. Lewis is so compelling. James Como demonstrates that Lewis was an *architecton*—a master builder—whose rhetorical skills enable his distinctly Christian mind to pierce the murkiness of modern thinking to excite the mind and embolden people to live authentic Christian lives. Daniel Estes follows this with an exploration of the integration of faith with all areas of life (something Lewis exemplified) by a careful exposition of Psalm 19. In chapter 6, Gene Fant highlights the theme of godly wisdom as it is witnessed in Lewis's most significant literary achievement, *Till We Have Faces*. The seventh chapter is an essay by Bruce Little, which puts C. S. Lewis and Francis Schaeffer in conversation, demonstrating that both men had a compelling interest in Christian evangelism that depended on the existence and discernibility of an objective reality.

In the eighth essay in this volume, Keith Callis considers the idea of disinterested love, especially as it is witnessed in *The Screwtape Letters* and *The Great Divorce*. Lewis points readers beyond themselves, showing that the Christian mind is about Christ, not the individual who has that mind. Lindsey Panxhi explores Lewis's concept of an Inner Ring in her essay in chapter 9. Panxhi shows how Lewis makes his prosaic concepts from his essay "The Inner Ring" real and compelling to readers through his fantastical novel *That Hideous Strength*. This is followed by my own essay that considers C. S. Lewis's ethics among men without chests in chapter 10. It is an attempt to show the dangers of scientism, which Lewis himself resisted, through the lenses of his essays in *The Abolition of Man* and the fictional world of *That Hideous Strength*.

Chapter 11 delves into Lewis's work on the Psalter, particularly comparing his approach to lament in *Reflections on the Psalms* to his posthumously published *Letters to Malcolm: Chiefly on Prayer*. Heath Thomas argues that Lewis's work on the Psalter has enduring value for Christians engaged in academic study on the subject, but that his writing on lament in *Reflections on the Psalms* needs to be corrected by his perspective on prayer in *Letters to Malcolm*. In the twelfth chapter, Leland Ryken offers literary criticism of a subject of common interest between C. S. Lewis and Michael Travers: the work of John Milton. Ryken writes about one of Milton's sonnets, "As Ever in My Great Task-Master's Eye," which focuses on life lived under the gaze of the savior and how that urges Christians toward faithfulness and energy in their labors. This was a common theme in the lives of both Lewis and Travers.

The book closes with an essay about the life and work of Michael Travers. Michael was a Christian gentleman in the most precise sense of that term. Like Lewis, he was a Miltonist. He loved the works of C. S. Lewis especially, produced exemplary scholarship on the Bible as literature, and wrote an excellent volume on the Psalms, which encourages devotional reading and careful literary interpretation. Michael was consistently kind to those who worked with him and patient in suffering, demonstrated by his faithfulness during the final stages of life, as he endured a painful form of cancer. Above all, Michael sought to embody the Christian mind by putting the glory of God and the interests of others above his own. This volume has been compiled in his honor. This is an honor that is, in the minds of the contributors, well-deserved.

## BIBLIOGRAPHY

Blamires, Harry. *The Christian Mind*. Grand Rapids: Family Christian, 2001.
Como, James. *Branches to Heaven: The Geniuses of C. S. Lewis*. Dallas: Spence, 1998.
Derrick, Stephanie L. *The Fame of C. S. Lewis: A Controversialist's Reception in Britain and America*. New York: Oxford University Press, 2018.
Jacobs, Alan. *Year of Our Lord 1943: Christian Humanism in an Age of Crisis*. New York: Oxford University Press, 2018.
Lewis, C. S. *The Abolition of Man*. San Francisco: HarperSanFrancisco, 2001.
———. *The Great Divorce: A Dream*. New York: HarperOne, 2001.
———. "Is Theology Poetry?" In *C. S. Lewis: Essay Collection and Other Short Pieces*, edited by Lesley Walmsley, 21. London: HarperCollins, 2000.
———. "Meditations on a Toolshed." In *C. S. Lewis: Essay Collection and Other Short Pieces*, edited by Lesley Walmsley, 607–10. London: HarperCollins, 2000.

Lewis, C. S., and E. M. W. Tillyard. *The Personal Heresy: A Controversy*. New York: HarperOne, 2017.

McGrath, Alister. *The Intellectual World of C. S. Lewis*. Malden, MA: Wiley-Blackwell, 2014.

Travers, Michael. "Myth Became Fact." Unpublished personal papers, n.d.

# 2

# Invitation to Glory

## C. S. Lewis's Apologetic of Hope[1]

*Michael E. Travers*

IN HIS APOLOGETICS AND fiction, C. S. Lewis invites his readers to hope for heaven and God. His great contribution is his reminder to twentieth-century Western culture, which has lost its mooring, of what it means to be humans who were made for God and to long for him all our lives. C. S. Lewis reminds readers that this longing for God, this hope of heaven, is the proper state for all of us in a fallen world. He offers to readers a vision of the Christian mind.

Our culture needs to remember what it means to be human: we are created in the image of God and for the purpose of praising God. At the very outset of his *Confessions*, Saint Augustine gives voice to the essential human need—and desire—to praise God:

> Great art Thou, O Lord, and greatly to be praised; great is Thy power, and of Thy wisdom there is no number. And man desires

---

1. While researching Michael Travers's biography, this article was uncovered as a previously unpublished conference paper and chapel address. It has been edited lightly to change formatting, style, and to prepare it for publication. This paper was delivered first to the C. S. Lewis Society of New York on November 22, 2013, at a conference commemorating the fiftieth anniversary of Lewis's death. It was later delivered as a faculty lecture on January 30, 2014, in the chapel of Southeastern Baptist Theological Seminary. The video of that chapel presentation is available here: https://vimeo.com/74760027

to praise Thee. He is but a tiny part of all that Thou hast created. He bears about him his mortality, the evidence of his sinfulness, and the evidence that *Thou dost resist the proud*: yet this tiny part of all that Thou hast created desires to praise Thee. Thou dost so excite him that to praise Thee is his joy. For Thou has made us for Thyself and our hearts are restless until they rest in Thee.[2]

Because we were made for God, we cannot be satisfied apart from him. Nothing in this world can satisfy the ultimate desire of the human soul to be satisfied in God. Human culture, particularly that inspired by Christianity, incarnates this desire for God in manifold ways, and, what is more, Scripture attests to it as well. The desire for God is a key element of the Christian mind.

The idea that we all desire God and hope for heaven is expressed in both the Old and New Testaments. In Ecclesiastes, the wisdom writer states that God has put "eternity into man's heart" (Eccl 3:11),[3] and evidences the implications of our desire for God in that nothing in this life ultimately satisfies the soul. The writer speaks of good things—such as work, food, and relationships—that we enjoy in this life, but he teaches that ultimate wisdom is to seek God and rest in him. Everything else is "vanity," or futility. The Psalmist writes that the ancient Hebrews longed for rest in the Promised Land. But, because of their unbelief and sin, they had to walk the wilderness pathways for forty years before they were allowed to enter that rest, and then it was only the next generation that was allowed to do so (Ps 95:1–11). In the New Testament, the writer of Hebrews applies the temporal rest of the ancient Hebrews in the Promised Land figuratively to the spiritual rest Christians have in Christ and then to the eternal rest we ultimately will enjoy in the new heavens and the new earth (Heb 3:7—4:11).

In this life, we are not yet at rest, and we cannot be at rest until our faith becomes sight in heaven. We hope for future glory. In the New Testament, the apostles often write of a hope that looks forward to eternity. The apostle Peter admonishes us to be "ready always to give an answer to every man that asketh you a reason for the hope that is in you" (1 Pet 3:15). Peter speaks this instruction to Christians, admonishing them to give a witness to non-Christians about heaven and eternity with God. For Peter, as for the other New Testament writers, this hope is not wishful thinking; rather, it is settled and certain hope, for it is predicated on the character of God as evidenced by the word of God—"Christ in you, the hope of glory," as Paul has it in

---

2. Augustine, *Confessions*, 3. Emphasis original.
3. All Scripture references in this chapter are to the King James Version.

Colossians 1:27. Paul speaks elsewhere of our hope in Christ, for Christ has paid the debt of our sins and granted us eternal life (see 2 Cor 1:10; 1 Tim 4:10). In the earthly life of Christ our longing for God is made concrete in the transfiguration, when Peter, James, and John see Christ revealed in all his glory. The transfiguration follows immediately after Jesus tells his disciples that he will come again in great glory, thereby prompting longing for that glorious kingdom; it is then that he is transfigured before the three men, and they are given a glimpse of the future and the one on whom their hope is founded. In Romans 8, Paul writes that the Christian's whole life is oriented toward this hope when we will be glorified in the presence of our Savior, Jesus Christ.

The Bible often expresses this hope in narrative form. Almost two-thirds of the Bible is narrative. From Genesis to Exodus, through the history books and prophets in the Old Testament, to the Gospels, the book of the Acts of the Apostles, and even the book of Revelation in the New Testament, the story of redemption is just that—a narrative. The writer of Hebrews symbolizes this life as a pilgrimage. He writes that we "desire a better country, that is a heavenly [one]" (Heb 11:16), and "for here we have no continuing city, but we seek one to come" (Heb 13:14). A pilgrimage is not just a wandering journey; rather, it is a teleological journey with a destination. For Christians, that destination is heaven with Jesus Christ, our ultimate beatitude. It is no accident, then, that the Bible incarnates a grand metanarrative that encompasses the whole of the created order and our place as humans in that story.

Giving voice to the Christian narrative of hope is what Lewis did in his writings at a time when others had lost sight of that hope. He presented a vision of the Christian mind. Austin Farrer writes of the voice Lewis gives to Christianity:

> It was this feeling intellect, this intellectual imagination that made the strength of his religious writings. . . . His real power was not proof [as in apologetics]; it was depiction. There lived in his writings a Christian universe that could be both thought and felt, in which he was at home and in which he made his reader at home.[4]

There is the note: Lewis invites his readers to come along home with him—to God and heaven. He knew that we longed for something beyond this world, and he invited us to join him in the search for our eternal home.[5]

---

4. Farrer, "In His Image," 384–85. Farrer was chaplain of Trinity College, Oxford, from 1935 to 1960, and a good friend of Lewis.

5. See Lewis, *Mere Christianity*, 143.

Lewis's method for inviting others to put on the Christian mind, through his prose, poetry, and narrative, was to put the metanarrative of the Bible on display.

## THE METANARRATIVE OF THE BIBLE

The Bible presents a metanarrative in four acts: first, God's creation of all that exists, including Adam and Eve; second, the fall of Adam and Eve into sin in the garden of Eden; third, the redemption offered sinful man in Jesus Christ, the "second Adam"; and fourth, the final eschatological consummation in glory of all things after Christ's return and the creation of a new heaven and a new earth. Seen in the light of the narrative superstructure, it becomes clear how longing and hope fit into the human experience. In broad brushstrokes it looks like this:

- **Creation:** In the original creation, in which everything was good, Adam and Eve had everything they needed, including perfect harmony with God and each other. Their joy was perfect and there was therefore no need for longing and hope.
- **Fall:** In the fall into sin, Adam and Eve were separated from God, estranged from each other, alienated from the natural creation, and fragmented psychologically even within themselves. In effect, they entered into exile. Because of their sin, Adam and Eve began to long for God, for "rest" in this life, and ultimately for reconciliation with God.
- **Redemption:** In Christ's sacrifice for our sins, Christians are restored positionally to a right relationship with God and given a guaranteed hope for heaven. The New Testament gives testimony to the fact that Christians' hope is set on Christ, and they long for heaven.
- **Re-creation/Eschaton:** At the end of all things, when the new heaven and the new earth are created and Christians are given their resurrection bodies, there will be no more need of hoping or longing, and faith will have become sight. We will have arrived at our destination. It will be transfiguration forever. It is this glory for which we were created; taking his cue from the apostle Paul, C. S. Lewis calls it a "weight of glory" (2 Cor 4:17).

All people—Christian and non-Christian alike—long for God, and it is easy to see how the grand biblical narrative provides the frame of reference for understanding this longing correctly. Because we are fallen, we hope for heaven.

C. S. Lewis often expresses this longing as hope. Hope requires three conditions: first, an undesirable present state that one wishes to leave behind; second, a future desirable state that is anticipated and possible; and, third, a time frame to move from present to future. In Lewis's fiction, where he provides this "apologetic of hope," as I have called it, Lewis frames his narratives in terms of *exile* (parallel to the fall in the Christian metanarrative); *longing*, which is the hope for redemption; *pilgrimage* or *journey*, which expresses the longing in narrative terms; *community*, or the hope partially realized here in this life; and *final arrival*, or the full eschatological glorification when the Christian's hope is realized and faith becomes sight.

## CREATION

Before we turn to the exile and longing which results in future glorification and rest, we need to look briefly at Lewis's narrative of creation in *The Chronicles of Narnia*, specifically in *The Magician's Nephew*. It is in this creation account that Lewis hints at the perfection and glory for which the characters in all of his fiction long. Echoing the biblical narrative in which God speaks the world into existence, Lewis has Aslan sing Narnia into existence. Aslan sings different notes and tones for each different creature or plant: some deep and earthy, some light and ethereal. The Cabby—and, it is hoped, the reader—finds Aslan's creative song "so beautiful he could hardly bear it."[6] Everyone who hears the song, other than Jadis the evil witch, finds that it evokes longing and joy in them. Wayne Martindale suggests that the creation account in *The Magician's Nephew* represents the "beatific vision" of the novel, filling the people with the glory of Aslan and evoking hope in them that they might live there in Narnia with him forever.[7] As far as *The Chronicles of Narnia* are concerned, this creation account provides the norm or baseline for the way things were meant to be in Narnia. Were it not for Jadis's introducing evil into the narrative, everyone would have lived in a perfect Narnia forever. But such a life was not to be: Jadis does introduce evil in Narnia, and all the characters from that point forward long to recover what they experienced briefly when it all began. Lewis provides an *inclusio*, or bookend, to *The Magician's Nephew* in the last book of the series, *The Last Battle*, where he narrates the re-creation of Narnia, now writ large and perfect. In the rest of the narrative of redemption—the rest of the invitation to glory—the characters remember the perfection of creation on the one

---

6. Lewis, *Magician's Nephew*, 106.
7. Martindale, *Beyond the Shadowlands*, 194–95.

hand, and hope to recover it on the other. They look backward in memory and forward in hope.

## EXILE

Exile is the condition of mankind that results from the fall—a desire that results from the separation of God, other people, the created order, and self. It is the product of sin. In fact, sin is in part an attempt to recover that oneness with God, only in the wrong ways. Sin takes such forms as greed and lust and finds expression in all kinds of behaviors, such as theft, fraud, sexual immoralities of all kinds, deceit, and lies—to name only a few. In Lewis's thinking, which is also Saint Augustine's, evil is the perversion of a good, the condition of being "bent," as he has it in *Out of the Silent Planet*. Screwtape says as much to Wormwood when he states that God made pleasures and, when the devils tempt humans to pleasure, they can only tempt them to enjoy pleasure in ways that pervert the ways God originally intended for them to be enjoyed.[8] Lewis puts it this way in "The Weight of Glory":

> At present we are on the outside of the world, the wrong side of the door. We discern the freshness and purity of morning, but they do not make us fresh and pure. We cannot mingle with the splendours we see. But all the leaves of the New Testament are rustling with the rumour that it will not always be so. Some day, God willing, we shall get in.[9]

Virtually all of Lewis's novels express this sense of elemental exile and separation and its concomitant longing. Lewis communicates the idea of exile in his apologetic works, as in *Mere Christianity* (in the appeal to a universal moral code), *The Abolition of Man* (again, the recognition of a universal moral code, the Tao), and *The Problem of Pain*. G. K. Chesterton, who was a significant influence on Lewis, writes in *As I Was Saying* that the fall into sin is "a view of life" that assures us "that happiness is not only a hope, but also in some strange manner a memory; and that we are all kings in exile."[10] Exile and hope are the Janus faces of our fallen condition—looking back in memory to Eden and forward in hope to heaven.

In *That Hideous Strength*, an extreme form of exile is conveyed in everything about the NICE (the National Institute of Coordinated Experiments) and Belbury in general, but it is in the pedestrian and dysfunctional marriage of Mark and Jane Studdock that the sense of separation is brought

---

8. Lewis, *Screwtape Letters*, 44.
9. Lewis, "Weight of Glory," 43.
10. Chesterton, *As I Was Saying*, 160.

to the fore. Marriage is intended to be a union and, ideally, in marriage, we are to find a reflection of the union of Christ with his church (cf. Eph 5:22–32), but neither Mark nor Jane see their marriage as an essential union; rather, they see it simply as the state of affairs for them. Jane interrupted her work on her doctoral dissertation of John Donne to marry Mark and now resents him for the delay. For his part, Mark lives for his career as a professor of sociology and longs earnestly to work his way first into the "Progressive Element" at Bracton College and, later, into the inner circle of the NICE and Belbury. Both seek for satisfaction in selfish ways; neither understands the Christian paradox that to live is to die and to lead is to serve, especially in marriage. Ironically, if they would give themselves to each other, they would become more fully human and fulfill their purposes in life. In this vein, Lewis states in *The Problem of Pain*, "From the highest to the lowest, self exists to be abdicated and, by that abdication, becomes the more truly self, to be thereupon yet the more abdicated, and so forever."[11] In their selfishness, however, Mark and Jane become dehumanized—especially Mark, who is helped along the way by the NICE's overt attempt to dehumanize, or "objectify," him, ultimately by getting him to desecrate a crucifix. Their hopes are twisted and thus, ironically, all they can experience is more exile and increasingly less satisfaction—a law of diminishing returns, as it were. Their sin is idolatry—bowing down to themselves rather than to God—and the result is hopelessness. Fortunately, both realize their error before it is too late, and the novel ends with the hope of a restored marriage.

The same trajectory of a good twisted into evil informs *The Chronicles of Narnia*. In *The Silver Chair*, the sense of exile fills most of the narrative. The story begins with Jill, Eustace, and Puddleglum journeying northward into an increasingly barren and hostile land, exiled, as it were, from the society and pleasures of Narnia in their quest to find and rescue Prince Rilian. Aslan has sent the three on this quest and has given Jill four signs to follow and obey. The novel is a classic quest narrative in which the protagonists travel far from home in order to accomplish a goal. In *The Silver Chair*, the journey takes Jill, Eustace, and Puddleglum "to the bottom of the world,"[12] reminding the reader of the harrowing-of-hell motif of the creeds of the church and such medieval literature as Dante's *Divine Comedy*. In effect, the heroes travel to "hell" to rescue a prisoner from the evil enchantments of the witch.

While they are under the earth, Jill, Eustace, and Puddleglum discover an Underworld, where the evil witch has trapped Rilian and plans to use

---

11. Lewis, *Problem of Pain*, 157.
12. Lewis, *Silver Chair*, 207.

him as her puppet prince when she conquers Narnia. Everything about the Underworld reveals it as a dystopian parody of Narnia itself where everything mimics Narnia but never matches Narnia's glory. There are artificial lamps instead of the sun, a pale city instead of Cair Paravel, and robot-like workers instead of willing and joyful Narnians. Nothing is real. Evil copies good, but can never quite get it right. At a turning point in the story, Puddleglum champions the rightness of Narnia against the dystopia of Underworld in a speech that rescues the heroes from succumbing to the witch's evil spell. He argues:

> Suppose we *have* only dreamed, or made up, all those things—trees and grass and sun and moon and stars and Aslan himself. Suppose we have. Then all I can say is that, in that case, the made-up things seem a good deal more important than the real ones. . . . That's why I'm going to stand by the play-world. I'm on Aslan's side even if there isn't any Aslan to lead it. I'm going to live as like a Narnian as I can even if there isn't any Narnia. So . . . we're leaving your court at once and setting out in the dark to spend our lives looking for Overland.[13]

Puddleglum's rejection of the pale mimicry that is evil and his declaration of faith in the rightful Narnia restore hope to the heroes: they kill the witch, escape the Underworld, and return to Narnia. There, the community of Narnians celebrates the end of Rilian's exile, the recovery of the rightful king to the throne, and the restoration of order to Narnia. Puddleglum's courage exposes the lie in the witch's temptations and reminds everyone that the Underworld is far from the norm. The celebration is not eschatalogical, however, for there are other Narnian tales to come, including *The Last Battle*, where exile and evil are given their final expression in the series and brought to the ultimate end.

## LONGING

Lewis called our innate yearning for heaven by various terms: joy, desire, *Sehnsucht*, and longing. Lewis reminds modern people what pre-modern Europeans knew instinctively from their Christian heritage: this world is not our home; we were made for heaven—what Lewis calls "the high countries" in *The Great Divorce* and our "true home" in *Mere Christianity*. He makes the point again in "The Weight of Glory":

---

13. Lewis, *Silver Chair*, 182.

> Apparently, then, our lifelong nostalgia, our longing to be reunited with something in the universe from which we now feel cut off, to be on the inside of some door which we have always seen from the outside, is no mere neurotic fancy, but the truest index of our real situation.[14]

Here, Lewis connects the longing for heaven with the fall, for he says we long to be "reunited" and we feel "cut off." Because of the fall and sin, we are exiled from our true home and long to return. In *The Problem of Pain*, Lewis considers the possibility that our silence about heaven may suggest that we really do not desire it. "But that may be an illusion," he states. "There have been times when I think we do not desire heaven; but more often I find myself wondering whether, in our heart of hearts, we have ever desired anything else."[15]

Longing for heaven is the proper state of things for us in this world. Longing is also there in *The Pilgrim's Regress*, where it is the voice of the island "from beyond the wood" that calls him onward.[16] Longing is there even in *Mere Christianity*, running throughout the book as the leitmotif and surfacing most fully in Book Three, "Christian Behaviour," in the chapter appropriately titled "Hope." There, as in "The Weight of Glory," Lewis writes of heaven as our "true country" and states that it is the purpose of his life to "keep alive in myself the desire of my true country, which I shall not find till after death . . . and help others to do the same."[17] And longing is front and center in Lewis's autobiography of his early years, *Surprised by Joy*, which traces the early hauntings of this longing until they are ultimately satisfied in the person and work of Jesus Christ. At the end of *Surprised by Joy*, Lewis calls these stabs of joy, these longings, "signposts" with "pillars" of silver and "lettering of gold" that point the way to heaven and to Christ himself.[18]

In his fiction, Lewis gives literary shape to the spiritual longing we all feel by casting it in the form of a narrative journey. Robert Palma notes, "Lewis was really inviting others to join him in his personal pilgrimage, one in which he was seeking to progress from affirmation to apprehension, and through it all and above all, worshipping God with his whole mind."[19] Lewis extends the invitation to join him in his pilgrimage to pursue the Christian

---

14. Lewis, "Weight of Glory," 42.
15. Lewis, *Problem of Pain*, 149.
16. Lewis, *Pilgrim's Regress*, 12.
17. Lewis, *Mere Christianity*, 137.
18. Lewis, *Surprised by Joy*, 290–91.
19. Palma, "C. S. Lewis's Use of Analogy," 100.

mind. Such is the theme of *The Voyage of the Dawn Treader*, where the narrative line is shaped throughout by longing.

## PILGRIMAGE/JOURNEY

In *The Voyage of the Dawn Treader*, King Caspian and his loyal subjects are sailing east from Narnia to find the seven lords who had never returned from their journey years before. At the same time in England, Lucy and Edmund and their cousin Eustace are on vacation from school. One day, they are drawn into a painting of the *Dawn Treader*, thus joining the Narnians on board the ship. The Narnian journey is a quest because it involves a voyage of discovery in unknown waters. For Reepicheep, however, the sea journey is much more than a search for seven lords. It is, rather, a spiritual quest that gives his whole life definition, for he longs to sail beyond the sunrise and come at last, perhaps, to Aslan's country. It is the fulfillment of the Dryad's prophecy spoken about him in his infancy:

> Where sky and water meet,
> Where the waves grow sweet,
> Doubt not, Reepicheep,
> To find all you seek,
> There is the utter East.[20]

Reepicheep's spiritual longing transforms the whole novel into a spiritual quest for everyone on board the boat and for the readers as well. Lewis states in one of his letters that "anyone in our world who devotes his whole life to seeking Heaven will be like R[eepicheep]."[21] Notice the intensity with which Lewis thinks of desiring heaven—devoting one's entire life to that end. Christians may not think of it all the time, but their lives are indeed purposeful, and living their lives purposefully moves them teleologically toward heaven. Heaven is their hope.

Reepicheep's quest for the "utter East" embodies this innately human desire that everyone senses and Christians understand so well. In another letter, Lewis writes that *The Voyage of the Dawn Treader* is about "the spiritual life (specially in Reepicheep)."[22] In his book on spiritual longing in Lewis's writings, *Into the Region of Awe: Mysticism in C. S. Lewis*, David C. Downing writes that the prophecy spoken over Reepicheep as an infant "evokes in the noble mouse a kind of Sweet Desire, like the piercing pleasure

---

20. Lewis, *Dawn Treader*, 21.
21. Lewis, *Letters to Children*, 45.
22. Lewis, *Collected Letters*, 3:1245.

the young Lewis felt on reading Longfellow's lines about Balder. If the young Lewis heard the call of 'Northernness,' Reepicheep might be said to be under the spell of 'Easternness.'"[23] Reepicheep is Lewis's "everyman" in this story.

As the quest draws to a close, the spiritual longings increase dramatically, as does the anticipation of something wonderful about to happen. Reepicheep declares his intentions to sail on:

> My own plans are made. While I can, I sail east in the *Dawn Treader*. When she fails me, I paddle east in my coracle. When she sinks, I shall swim east with my four paws. And when I can swim no longer, if I have not reached Aslan's country, or shot over the edge of the world in some vast cataract, I shall sink with my nose to the sunrise and Peepiceek will be head of the talking mice in Narnia.[24]

The last three chapters of the novel are filled with glorious longings and joys for all the travelers. As they approach the "utter East" of the world, it seems that every one of their senses is heightened. They see new constellations every night, and the voyagers believe their sense of sight is improved for they can look at brighter and brighter lights. They smell fragrances they have never before experienced. After Lord Ramandu and his daughter sing, they hear voices in the air "which took up the same song that the Lady and her Father were singing."[25] They taste the water, now fresh and not salt, and exclaim, "It is sweet. That's real water, that."[26] Everything is preternaturally alive—all intense and glorious—as their hope to see Aslan's country comes closer and closer to realization. These are all scenes in which nature is numinously keen and more beautiful than ever, thus heightening the reader's hope for heaven.

In Lewis's fiction, it is the ordinary world as the characters know it that is made numinous, and this is a reflection of his understanding of Christian teaching in Romans 8. In *Surprised by Joy*, Lewis speaks of his imagination being "baptized" by reading George Macdonald; in Macdonald's writings, Lewis "saw the common things drawn into the bright shadow."[27] The world as we know it will be remade, and it is this reality that is the way nature was prior to the fall and will be again after the re-creation in the eschaton. In this fallen world we inhabit, longing for heaven is the proper condition of the human soul, and the most natural way for that longing to be expressed

---

23. Downing, *Into the Region of Awe*, 137.
24. Lewis, *Dawn Treader*, 213.
25. Lewis, *Dawn Treader*, 205.
26. Lewis, *Dawn Treader*, 228–29.
27. Lewis, *Surprised by Joy*, 222.

in words is in the narrative form of the quest, or pilgrimage, in search of the city where people can live in unity and harmony.

## COMMUNITY

While the hope for heaven will not be realized in its entirety until we enter it after death, there are glimpses of the hoped-for rest even here and now in this life. Scattered throughout Lewis's fiction are communities of people who understand the true condition of their lives and who, together, incarnate little havens in their gatherings. This side of death, we are not left destitute of times of rest. In these communities in Lewis's novels, people live together in unity and harmony, embodying the Christian mind; they serve each other joyfully; and they await ultimate rest in heaven.

One such community is found in the last novel of Lewis's space trilogy, *That Hideous Strength*. Throughout the novel, Mark and Jane Studdock have tried to fulfill themselves each in their own professions. Mark has chosen a dangerous path and finds himself drawn increasingly into the National Institute for Coordinated Experiments (NICE). Ironically, while associated with the NICE, Mark becomes more and more a puppet of the organization's leader and less and less an individual person. The NICE is what Lewis calls elsewhere a "collective"—a mob rule where individuals are sublimated into the masses and become impersonal pawns.[28] Jane's story, on the other hand, takes an entirely different trajectory. Through a series of events which she does not orchestrate intentionally, she ends up at St. Anne's on the Hill where an unlikely gathering of very different people find unity and hope in the community they create.

Lewis develops the experiences associated with the community at St. Anne's on the Hill in two chapters, "The Descent of the Gods" and "Venus at St. Anne's." The effect of elongating the narrative like this is to intensify the reader's anticipation of hope, joy, and the harmony of a healthy community. In "The Descent of the Gods" chapter, Jane and others experience a delicious sensation which delights their senses. "How warm it was," Jane reflects, "how comfortable and familiar."[29] Her senses, like those of the travelers on the *Dawn Treader*, are preternaturally keen; and simple, everyday pleasures become intensely pleasant. The whole community of St. Anne's is affected. Even their language is transfigured into something like a prelapsarian form of language in which every word is meaningful (as language was

---

28. Lewis, *That Hideous Strength*, 22–23, 173.
29. Lewis, *That Hideous Strength*, 322.

meant to be), harmonious, and eloquent.[30] Their laughter also takes on significance, and finally, "their love for one another became intense."[31] All of these changes of everyday experience into something more intense and meaningful point to a deep, primal unity among the people at St. Anne's, and hint briefly at the joys of heaven to come.

As he does throughout the novel, Lewis alternates Jane's experiences at St. Anne's with Mark's difficulties at Belbury, contrasting Jane's joys with Mark's terrors and thereby heightening them both. At this point in the narrative, Lewis interrupts the joys and pleasures of St. Anne's by inserting a chapter about Mark at Belbury, thus increasing the reader's anticipation of the final chapter, which is set largely at St. Anne's. When readers come to the final chapter of the book, they are filled with hopes for millennial and heavenly longings and joys. On the one hand, Belbury descends into Babel-like chaos and murder, and on the other, the people at St. Anne's prepare for a grand celebration. Everyone at St. Anne's is transfigured. Even the animals take part in the "gloria" of the moment. At St. Anne's, it is as if the whole creation is redeemed and restored. The isolation and exile brought about by the fall of Adam and Eve into sin are briefly reversed as harmony and joy are restored. The chapter can be understood in millennial terms, for here, as it were, the wolf lies down with the lamb. Finally, at the end of the chapter and the book, Jane and Mark are reunited in what appears to be a restored, and even redeemed, marriage. The last chapter of *That Hideous Strength* constitutes a beatific vision full of hope for those involved.

Indeed, the images of music and dance in this scene are appropriate expressions of Lewis's idea of what a healthy community is supposed to be like—comprised of individuals who serve each other, yet paradoxically do not lose their individuality in such service. The parallel images of community in the Bible are the body, the building, and marriage, all of which symbolize the church. In these three biblical images, there are separate parts or persons, each with its own identity and function, yet the parts serve the whole. Husbands and wives fulfill different functions, but both work together to form a marriage—a sum greater than its parts. So it is for Christians, each gifted uniquely, yet each serving the church, or the "body of Christ." In effect, the faithful communities on this earth prefigure the full community in heaven, when faith will have become sight.

---

30. Lewis, *That Hideous Strength*, 321.
31. Lewis, *That Hideous Strength*, 322.

## ARRIVAL/ESCHATON

The final and climactic event in the biblical metanarrative is the eschatological new heaven and new earth seen in the book of Revelation. All of the earlier events, from creation through the fall and on to the little communities of faith on earth, point to this final act when God makes everything new and faith becomes sight for believers. The apostle John writes of the "marriage supper of the Lamb" when Christ receives his "bride" (all believers, the church) (Rev 19:6–9). With the words, "Behold, the tabernacle [dwelling place] of God is with men," John introduces the picture of the New Jerusalem descending from heaven (Rev 21:3). What follows this glorious declaration is the familiar heavenly imagery of gates and streets of gold; the point is that Paul's prediction in Romans, chapter 8, of a redeemed creation comes true in this eschatological image: God is with man; thus, faith becomes sight, and the dwelling place of God is with man. Lewis points the way.

In *The Great Divorce*, Lewis has his imaginary characters—representative souls from hell—take a bus ride to the gates of heaven. At the start of the book, Lewis emphasizes that he is not attempting to present his picture of what heaven in fact might look like, but rather, he is putting before readers the fact that they must choose heaven or hell.[32] The imagery Lewis uses to figure forth heaven in the book is intended to demonstrate heaven's "otherness" and its transcendent beauty. The narrator's first impressions of the "High Countries," as Lewis calls the setting before heaven's gates, is that "[t]he light and coolness that drenched me were like those of summer morning; early morning a minute or two before sunrise, only that there was a certain difference. I had the sense of being in a larger space, perhaps even a larger *sort* of space, than I had ever known before."[33] In contrast to the grey town (hell), everything here is full of light and is diamond-hard, which is Lewis's way of stating that heaven is more real than earth. Earth is the "Shadowlands," while heaven is the Reality that the Shadowlands figure forth. *The Great Divorce* presents a series of dialogues of "Ghosts" from hell (as they are called) being given an opportunity to enter heaven; while it does not describe Lewis's idea of what heaven looks like, it most emphatically asserts the reality and beauty of heaven. Here, faith becomes sight for a few of the "Ghosts" as they choose to enter heaven.

I have already mentioned the beatific vision at the end of *That Hideous Strength* in the discussion of communities of faith and hope in this life, and this community has millennial touches that suggest the full glorification of

---

32. Lewis, *Great Divorce*, x.
33. Lewis, *Great Divorce*, 19–20. Emphasis original.

heaven to come. The community of faith in this life spills over into beatific vision of the next life, in heaven.

Lewis brings these many motifs together at the end of the *The Last Battle*, which concludes the history of Narnia. There is a new heaven and a new earth brought into being; and all things finally fulfill the purpose of their creation—they praise Aslan. The conclusion of *The Last Battle* is both beatific and doxological. At the end of all things, the scene is set in a stable. Lucy remarks on how appropriate it is that things should end in a stable. She declares, "In our world, too, a stable once held something inside it that was bigger than our whole world."[34] Lucy connects the eschaton with the incarnation. Theologically, the incarnation of God in Jesus Christ of Nazareth began the redemption and restoration that would come in the eschaton, for in Christ God dwelled with men (John 1:14), and, because of that, he will redeem the whole creation at the end of things. Lucy's comment forms an *inclusio* to the whole series of Narnian tales, linking *The Magician's Nephew* with *The Last Battle* and framing all the other tales within them.

At the end of all things in Lewis's narrative, there is a new heaven and a new earth created over against the de-creation of Narnia going on outside the stable door. It is not so much a "new" Narnia in *The Last Battle* as it is "the real Narnia." Like the Professor in *The Magician's Nephew* before him, Lord Digory states to Lucy: "It's all in Plato, all in Plato."[35] This is a clear allusion to Plato's Cave. Everything is recognizable as "Narnia." The narrator elaborates, "The difference between old Narnia and the new Narnia was like that. The new one was a deeper country: every rock and flower and blade of grass looked as if it meant more. I can't describe it any better than that: if you ever get there you will know what I mean."[36] The "real Narnia" is where all the Narnians belong: "This is the Land I have been looking for all my life," the Unicorn cries, "though I never knew it till now."[37] Creation has been redeemed and restored, and it is now their proper and permanent home.

There is a new heaven at the end of things as well. In the final chapter of the book, "Farewell to Shadowlands," all the true Narnians enter into the eternal Narnia. Again, everything is recognizable, but now it is all changed. Everything is bigger; the Narnians can do superhuman feats such as swim up the Great Waterfall; all the dead Narnians are alive again; Reepicheep welcomes them home. Everything evil is undone, and everything good is eternal. Of course, the new earth and the new heaven are one and the

---

34. Lewis, *Last Battle*, 161.
35. Lewis, *Last Battle*, 195.
36. Lewis, *Last Battle*, 196.
37. Lewis, *Last Battle*, 196.

same—the real Narnia, the archetype of which the Shadowlands Narnia is the ectype. All of the Narnians' hopes from the earlier novels are realized in the real Narnia such that they no longer have to hope for and anticipate true joys. At the end of all things, faith becomes sight. They have arrived in their "true country."

It is not just the new earth and the new heaven that makes the new Narnia the real Narnia; it is Aslan who makes it so. Aslan is there, and everyone praises him. It is eternal doxology. Lucy senses it when Lord Digory tells her about the stable door, for "[s]he was drinking everything in more deeply than the others."[38] This is a fitting end for Lucy, for it was she who entered Narnia first, she who returned on the *Dawn Treader*, and now she who sees the real Narnia for what it is in truth. And it is Lucy who is the first to worship the risen Aslan in *The Lion, the Witch and the Wardrobe*. In the end, however, Lewis leaves it to Emeth—the last one to recognize Aslan for who he is as the Lord of lords and King of kings—to describe the risen and glorified Aslan. Emeth declares,

> The speed of him was like the ostrich, and his size was an elephant's; his hair was like pure gold and the brightness of his eyes like gold that is liquid in the furnace. He was more terrible than the Flaming Mountain of Lagour, and in beauty he surpassed all that is in the world even as the rose in bloom surpasses the dust of the desert. Then I fell at his feet.[39]

For the reader with the eyes of Saint John, this description of Aslan evokes worship and glory because it echoes the description of the risen and glorified Jesus Christ in the book of Revelation:

> Then I turned to see the voice that was speaking to me, and on turning I saw seven golden lampstands, and in the midst of the lampstands one like a son of man, clothed with a long robe and with a golden sash around his chest. The hairs of his head were white, like white wool, like snow. His eyes were like a flame of fire, his feet were like burnished bronze, refined in a furnace, and his voice was like the roar of many waters. In his right hand he held seven stars, from his mouth came a sharp two-edged sword, and his face was like the sun shining in full strength. (Rev 1:12–16)

---

38. Lewis, *The Last Battle*, 161.
39. Lewis, *The Last Battle*, 188.

Instantly, John falls at Jesus's feet and worships him—the proper response to such a being! So it is in the real Narnia; Emeth falls at Aslan's feet. It is "heaven" because Aslan is there, and he will never leave again.

## CONCLUSION: AN INVITATION TO GLORY

C. S. Lewis reminds readers in the twentieth and twenty-first centuries of a truth that premodern western people knew as part of their culture and we have largely forgotten today: we were created to worship God. Lewis encourages his readers to worship God again—that is, to put on the Christian mind. He invites them to accept that "weight of glory." Lewis embodies the heart of Christianity in this invitation, for the metanarrative of the Bible tells the same story: creation, fall, redemption, and re-creation. Lewis incarnates this metanarrative in his apologetics, his poetry, and his fiction. It is by developing a Christian mind that Lewis fulfills his role as worshiper.

For Lewis, the original creation is the normative mode of existence for human beings, in fellowship with each other and God. In this created condition, there was no need for longing to escape and go to heaven, no need for hope, for all things were as they should be. Lewis invites his readers in all of these books to participate in the glory of things as they were meant to be. In the fall into sin, however, humans were plunged into a pathological condition, producing a sense of exile because we were cut off from God and therefore long to be reunited with him. It is this undesirable state of sin and exile that forms the foundation of Lewis's apologetics and fiction. Our innate longing for a remedy finds expression in his novels, in the form of a pilgrimage, or quest—a journey that inherently incarnates longing and hope in its form and structure. This longing is for renewal of all that has been tainted by sin; it is a longing for a new life.

Lewis's fiction provides descriptions of this coming renewal, which begins with a sense of release from sin's effects. He expresses the sense of beginning a new and glorified life in heaven this way in *The Last Battle*:

> "There *was* a real railway accident," said Aslan softly. "Your father and mother and all of you are—as you used to call it in the Shadowlands—dead. The term is over: the holidays have begun. The dream is ended: this is the morning."
>
> And as He spoke He no longer looked to them like a lion; but the things that began to happen after that were so great and beautiful that I cannot write them. And for us this is the end of all the stories, and we can most truly say that they all lived happily ever after. But for them it was only the beginning of the real story. All their life in this world and all their adventures in

Narnia had only been the cover and the title page; now at last they were beginning Chapter One of the Great Story, which no one on earth has read, which goes on forever, in which every chapter is better than the one before.[40]

All of Lewis's writings encourage his readers to long for God and to hope for heaven; this is a central characteristic of the Christian mind. And it is fitting that this is so, for the longer we live in communion with Christ, the more we long to see him face to face. Lewis knew that longing well and his works form what I call in my title "an apologetic of hope."

I close this essay in a manner of which I think C. S. Lewis would approve. I offer an invitation to glory in the language of the apostle Paul's benediction to the Romans: "Now the God of hope fill you with all joy and peace in believing, that ye may abound in hope, through the power of the Holy Ghost" (Rom 15:13).

## BIBLIOGRAPHY

Augustine. *Confessions*. Translated by F. J. Sheed. Indianapolis: Hackett, 2006.

Chesterton, G. K. *As I Was Saying*. Grand Rapids: Eerdmans, 1985

Downing, David C. *Into the Region of Awe: Mysticism in C. S. Lewis*. Downers Grove: InterVarsity, 2005.

Farrer, Austin. "In His Image." In *Remembering C. S. Lewis*, edited by James Como, 383–86. San Francisco: Ignatius, 2005.

Lewis, C. S. *The Collected Letters of C. S. Lewis*, edited by Walter Hooper. 2 vols. New York: HarperCollins, 2004.

———. *The Great Divorce*. New York: HarperCollins, 2001.

———. *That Hideous Strength*. New York: Scribner, 1994.

———. *The Last Battle*. New York: Harper Trophy, 1994.

———. *Letters to Children*. New York: Scribner, 1996.

———. *The Magician's Nephew*. New York: Harper Trophy, 1994.

———. *Mere Christianity*. New York: HarperCollins, 2001.

———. *The Pilgrim's Regress*. Wade Annotated Edition. Edited and introduced by David C. Downing. Grand Rapids: Eerdmans, 2014.

———. *The Problem of Pain*. New York: HarperCollins, 2000.

———. *The Screwtape Letters*. New York: Simon & Schuster, 1996.

———. *The Silver Chair*. New York: Harper Trophy, 1994.

———. *Surprised by Joy: The Shape of My Early Life*. San Francisco: HarperOne, 2017.

———. *The Voyage of the Dawn Treader*. New York: Harper Trophy, 1994.

———. "The Weight of Glory." In *The Weight of Glory*, 25–46. New York: HarperCollins, 2001.

Martindale, Wayne. *Beyond the Shadowlands: C. S. Lewis on Heaven and Hell*. Wheaton: Crossway, 2005.

Palma, Robert J. "C. S. Lewis's Use of Analogy in Theological Understanding." In *Seven: An Anglo-American Literary Review* 22 (2005) 89–102.

---

40. Lewis, *Last Battle*, 210–11.

# 3

## "The Intolerable Compliment"

Desire and Love in *The Chronicles of Narnia*

### Elizabeth Travers Parker

MY FATHER LOVED TEACHING C. S. Lewis to undergraduates and graduate students. Himself a convert to Christ in much the same manner as Lewis, my dad believed that Lewis's stories and nonfiction could guide readers to important questions, moments of self-realization, and reckoning with the claims of Christ. Teaching Lewis was, for my father, pre-evangelism—presenting texts that could train the minds and hearts of students to think and love like Christ.

The heart of my father's attraction to Lewis's type of evangelism was, appropriately, its source in "the intolerable compliment" of God's love in the incarnation. The crucifixion saved my dad, and the incarnation "baptized his imagination." The incarnation of Christ provided everything my father needed as a Christian literary scholar and for the life of the Christian mind. It provided the aesthetic framework for the way he read and taught texts; it provided a reasonable and beautiful explanation for the significance of words; and it gave him a reason to read and teach imaginative fiction as a Christian "in wartime" when other defenses against attacks on Christianity might have been more highly prized. Most importantly, God the Father's extraordinary act of love in the eternal enfleshment of Jesus Christ taught my father—as it teaches every Christian believer—how to love, and he found that Lewis's imaginative fiction warmed his heart and drew him to the Beloved.

Because of his love for C. S. Lewis's writings, my father had long wanted to write a book on them, and when he passed away, he left behind a wealth of notes for teaching and writing. One of these items included a document in which he had sketched out a book entitled "'The Intolerable Compliment': Desire and Love in the Fiction of C. S. Lewis." The ideas and lines of thought are in their first stages, but there is an implicit and important argument embedded in them that I will pursue and extend: that Lewis's imaginative fiction is incarnational, mediating the divine act of love—kenosis—and inviting readerly participation in that divine love.

## "SEEING IN PLACE"

Lewis's "fairy stories" form his readers' habits of mind by forming their desires, teaching us what to love and how to be loved. In "On Three Ways of Writing for Children," Lewis identifies two types of longing when reading fantasy or fairy stories—one for wish-fulfillment, for the things that might become or "should" be true if we had a lucky break, and one for those things beyond reach, the desire for which makes all things more enchanted. The first Lewis calls a disease, and the second he calls *askesis*, or spiritual exercise.[1] Lewis does not explicitly elaborate on his choice of term, but the entire project of his essay is to show how fairy story does and can teach. It does not teach by moral but by image, and in this respect, Alan Jacobs's comparison of Lewis's term to the *Spiritual Exercises* of Ignatius of Loyola is apt.[2] Ignatius constructed the *Exercises* around intentional actions of the spiritual imagination in furnishing the mind's eye with the places where Jesus Christ lived and acted. As Jacobs notes, the "success of many of the *Exercises* depends on the mediator's ability to 'see in place,' to visualize a spiritual truth and thereby make it more real."[3] Likewise, Lewis repeatedly says that his fiction stories began with an image,[4] and while the image created the need for a plot, plot did not drive the story: the image did. Thus, the *Chronicles*, "with their elaborate complement of images, contribute to an *askesis*, a spiritual exercise. They are a kind of training in how to long, and what and whom to long for."[5] As training, or exercise, fairy story of the

---

1. Lewis, "On Three Ways," 30.
2. Jacobs, "*Chronicles of Narnia*," 278–79.
3. Jacobs, "*Chronicles of Narnia*," 278.
4. Lewis, "Fairy Stories May Say Best," 35.
5. Jacobs, "*Chronicles of Narnia*," 279.

kind that Lewis writes is deliberately pedagogical. Lewis has an educational project in mind when he writes, and his "teaching methods" are intricately connected with his vision of what literature *is*. What literature *is* to Lewis is, in turn, directly related to his beliefs about God in the world. In short, to read Lewis's fairy story in the *Chronicles* is to participate in a seamless moral, spiritual, intellectual, and literary world.

If we take Lewis's own description of fairy story, as well as Jacobs's comparison to the imaginative and contemplative work of the Ignatian *Spiritual Exercises*, we might then need to ask *how*. How do we read the *Chronicles* as *askesis*? How do the novels teach? What is the nature of the exercise for the reader? Again, Jacobs may be helpful. He points back to the images, which Lewis says are the only moral teaching tool he uses. But even these, Lewis argues, teach by reverberating with whatever spiritual chords have already been struck in the reader's life.[6] The image of the faun, the lion, and the witch "may be experienced simply as interesting or beautiful pictures . . . , [but] understood more deeply and fully . . . [they] contribute to an *askesis*."[7] To begin our spiritual training, we should start by contemplating the vivid, literary images that make Lewis's fairy stories come to life.

Alongside the iconic images of Aslan bounding into the story, Lucy wondrously stepping through the wardrobe, the lamppost in the snowy wood, and the faun taking tea, Lewis's fiction is known for its landscapes, and these are the images I want to contemplate. Each story in the *Chronicles* possesses a dominant sense of landscape, which contributes to the atmosphere and what Lewis would call the "theme" (imaginative vision) of the story.[8] In *The Lion, the Witch and the Wardrobe*, of course, this landscape is the white, wintry forest of Narnia. The landscape changes dramatically to spring as Aslan approaches, but while the landscape of spring dominates the *telos* of and the turn in the story, the winter landscape dominates the reader's imaginative first sight of Narnia and gives the story its sensibility. Similarly, *The Horse and His Boy* is dominated by hot, desert Calormen, and, again, while the story ends in Archenland, the "otherness" of Calormen (with regard to all that we know as "Narnian") governs the story's imaginative vision. Each of the seven books possesses a "ruling spirit," available in and incarnated by the landscapes. These landscapes, in turn, train readers in the transcendent.

---

6. Lewis, "On Three Ways," 33. Also referenced by Jacobs in "*Chronicles of Narnia*," 278.

7. Jacobs, "*Chronicles of Narnia*," 278.

8. Lewis, "On Stories," 18.

Michael Ward has likewise noted the presence of a "ruling spirit" in Lewis's Narnian world. In his blockbuster of literary criticism, *Planet Narnia*, he locates the "ruling spirit" of each story in Lewis's appropriation of the medieval cosmos. Ward attends to the range of imagery in the books, connecting each to one of the seven planets in medieval cosmology. In *The Lion, the Witch and the Wardrobe*, for example, he links to Jupiter, or Jove, foregrounding the restoration of joviality and rightful rule in the arrival of Aslan and the Sons of Adam and Daughters of Eve. The spirit of Jupiter, argues Ward, superintends the entire story.[9] He explicates the subsequent stories in the series similarly. At the end of his study, Ward gestures toward a more fundamental, theological narrative at work in Lewis's use of the cosmos. C. S. Lewis's fairy stories are not constructed, first, by a beloved and exquisite cosmology. This is one true narrative of many at work in the stories. Rather, Lewis presents "participatory deification . . . of the children in the divine nature" and a sophisticated Christology in which "Aslan . . . is not just incarnate as an identifiable, locatable character; he is also discarnate as the Word who sustains the cosmos of each romance."[10] Here, at the end of his study, Ward gestures toward the incarnational quality of Lewis's fiction, and I take up that conversation here, arguing that Lewis's fairy stories are constructed, first and foremost, to be incarnational and, as incarnational, they transpose the transcendent and ineffable into lower forms. If Lewis's cosmology is the "Deep Magic" of his fiction, then his incarnational poetics is the "Deeper Magic from Before the Dawn of Time."[11]

## INCARNATION AND TRANSPOSITION

Along with Ward, many other scholars have noted the centrality of Christ's incarnation in C. S. Lewis's thought, and my project is not to unseat them but to shade the outlines of the conversation. Peter Schakel notes Lewis's "moral imagination" in intentionally crafting his fiction not as fable—which ends with an explicit moral—but as fairy tale in which the universe itself is inherently moral and the images instruct implicitly rather than explicitly (as in "On Three Ways of Writing for Children").[12] For Schakel, the divine mysteries, like the incarnation, draw a line from Lewis's fiction to theological doctrine that provides the ground of moral events in the worlds he creates. Everything moral in Lewis's fictional universes can be traced back to the

---

9. Ward, *Planet Narnia*, 42–76.
10. Ward, *Planet Narnia*, 237.
11. Lewis, *Lion, Witch, and the Wardrobe*, 152–53.
12. Schakel, *Imagination and the Arts*, 175–76.

"embodiment" of "divine mysteries": sacrifice, selflessness, obedience, and so on.[13] As Lewis writes in *Miracles*,

> The central miracle asserted by Christians is the Incarnation. They say that God became Man. Every other miracle prepares for this, or exhibits this, or results from this. Just as every natural event is the manifestation at a particular place and moment of Nature's total character, so every particular Christian miracle manifests at a particular place and moment the character and significance of the Incarnation.[14]

Likewise, Gregory Wolfe scrutinizes Lewis's use of language in the Space Trilogy, arguing that language has the capacity to reunite the soul and the body, an activity that reflects the Incarnation.[15] Other writers, like James Como[16] and Thomas Werge,[17] emphasize the sacramental character of Lewis's secondary worlds, urging an emphasis on the "real presence" of the divine and, therefore, a literal participation in the same.[18] Regardless of emphasis, Lewis's specifically Christian view of literature's form and function begins and ends with the incarnation of Christ.

Lewis explains himself in his chapter on "Transposition" from *The Weight of Glory*, providing a philosophical and theological framework for understanding how landscapes, as a thoroughly natural entity in his fiction, can function as an "incarnational" literary device. In "Transposition," Lewis argues that there is a necessary continuity between the natural and the spiritual. Although this seems like a dilemma, for that would mean that there is nothing in language or emotion that "has not been borrowed from Nature,"[19] Lewis looks for a way to both defend the distinction be-

---

13. Schakel, *Imagination and the Arts*, 176.

14. Lewis, *Miracles*, 131.

15. Wolfe, "Language and Myth," 73.

16. In Como, *Branches to Heaven*, he refers to Lewis's "literary sacramentalism," which is quite close to the narrative mode I am trying to emphasize here (132). Lewis, he argues, thought that "the imagination, when kindled by a beam of sacramental longing, encounters holiness. That is its baptism; and that is precisely the 'dialectic of desire' that Narnia seems to occasion. With nothing less than our spiritual destiny at stake, its Joy calls us home" (130). Como concludes that the sacramentalism of the Narnian drama "mediates reality" and "compel[s] us to see and know by way of mediation" (134). Thus, they teach us not only how to interpret our own physical world (for "this world figures the next"), but they also instruct us in the very process by which such figuring occurs (134).

17. Werge, "Sanctifying the Literal," 76–85.

18. See also Payne, *Real Presence*.

19. Lewis, *Weight of Glory*, 95.

tween natural and spiritual *and* to account for the apparent collapse. The answer is found in what he calls "transposition," where the higher is "transposed" into the lower, and the lower, in turn, is incomprehensible without the higher. This activity is obvious, Lewis says, in the relationship between bodily sensation and emotion. The bodily sensation that we feel for joy is the same we feel in anguish. Bodily sensation, he concludes, is a lower form of expression—a language with fewer words—whereas emotion is a higher form of expression—a language with a richer, more precise lexicon. Emotional life, as richer and more varied than the life of bodily sensation, is three-dimensional, but its three-dimensionality is collapsed into the two-dimensional life of the body just as ideas are collapsed into words and the world around us is collapsed into a sketch or painting. Lewis, importantly, figures transposition as a kind of descent: the higher accommodates itself in the lower.

Lewis entertains three possible ways to interpret the descent of the higher into the lower: symbol, sacrament, and something beyond sacrament, which he does not name and which I am calling "incarnation." Lewis rejects symbol as a descriptor because it does not imply any necessary relationship between the sign and the signified. Written words, he says, are mere symbols of spoken words, and there is no necessary relationship between the sign and the sound. This is true for language, but what about images? Pictures represent by being a part of the world and by possessing a necessary relationship to the world. "If I had to name the relation," writes Lewis, "I should call it not symbolical but sacramental."[20] Lewis quickly qualifies his statement:

> But in the case we started from—that of emotion and sensation—we are *even further beyond mere symbolism* [emphasis mine]. For there, as we have seen, the very same sensation does not merely accompany, nor merely signify, diverse and opposite emotions, but becomes part of them. The emotion descends bodily, as it were, into the sensation and digests, transforms, transubstantiates it, so that the same thrill along the nerves *is* delight or *is* agony.[21]

The relationship between emotion and sensation exceeds the symbolic and the sacramental. One might use the term "transubstantiation," since Lewis himself uses it, but that risks potentially confusing and vexed conversations about the distinctions between "sacramental" and

---

20. Lewis, *Weight of Glory*, 102.
21. Lewis, *Weight of Glory*, 102–3.

"transubstantiation." Thus, I suggest that what Lewis reaches for here, and what he comes to later in the essay, is "incarnation."

As "incarnation," transposition makes possible the fulfillment of human nature, not the destruction of it. Although the fulfillment may feel very like destruction, says Lewis, "every negation will be only the reverse side of a fulfilling."[22] Fulfillment occurs when a preexisting "Spiritual Reality," as Lewis calls it, "gives [a] natural act a new meaning, and more than a new meaning: makes it in a certain context to be a different thing."[23] Lewis shows his Augustinianism quite plainly here. The spiritual precedes the natural, and when the human heart longs for eternity, it longs for something it has already known and still knows. The longing is an act of memory.[24] This same rule may apply to the incarnation of Christ, and Lewis draws a hesitant line to it before bowing his head to "the verdict of real theologians."[25] Transposition can give us no help in understanding or conceiving of the incarnation if it is merely symbol. However, if, as Lewis has argued, the Spiritual Reality gives new meaning, and even a new shape, to nature, then it might be helpful.

As Lewis transitions from his general discussion of transposition as a natural rule and into the theological, he shifts registers subtly but tellingly. Until this point in the essay, he has imagined transposition as an act of "descent" where higher, richer things accommodate themselves to the lower and simpler. When he speaks of the Incarnation of Christ, however, he speaks of it as an "ascent" in which the "lower reality can actually be drawn into the higher and become part of it. The sensation which accompanies joy becomes itself joy; we can hardly choose but say 'incarnates joy.'"[26] The higher may accommodate itself *in* the lower as a general rule, but if the incarnation has anything to do with transposition, then the lower may be *transformed* by being taken into the higher.[27]

Descent and ascent form the dynamic tension of love and desire at the heart of the incarnation of Christ. In the incarnation, says poet George Herbert,

---

22. Lewis, *Weight of Glory*, 109.
23. Lewis, *Weight of Glory*, 112.
24. See Augustine's *Confessions*, book 10, for his discourse on human memory.
25. Lewis, *Weight of Glory*, 113.
26. Lewis, *Weight of Glory*, 113.

27. The Athanasian Creed states that Christ is "One, not by the conversion of the godhead into flesh, but by taking of that manhood into God." C. S. Lewis knew the Athanasian Creed and uses it in *Reflections on the Psalms* (135) to defend the spiritual and biblical principle he earlier explicated in *The Weight of Glory* as "transposition."

> The God of power...
> Resolv'd to light[28]; and so one day
> He did descend, undressing all the way.[29]

Likewise, the apostle Paul writes in his letter to the Philippians that Christ "made himself of no reputation, and took upon him the form of a servant, and was made in the likeness of men: and being found in fashion as a man, he humbled himself and became obedient unto death" (Phil 2:7–8). Christ's descent is the great sacrifice, and in it he sets in motion the earthly course of his love for the creaturely. Descent is only half the internal movement of the incarnation, however. God descends in love to become man so that he might reascend, taking up human nature and placing it, in his own person, at the right hand of God. In ascent, Christ initiates and models the progress of the human soul in desire towards its maker. Thus, the incarnation of Christ is a double act of mediation, in which the divine nature is accommodated to humanity by being fully united to it and in which humanity is "taken up" to the presence of the divine.

## LANDSCAPE AND INCARNATION

Lewis's fairy story landscapes enact and embody this same dialectic of descent and ascent, love and desire. Their capability of doing so comes from Lewis's belief that the geography of the natural world communicates the ineffable.[30] The barren wastelands of Ettinsmoor, exotic Calormen, the long stretch of lonely islands in the Eastern Sea, the homely houses of the Beavers and Mr. Tumnus, Aslan's How—each carefully crafted landscape is a fitting and beautiful mark of a transcendent reality, instructing readers in the holy descent of divine love toward the creaturely in the incarnation and in the ascent of human desire to the divine. Nature is an appropriate vehicle for this activity because of the doctrine of creation: in the biblical account of creation, God spoke creation and the creaturely into being as an overflow of the divine self and divine love. All creation, as a "spoken" entity, functions as a contingent sign of God himself. He is both separate from nature and the ground of it. He is both transcendent and immanent. He both ascends from nature and descends to nature. By contemplating and attending to Lewis's landscapes in the *Chronicles*, readers' minds are instructed by a concerted effort of imagination (*askesis*) and a process of gradual revelation that draws readers into the experience of divine encounter available through the

---

28. Herbert likely means "alight" here.
29. Herbert, "Bag," ll. 9–12.
30. Lewis, *Reflections on the Psalms*, 76–89.

natural world via transposition. Thus, Lewis's landscapes in the *Chronicles* mimic the pedagogy of the revelation of God, in which "God communicates himself to man gradually,"[31] unveiling and incarnating the gospel story of alienation and reconciliation to God.

Landscapes exert great pressure on the human imagination. In the well-known boat-stealing scene from *The Prelude*, Wordsworth describes "a huge peak, black and huge," that "upreared its head" from "behind that craggy steep."[32] It seemed, to his boyish conscience in the darkness on the water, that the mountain "measured motion like a living thing" and "strode after me."[33] The image of the bigger peak emerging from behind an already monstrous crag feels heavy and foreboding. Wordsworth's sensation of being pursued is understandable given the massive weight of the peak and its sudden, incongruous movement from behind the crag in the dark. As several scholars have noted, Lewis participates in and modifies this Romantic idea of nature.[34] In "On Stories," he talks about the specificity of a story's excitement and sense. "*Jack the Giant-Killer* is not," writes Lewis, "in essence, simply a story of a clever hero surmounting danger. It is in essence the story of such a hero surmounting *danger from giants*. . . . The whole quality of the imaginative response is determined by the fact that the enemies are giants. That heaviness, that monstrosity, that uncouthness, hangs over the whole thing."[35] He compares this feeling to experiences he has had in nature, saying, "I have seen landscapes (notably in the Mourne Mountains) which, under a particular light, made me feel that at any moment a giant might raise his head over the next ridge. Nature has that in her which compels us to invent giants: and only giants will do."[36] That thing in nature "which compels us" is not a vague *anima mundi* but the particularity and distinct

---

31. *Catechism of the Catholic Church*, 53.
32. Wordsworth, *Prelude*, 1.377–80.
33. Wordsworth, *Prelude*, 1.384–85.
34. Carnell, *Bright Shadow of Reality*. Carnell considers the boat-stealing scene as an example of Wordsworth's ambivalence about the continuity of the spiritual and natural (16–17). Humanity "senses the divine but is separated from it also" because of its defects. Carnell's study traces the origins of Lewis's notion of *Sehnsucht* in Romanticism, as well as Lewis's own contribution to the theme in reenchanting it with the immanence of the divine.
35. Lewis, "On Stories," 8.
36. Lewis, "On Stories," 8.

inscape[37] of the Mourne Mountains or the wastes of Ettinsmoor or any such specific and coherent landscape.[38]

Far from separating the creaturely from the divine, the great force of nature's infinite particularity (the pressure "which compels"), draws creation and the creaturely into communion with the divine. Creation is both the outflow of divine love and the ladder of creaturely desire that leads to the divine. To follow this dialectic in Lewis's fairy tale landscapes, and for the sake of simplicity, I read the landscapes of the *Chronicles* within the narrative framework of exile, longing, and return. Narratives of exile draw readers into a descent, narratives of longing are experiences of ascent, and narratives of return implement both motions in a simultaneous counterpoint as the two are united in fulfillment. Exile, longing, and return also easily map onto the progression of Christ's incarnation and, I hope, clearly demonstrate the activity of transposition, its theological analogy in the incarnation, and its literary significance in fairy story and fantasy.

## THE LANDSCAPE OF EXILE: *PRINCE CASPIAN*

Exile can be both a spiritual condition of alienation and a physical condition of absence. In both cases, exile is a condition of privation and want when an absolute good—a place of belonging—is withheld or missing. Narratives of exile are characterized by chaos, wandering, and irresolution. Take, for instance, Homer's *Odyssey*. Odysseus's travels are a study in disorder. The plot itself is nonlinear, emphasizing the chaotic journey, and Odysseus and his men repeatedly demonstrate the want of order and of a fitting connection between character and place. Every place and landscape they encounter is a threat to peace and resolution: on Aeaea, Odysseus's men are transformed into pigs; in the land of the dead, Odysseus is beset by the shades of the dead begging for news of the living; on Thirinacea, the sailors invite the wrath of Zeus by slaughtering the cattle of the Sun; and so on the tale of woe goes. When Odysseus returns home, his house, land, and family are likewise in chaos, and peace is threatened. In disguise, he restores order, banishing

---

37. Gerard Manley Hopkins created and uses this term to describe the "landscape" of being—the unique design of an individual self. I borrow it here as a helpful shorthand with similar theological resonances as Lewis's own depiction of nature in his fiction.

38. In *Surprised by Joy*, Lewis writes that the stabs of joy he felt from his experiences with nature simply reminded him of his unnamable desire. He did not love nature with a "studious love," like "a botanist or an ornithologist" (78). Rather, he tells the reader that "it was the mood of a scene that mattered to me; and in tasting that mood my skin and nose were as busy as my eyes" (78). He finds that nature, like music and poetry and human love and everything else he tries, is simply a spark for Joy, not Joy's self or Joy's object.

Penelope's suitors and reestablishing his place in Ithaca. The reader's desire for consolation is piqued by Odysseus's ongoing exile and is fulfilled by Odysseus's return to and restoration of Ithaca. In narratives like this, readers experience disorientation and alienation in order to arrive at this desire for reconciliation and belonging. Stories where characters are absent from their homeland or are alienated from some kind of national, social, or spiritual history are both preparatory and painful, creating the space from which longing emerges.

*Prince Caspian* is one such story.[39] Rather than recounting ancient history from the beginning of the story, Lewis begins the action *in medias res*, only later using a key character, Trumpkin the dwarf, to recount the history of Narnia since the reign of the four Pevensie children. Lewis begins *in medias res* because the narrative form fits the narrative purpose: *Prince Caspian* is a story about history, the loss of history, the alienation from a national history, and the reconstruction of history. By embedding this history as a flashback narrative within a present and active narrative, Lewis recreates the act of history-making for readers.

This narrative strategy invites readers to experience the alienation of the Pevensie children upon returning to a Narnia hundreds, perhaps thousands, of years older than the one they left behind. The changed landscape of their beloved Narnia emphasizes their disorientation. Everything as they knew it has been changed beyond recognition. Readers know the Pevensies have reentered their favorite world because we are reading the *Chronicles of Narnia*, but the Pevensies do not. Readers experience this disjunction between our own assumptions and the character's disorientation forcefully in *Prince Caspian*. We know where we are, but at the same time, we inhabit the Pevensies' confusion with them, seeing the landscape through their eyes.

The altered landscape of Narnia alienates the Pevensie children from a place they consider "home." Their physical alienation from their homeland, as they remember it, imitates the pain of the soul's spiritual alienation as it remembers, often without words or pictures, that "here we have no lasting city" (Heb 13:14, ESV). This connection between the physical and the spiritual is not accidental in any of Lewis's post-conversion writing. Schakel clarifies that Lewis, after conversion, "regarded the ultimate purpose of the imagination—like that of romantic longing at the end of *Surprised by*

---

39. See Schakel, *Imagination and the Arts*, 70–88. Schakel argues that Lewis was preoccupied with the way readers experience stories. Good readers, Lewis thought, inhabit the stories they read. They leave themselves behind and immerse themselves in the world and craft of fiction. Writers bring readers along, positioning themselves and the reader along the way in the narrative so that the reader's experience of the unfolding story is coherent and enthralling.

*Joy*—as bringing one to a vision of God."[40] For Lewis, seeing the face of God required a spell in the Shadowlands, the lands of exile. [41]

As the Pevensies journey further into Narnia, they discover the ruins of an old castle and, adjacent, an ancient apple orchard. The narrative process Lewis constructs as the children piece together the evidence that this is *their* castle and apple orchard mimics the process of uncovering and reconstructing the past through memory—a pivotal activity of the soul in its progress toward the vision of God.[42] As noted, the landscape has sufficiently changed that the children do not immediately recognize the world they have entered as Narnia. They walk through the woods, to the inlet, up a stream, and find themselves in an overgrown orchard next to a ruinous stone wall. As they go, they piece together its history. Writes Lewis,

> [The children] all got up and began to follow the stream. It was very hard work. They had to stoop under branches and climb over branches, and they blundered through great masses of stuff like rhododendrons and tore their clothes and got their feet wet in the stream. . . . They panted up the steep bank, forced their way through the brambles, and found themselves standing round an old tree that was heavy with large yellowish-golden apples as firm and juicy as you could wish to see.[43]

The first sight of the apple tree—an image resonant of the life-giving apple tree in *The Magician's Nephew*—comes after some difficulty. Their way through the brambles contrasts to the magical wonder of their entrance, hundreds of Narnian years earlier, through the wardrobe door. Rather than an incredulous, wonder-filled entrance to a land of exquisite (although perilous) snow, the children "blunder," "pant," and "force" their way through

---

40. Schakel, *Imagination and the Arts*, 22.

41. See Daigle-Williamson, *Reflecting the Eternal*. The influence of Dante on Lewis is profound, and the Beatific Vision forms a crucial part of reading Lewis's fictional landscapes, especially through the lens of exile, longing, and return.

42. Como also recognizes the importance of this particular section from *Prince Caspian* in an understanding of Lewis's personal brand of literary sacramentalism. In this scene, argues Como, the children "perfectly exemplify the symbolic importance of the fantasy protagonist." The children and the reader have to learn to see "theogonically," that is to recognize that "they are gods—or angels—once again and know themselves as such." Thus, the children exemplify that living itself "is an interpretive, critical enterprise." See Como, *Branches to Heaven*, 136. While I agree with the fundamental claims Como is making here, I clarify, and thus extend, his argument here by asking for more specifics: What does Lewis use to reify this interpretive process? What is the goal and nature of this process for the children and, by extension, the reader?

43. Lewis, *Prince Caspian*, 9–10.

the wild, overgrown landscape. The wildness of this landscape is less pastoral than ominous, a reminder that Narnia is not a land at ease or at peace.

The Pevensies's ability to read the riddle of the ancient ruins and the landscape correctly comes from their past in Narnia and their years walking the footprint of Cair Paravel day after day. They, very unconsciously, comprehend the unique relationship between the landscape and the ruins because they have already known this place as home. While surveying the apple tree, Edmund and Susan are the first to recognize that they are looking at an orchard from "long, long ago, before the place went wild and the wood grew up." Still not recognizing where they are, the children push through a large apple tree, breaking some of the branches, and through an arch in the stone wall. "In here," writes Lewis, "there were not trees, only level grass and daisies, and ivy, and grey walls. It was a bright, secret, quiet place, and rather sad."[44] The children again emerge, this time not from the wild wood to an overgrown apple orchard, but from an apple tree and an archway to a green space, enclosed by ancient walls. Here the chapter ends, rather abruptly, as the children stretch their limbs. Lewis disrupts the narrative flow with two strokes: the change in scenery from dense overgrowth to a garden-like space and the quick end to the chapter. The disruption signals a change, both in the landscape and in the narrative. The children have not just emerged into a garden, they have turned an important narrative corner in their attempt to reconstruct the history of the place they are exploring: the children recognize the garden as a courtyard and, thus, what they are exploring as a ruined castle. A passing traveler at such a ruin would struggle to piece together the footprint. Half walls, missing roofs, crumbling or absent doorways, overgrown weeds, and underbrush would all conspire to hide the purpose of each walled segment. A traveler with more imagination and history would have better success. A traveler with firsthand knowledge would quickly and instinctively know how to read the ruins.

The landscape of occupied Narnia, ruinous and overgrown, invites the reader to participate, with the children, in an act of recovery. Acts of recovery are acts of love.[45] Thus, the landscape of Narnia at the beginning of *Prince Caspian* both incarnates the motion of love in exile and recovery

---

44. Lewis, *Prince Caspian*, 11.

45. See McGrath, *Intellectual World of C. S. Lewis*, 13–14. McGrath finds resonances with the medieval practice of *ars memorativa* in Lewis's autobiography, *Surprised by Joy*. He points to Dante as one of the finest practitioners of this genre in the *Vita Nuova*. Dante's masterpiece "concerns the retrieval and transformation of memory, offering a means by which the retrieval of the past acts as a key to unlock the meaning of the pilgrimage of life" (13). McGrath rightly locates the origin of this high art in Augustine's *Confessions*.

and echoes the incarnation itself in Christ's self-imposed exile to recover creation. Exile creates the space from which desire emerges, just as desire emerges from an experience with love.

The incarnation is the manifestation, or revelation, of God's love. For Lewis, the love of God toward his people was a full-fledged love and not a cheap sentimentality.[46] Sentiment, or what Lewis calls "a senile benevolence," is superficial. It is pleased with the loved one and makes much of his or her lovable qualities. Sentimentality, or indiscriminate benevolence in Lewis's terms, has no purpose outside of its own expression. It is often its own justification, though sometimes it seeks personal gain or pleasure in praising the beloved. To be sure, the object of such affection may become vain when he or she basks in the sentiment shown. Either way, the result is not pretty.

Love, on the other hand, places the object of affection first and wants the best for the person loved. Because this kind of love wants the best for the beloved, it is a paradoxical love. It wishes what is the appropriate "best" for the beloved, which is nothing short of his or her perfection. Such perfection is not always easily attained. This kind of love, which finds its supreme expression in God's *agape* love for his people, is not satisfied with mere sentiment and appreciation of lovable qualities; rather, this kind of love loves enough to want the beloved to reach his or her full potential.

In *The Problem of Pain*, Lewis uses several analogies for God's love for his people. Lewis compares this kind of divine love to a man's love for a dog in that the man wishes to make the dog more lovable. The dog must change if it is to respond to the love the man offers it.[47] Lewis then speaks of this love in a biblical image—namely, the love of a father for his son in that it teaches the loved one obedience. God is the father, we are the sons—and we learn to love by obeying. Again, the father's loving guidance of the son requires changes in the son's character if he is to become what he was intended to be.[48] A third analogy Lewis uses is another biblical analogy, and that is the love of a man for his wife. A man loves his wife so completely that he wishes her to become all that she was made to be.[49] In the language of Paul's Epistle to the Ephesians, this kind of love perfects the beloved so she has no impurities or imperfections. God *will* make his people holy. The common ground in all these analogies is that love—God's love—changes

---

46. This sentence begins a section adapted from Michael Travers's unpublished notes for a study on love in C. S. Lewis's writings.

47. Lewis, *Problem of Pain*, 35.

48. Lewis, *Problem of Pain*, 36–37.

49. Lewis, *Problem of Pain*, 37–39.

the beloved for the better. It does not leave the beloved the way he was to begin with; rather, it perfects the beloved so that he is more fully what he was made to be. God's love is not sentimental benevolence; it is a sanctifying love, a recovery, that will bring us to heaven, our final home in any event.[50] This recovery, reenacted by characters and readers in *Prince Caspian*, points forward to fulfillment in a return, a homecoming.

## THE LANDSCAPE OF LONGING:
### *THE VOYAGE OF THE DAWN TREADER*

In the gap between exile and return lies longing. Longing emerges from an experience of loving or being loved. Sometimes the two may be so interconnected as to be indistinguishable. At other times, the two related events may be separated by a great span of time. In either case, longing contains within it both that which looks backward with the eye of memory to an almost unconsciously remembered moment of love and that which looks forward with the eye of hope to an anticipated moment of union or reunion. Hence, scholars studying Lewis's interpretation of *Sehnsucht* (which he translates as "Joy") often refer to its relationship to the English word "nostalgia."[51] While "nostalgia" does not give full access to the richness of the German word, it does allow access to the kind of bittersweetness and melancholy that emerge from an experience with "Joy." Carnell defines *Sehnsucht* as a "sense of separation from what is desired, that longing which always points beyond."[52] Carnell draws this definition from his synthesis of Lewis's many thoughts on the subject, but one particular definition from Lewis himself seems to echo loudly in Carnell's definition: in *Surprised by Joy*, Lewis writes that *Sehnsucht* is an "unsatisfied desire which is itself more desirable than any other satisfaction."[53] From these two descriptions, the defining characteristics of *Sehnsucht* seem to be that the experience of desire produces a desire for itself and that desire magnifies the sense of separation from the desired. The one who desires finds himself or herself on a "compulsive quest, which brings with it both fleeting joy and the sad realization that one is yet separated from what is desired."[54] *Surprised by Joy* tells the story of Lewis's realization that Joy itself is not the object. Although he spent his early life longing for repeated experiences of Joy, thinking that repetition would satisfy the desire,

---

50. This ends the section adapted from Michael Travers's unpublished notes.
51. For one, see Carnell, *Bright Shadow of Reality*, 15.
52. Carnell, *Bright Shadow of Reality*, 23
53. Lewis, *Surprised by Joy*, 17–18
54. Carnell, *Bright Shadow of Reality*, 22.

he recognizes that the experience is by nature unsatisfiable. It must always point not just beyond but beyond itself. "All Joy reminds," writes Lewis. "It is never a possession, always a desire for something longer ago or further away or still 'about to be.'"[55] The longing for union and reunion takes the form of a quest, with Love itself as the object.

Narratives of longing are usually characterized by physical or spiritual journeys, and they are most often about the journey itself, not necessarily its accomplishment. While the reader expects consolation in the successful completion of the quest, the reader's sense of the story is shaped by the line of yearning drawn out in the journey. Because longing is often imagined as a quest or journey, it is innately connected to geography and, thus, to landscape. Whether physical or spiritual, journeys progress—that is, they depend upon forward motion—and they progress linearly—that is, along a horizontal line of space and time. Even stories that chart a figurative journey, whether by allegory, symbol, or some other literary framework, do so along a horizontal plane, charting a geography of the soul or mind if not of the physical land. Likewise, these quests often take place between "worlds." They occur along borders and within hinterlands—the "negative spaces" on maps, like wildernesses, unnamed or remote territories, and seas. Because they take place away from domestic or "civilized" spheres, they also tend to be lyrical, blurring the line between prose fiction of event and poetic language of experience.[56]

*The Voyage of the Dawn Treader* fits this description neatly: the title itself points to the matter of the story, the journey, and the journey takes place in a ship upon the sea. It progresses along a linear plane, laid out for the reader via a series of geographical markers, but it also incarnates a spiritual journey of ascent, compressing the two planes into one. The journey has a *telos*, especially for Reepicheep, but that end is nebulous for most of the story, and the matter of the story itself does not necessarily depend upon a clearly defined, hard-edged object. For all the passengers on the *Dawn Treader*, the journey across the landscapes of the novel—the sea and its islands—prefigures devotional experience in the process of *theosis*.[57] Readers

---

55. Lewis, *Surprised by Joy*, 78.

56. Carnell sketches a brief history of the literature of longing in the early chapters of *Bright Shadow of Reality*. To his list of examples, I would also list *Moby Dick* and *The Rime of the Ancient Mariner* as two of the finest examples in all of literature and a perfect blend of lyricism, journey, melancholy, and, even, ecstasy.

57. *Theosis* refers to the Eastern Orthodox doctrine of deification (becoming like God) via the three stages of purgation, illumination, and union with God. Scholars debate the extent to which Lewis believed in a kind of deification of believers, and Lewis makes several statements in *Mere Christianity* and *The Weight of Glory* that might be read as such. Here I use the term to point to a progressive spiritual process of union

and characters ascend by means of purgation and illumination—terror and joy—as they progress across the landscapes.

The *Voyage* initiates the devotional experience by inviting readers to a threshold from which desire emerges. The story takes place upon the sea, and it begins along a border. Like four of the other Narnia stories,[58] the events in Narnia are framed by brief events in this world. The *Voyage* is also literally encased in a frame. The children enter Narnia through a framed painting of a ship hanging in Lucy's bedroom at her aunt and uncle's house. At the beginning of the story, while still in this world, Lucy and Edmund talk about returning to Narnia. They long to repeat a remembered experience of the Joy they felt during visits to their once and future kingdom. "The question is," Edmund says, "whether it doesn't make things worse, *looking* at a Narnian ship when you can't get there."[59] Their reverie is interrupted by Eustace, who priggishly teases them about the picture and for talking about Narnia. Lucy likes the picture, she tells Eustace, because "the ship looks as if it was really moving. And the water looks as if it was really wet. And the waves look as if they were really going up and down."[60] The tangibility of the scene stirs something in Lucy that she calls Narnia.

The picture of the ship, with its prow shaped like a dragon and its square sail, provokes an unsatisfiable desire in the pair, but the two have no power to satisfy this desire. Aslan alone possesses that power. There are hints, however, that the longing of the children has a great deal to do with their response to Aslan's call. In *The Silver Chair*, for example, Aslan tells Jill, "you would not have called to me if I had not been calling to you."[61] Although *The Silver Chair* was written after and takes place after the *Voyage*, Aslan's statement to Jill reverberates back across this scene as Lucy and Edmund gaze yearningly at the painting. Their act of memory is also an act of hope, both emphasizing the divide between worlds and reaching forward in response to Aslan's call. By nesting the Narnia events within external events, and framing them so self-consciously, Lewis narratively enacts the displacement characteristic of longing and establishes a threshold, or border,

---

with God that occurs throughout the devotional experience of this life. This devotional experience is comprised of periods of purgation and illumination, to be sure. To use the term "sanctification" instead would be to lose the importance of "union" in Lewis's conception of the spiritual life.

58. Lewis, *Magician's Nephew*; Lewis, *Lion, the Witch and the Wardrobe*; Lewis, *Prince Caspian*; and Lewis, *Silver Chair*. *The Horse and His Boy* and *The Last Battle* are the only two stories that begin with events in Narnia.

59. Lewis, *Voyage of the Dawn Treader*, 4.

60. Lewis, *Voyage of the Dawn Treader*, 6.

61. Lewis, *Silver Chair*, 19.

from which longing extends forward throughout the narrative.[62] With this, Lewis also reenacts the Christian longing for a return to and union with the Father. The reality that frames Narnia in the novels is itself framed by a deeper reality, a narrative embodiment of the frame of Christian devotional experience.

Two landscapes dominate the voyage: the sea and the islands. The Eastern Sea draws the voyagers on and on into the unknown. Readers and characters alike experience the suspense of the sea's emptiness—its opaque surface, forbidding depths, and tracklessness. The sea, too, is unchartable without the sun, moon, and stars, and in order to stay on course, Drinian, the ship's captain, must look up to them, not ahead to the next invisible island. Thus, with no sense of what is ahead of them, readers and voyagers are drawn on from island to island, scattered junctures of both testing and delight.

The journey is episodic and lateral, a fictional incarnation of the process of *theosis*. Although the primary motion of longing, as an expression of desire, is ascent towards the numinous, longing also occurs laterally in the physical journey of the *Dawn Treader*, transforming into physical ascent only at the finish when Reepicheep is caught up at the World's End. Rather than a Dantean ascent through a physical hierarchy of realms, Lewis reenacts the devotional experience as a lateral progression across a plane.[63] While spiritual longing draws the soul upward to the divine in an ascent, the voyager experiences this ascent as a lateral progression punctuated by intense moments of joy and, sometimes, terror. Both sensations inform one another: Joy is shaped by terror and terror by joy.

Each of the islands communicates joy or terror to the travelers to varying degrees, some more intensely than others and some in equal mixture. However, the visit to the Dark Island, "where dreams come true," is the clearest moment of terror in the story, and the visit to Ramandu's Island is the clearest moment of Joy, until the voyagers reach the sweet waters of the Utter East. The visit to the Dark Island tests the courage and fortitude of the ship's inhabitants, incarnating the "dark night of the soul" in the land

---

62. The other four framed stories in the series follow this same pattern. The character of that nostalgia and longing may be different, but its end is the same. As for the two unframed stories, Lewis uses different narrative techniques to draw out longing. In *The Horse and His Boy*, he uses speech—the high speech of chivalric romance for the Narnians and the vivid, courtly speech of Middle Eastern nobility for the Calormenes—and in *The Last Battle* he uses parody and inversion, which I discuss later.

63. See Simon, "On Love," 155. Simon notes the difference between the "intricate hierarchical structure of Dante's hell, purgatory and heaven compared with the flatness of Lewis's hell and heaven" (155). Lewis's hell and heaven in *The Great Divorce* are, rather, characterized by distance rather than by hierarchy.

itself. The landscape of the Dark Island is virtually unknown, except that it seems mountainous. Otherwise, it is shrouded in a thick, black mist that makes it impossible for the characters to see the island's geography. The blackness of the Dark Island intensifies the uncertainty of the sea voyage. Yet, the blackness is not empty. Instead, the darkness of the island suffocates the voyagers with dread and despair. Lord Rhoop, whom they rescue in his desperate attempt to escape the island, is a "broken man," a poignant image of a crushed spirit. Lewis's images purposefully invite readers to elide the crushing darkness and the crushed spirit of Lord Rhoop. To modify one of Lewis's statements, there is that in the landscape of the Dark Island which compels us to invent nightmares.

On the other hand, the visit to Ramandu's Island consoles readers and characters at a similarly crucial juncture, just as the voyagers begin to think they will never reach the end of the journey and just as uncertainty weighs heaviest on them. Interestingly, Lewis tells readers very little about the geography of Ramandu's Island, yet the island is no less evocative than the others and certainly more evocative than some. He tells readers that the travelers proceed into the heart of the island along a "level valley," but that there is no road, just "fine springy turf dotted here and there with a low bushy growth which Edmund and Lucy took for heather."[64] The only other details we know about the island are the sleepers, the stone table, and the hill from which Ramandu emerges. However, the landscape is dominated by the numinous because it harbors a magic that seems both deadly and desirable. Until the travelers meet Ramandu, for example, they question the safety of the food spread out on the table: did this food possess some magic enchantment that sent these men into a deep, unending sleep? Ramandu allays their fears, offering perfect rest in two forms: dreamless, healing sleep and a daily, magically renewed feast. Here, Ramandu the star, himself daily renewed, provides travelers with the two commodities they most need to soothe their minds and restore their bodies from the trials of the journey. Yet, despite this consolation, Ramandu also heightens the sense of the unfamiliar, ancient magic that pervades the island. This is a strange and unknown place, a fitting occupant of the world's farthest extremity. It is a place both immediately compelling and beyond what the voyagers have yet known.

Joy and terror accompany one another in Lewis's notion of *Sehnsucht*. Longing "stirs and troubles [the reader] . . . with a dim sense of something beyond his reach and, far from dulling or emptying the actual world, gives it a new dimension of depth."[65] Aslan embodies the joy and terror of longing:

---

64. Lewis, *Voyage of the Dawn Treader*, 165.
65. Lewis, "On Three Ways," 29–30.

he is at once playful and majestic, comforter and king, utterly necessary and completely unsafe. As the Beavers tell the four Pevensies in *The Lion, the Witch and the Wardrobe*, "Who said anything about safe? 'Course he isn't safe. But he's good."[66] Likewise, Orual, in *Till We Have Faces*, trembles as the god approaches:

> Each breath I drew let into me new terror, joy, overpowering sweetness. I was pierced through and through with the arrows of it. I was being unmade. I was no one. . . . The earth and stars and sun, all that was or will be, existed for his sake. And he was coming. The most dreadful, the most beautiful, the only dread and beauty there is, was coming.[67]

Terror arises from a sense of alienation from the divine, the unknowability of the journey's end, and the dread weight of divine glory; joy arises from the growing awareness that the unknowable is also the uncontainable, the irresistible, and the inexorable. Thus, the great cost of alienation from the Father is also the consolation, the motivation that propels his creatures towards him.

## THE LANDSCAPE OF RETURN: *THE LAST BATTLE*

If Lewis's landscapes of exile perform an act of recovery (using a narrative "descent in love") and his landscapes of longing perform the devotional experience (using a narrative "ascent by desire"), how do his landscapes perform the natural act of return and union that should fulfill love and desire? How does Lewis transmute love and desire, descent and ascent, into union? To answer these questions, we must turn to the final story in the *Chronicles*: *The Last Battle*. While each story in the series enacts this pattern of exile, longing, and return, or union, in microcosm, the macrocosmic arc of the stories is resolved in *The Last Battle*, making it the best place to start for an ending to this study.

*The Last Battle* incarnates the activity of return and union using a surprising narrative device: parody and inversion. As I have demonstrated, Lewis's narrative devices shape readerly action: in *Prince Caspian*, the story begins *in medias res*, calling readers to an act of historical recovery; in *The Voyage of the Dawn Treader*, Lewis uses a framing technique that self-consciously calls readers to the devotional process of *theosis*. In *The Last*

---

66. Lewis, *Lion, the Witch and the Wardrobe*, 75–76.
67. Lewis, *Till We Have Faces*, 307.

*Battle*, parody and inversion invite readers to participate in the unmaking of Narnia and, paradoxically, the final union of love and desire.

Parody subverts and conceals its object and in so doing presents an inverted version of that object. As a result, parody is a process of unmaking. This approach fits the content of *The Last Battle* because it is, at first, a story of destruction—the destruction of creaturely relationships, a kingdom, and eventually an entire world. *The Last Battle* parodies and inverts the established laws and characteristics of the Narnia Lewis shaped in the previous six books, especially the fundamental law of Narnia, freedom. The law of freedom undergirds Aslan's creation of Narnia in *The Magician's Nephew* and governs creaturely relationships throughout the series, including the commerce between creatures and the land: Lewis's landscapes possess agency, making them participants in the freedom granted to the creatures by Aslan in *The Magician's Nephew*. This story charts the slow unraveling of freedom, both for creatures and for the landscapes, as Shift the Ape exploits and manipulates it for his own end.

Shift the Ape wreaks a havoc on Narnia unlike any other. Narnians have endured internal threats and external threats, but they have never encountered as subtle an evil as Shift. Shift's project of unmaking begins in the first chapter when he and Puzzle the Donkey find a lion skin floating in Caldron Pool. Shift convinces Puzzle to put on the lion skin, turning the donkey into a parody of Aslan. As the story progresses, Puzzle's hapless performance as Aslan is not, as Shift promised him, innocent and well-meaning. Instead, it maliciously uses Aslan's character and power against the Narnian creatures, inverting all their known history and beliefs about him. Twice characters express a desire to have died before they witnessed the return of Aslan because, they say, he has turned out to be much different from what they were taught to believe. Shift strikes at the root of Narnian belief—their established and inherited tradition—by remaking it for his own ends. Likewise, Shift unmakes Narnian law and order. He dresses himself in fine clothing, parodying the Daughters of Eve and Sons of Adam, the rightful rulers of Narnia. He insists that he is a man, not an ape, claiming his right to speak for Aslan as one of the humans Aslan ordained to care for and steward the world he created. Shift's unmaking is total, extending to all other realms of created order: he turns work into slavery, freedom into fear, and enemies into friends.

Shift's project to unmake Narnia is apparent in the startling transformation of the landscape under his new brand of economy and rule. The first landscape in the story is, as mentioned, Caldron Pool, on the very western edge of Narnia. Caldron Pool reminds readers of the woodland pools between the worlds in *The Magician's Nephew*. These pools between the worlds were portals from one place to the next, and through one of these Jadis, the White Witch, entered Narnia before it began. Caldron Pool, too, becomes a portal of sorts. Situated on the western border, the pool collects the water that pours down from the mountains beyond the Western Wild. A waterfall "keeps the pool always dancing and bubbling and churning round and round as if it were on the boil."[68] Puzzle the Donkey pulls the lion skin from this pool, setting in motion the chain of events that begin on the farthest western border of Narnia and work their way in to its very center.

Shift's new economy then extends to the woods along the Lantern Waste, recalling Lucy's first entry into Narnia in *The Lion, the Witch and the Wardrobe* and Digory's tree in *The Magician's Nephew*. Again, however, Lewis inverts his original narrative as the Lantern Waste is, literally, laid waste. The Dryad who arrives to tell King Tirian the news dies in front of him as someone far away in the wood fells her tree. In rage, Tirian and Jewel the Unicorn leave for the Lantern Waste to confront this evil. As they arrive, they see a ghastly sight:

> When they had reached the top of it [the rise] they could see right into Lantern Waste itself. And the King's face turned white when he saw it. Right through the middle of that ancient forest—that forest where the trees of gold and of silver had once grown and where a child from our world had once planted the Tree of Protection—a broad lane had already been opened. It was a hideous lane like a raw gash in the land, full of muddy ruts where felled trees had been dragged down to the river. There was a great crowd of people at work, and a cracking of whips, and horses tugging and straining as they dragged at the logs.[69]

Lewis describes the land like a body. The land stretches out, prostrate and wounded. As if to underscore the land's embodiment, Lewis invokes the wounded bodies of the whip-driven horses, their backs no doubt bearing furrows like the muddy ruts in the land. In contrast to the wounded land and creatures, Lewis recalls the Tree of Protection, now seemingly ineffective and perhaps even itself now felled.

The crucifixion of the Narnian landscape, to use a deliberately provocative word, initiates and incarnates fulfillment. Although the land is slowly and steadily being destroyed by Shift's new economic program of progress, Lewis renarrates this destruction as fulfillment by turning parody itself inside out. Although Shift, Puzzle, and the Calormene slave-drivers mock the

---

68. Lewis, *Last Battle*, 2.
69. Lewis, *Last Battle*, 20–21.

fundamental laws of Narnia, Lewis, again, sets a deeper magic to work, and what seems like destruction becomes, in Aslan's hands, transformation.

Aslan completes the unmaking of Narnia, transforming destruction into fulfillment and union. Unlike Shift, Aslan possesses the authority to end the world he created. In chapter 14, "Night Falls on Narnia," Lewis writes that the whole land is covered in darkness and all that can be seen are shapes of trees, the stars above, and another looming, growing black shape—the outline of Father Time, whom Jill and Eustace had seen below ground in *The Silver Chair*. Strikingly, everything in this scene is observed only in negative. The onlookers only know that trees exist and that Father Time has raised his horn because these shapes obliterate the stars, the only light available. The only contrast is between darkness and deeper darkness, not even between light and shadow. Although the land is preternaturally dark, it deepens as the sky loses its stars. "Immediately the sky became full of shooting stars," writes Lewis. "Even one shooting star is a fine thing to see; but there were dozens, and then scores, and then hundreds, till it was like silver rain: and it went on and on."[70] Left behind is not just darkness, which is a something, but "simply emptiness,"[71] a nothing. This encroaching emptiness does not strike the characters or the reader with fear. Aslan is not performing a violence upon the land. Instead, he is performing an act of collection, gathering the exiles together and to himself. Writes Lewis, "All the stars were falling: Aslan had called them home."[72] Narnia has been unmade, and in its unmaking it has become what it always was: a shadow of the real Narnia.

The landscape of the New Narnia completely inverts the mockery that Shift had made of Aslan and Narnia. It also completes the narrative we have been considering in this study, fulfilling the longing evoked by the journey in *The Voyage of the Dawn Treader* and giving back to Narnia its history, like an exile returning home. However, true to transposition, Lewis does not merely return Narnia's exiles to their home and give them their three wishes. Instead, the landscape of the New Narnia in *The Last Battle* shows longing and exile transmuted into something far greater. In the New Narnia, the land draws the characters "further up and further in" in an eternal ingress and ascent. The movement of the characters in the New Narnia is both lateral, as it was in *The Voyage of the Dawn Treader*, and vertical. The spiritual ascent of desire in *The Voyage of the Dawn Treader*, compressed to a lateral physical plane because of its role as an image of the devotional experience *in life*, is

---

70. Lewis, *Last Battle*, 150.

71. Lewis, *Last Battle*, 151.

72. Lewis, *Last Battle*, 151.

transmuted into an eternal and eternally fulfilling vertical ascent into the layers and up the heights of the New Narnia. Likewise, one of the greatest delights of the New Narnia to the characters is the discovery that the land is their remembered home, but somehow more so. Far from the experience of the four Pevensies reentering Narnia in *Prince Caspian*, piecing together the land's puzzle in an attempt to recover a long-lost history, the characters in *The Last Battle* find the landscape changed not *beyond* recognition but *into* recognition as they ascend the interior layers of the New Narnia. In *The Last Battle*, as in *The Great Divorce*, Lewis imagines spiritual restoration and union with God as eternally fulfilling desire—we perpetually ascend and perpetually arrive at union with God while he perpetually descends in loving union with us.

Readers participate in the unmaking and transformation of Narnia in *The Last Battle* by reading the story *through* the others. The events of *The Last Battle* become comprehensible in light of the previous six books because they first invert them then transmute them. Thus, we read the text beneath the text—the work of Aslan underneath the parody of Shift and Puzzle—as we read the hand of Providence. Readers are pulled into an act of trust and contemplation, an act of collection, as we see the events of the previous six novels come to fruition and raise our own love of Narnia to a kind of spiritual sight beyond itself. As a result, Lewis is able to create a sense of the story he has told in the *Chronicles* as a perpetual one, drawing us "further up and further in" to the narratives we have loved and, now, love more.

## "THE INTOLERABLE COMPLIMENT"

Lewis's fairy story landscapes reenact and embody the incarnational dialectic of descent and ascent via self-conscious transposition. The altered landscape of Narnia in *Prince Caspian* transposes Christ's self-imposed descent in the incarnation, inviting readers to participate, narratively, in the act of exile and recovery. By placing characters and readers into the story *in medias res*, Lewis summons them to reconstruct both story and landscape, activating memory and recovering a long-lost history. *The Voyage of the Dawn Treader* transposes Christ's bodily ascent, in which he carries human nature up to God, leading readers to participate, narratively, in the act of longing and *theosis*. Here, readers and characters undergo a separation, through the narrative framing device, and progression, through fleeting, episodic spots of joy and terror, reenacting the ascent of the Christian soul in unsatisfied desire for God. *The Last Battle* transposes the final compression of these dual motions in Christ's eternal relationship with the Father, drawing readers to participate in an act of union with, and return to, God. Through parody and inversion, readers partake in the final unmaking and transformation of the Narnian landscape.

Thus, Lewis's fairy stories for children resist teaching by moral or by example. Instead, his images and narrative choices incarnate the motions of divine love and human desire, requiring readers to participate actively in the telling of the tale. In this activity, our practices shape our thinking and our loves. As in the Ignatian *Spiritual Exercises*, the formation of spiritual habits orders the Christian mind and affections rightly: "just as taking a walk, traveling on foot, and running are physical exercises, so is the name of spiritual exercises given to any means of preparing and disposing our soul to rid itself of all its disordered affections and then, after their removal, of seeking and finding God's will in the ordering of our life for the salvation of our soul."[73] Lewis's fairy stories likewise form habits through narrative and readerly practice, and as they are formed, readers learn what to love and how to be loved. Landscapes like those explored in *Prince Caspian, The Voyage of the Dawn Treader*, and *The Last Battle* cultivate certain habits of the heart as readers patiently piece together the altered terrain of Narnia, embark hopefully on an unknown journey across a blank sea, or trust in the goodness of Aslan as the whole Narnian countryside is turned inside out.

Lewis deliberately chose fairy story as the *literary* landscape within which to set his adventures. If landscapes define the mood, setting, and the form of events in a story, then genres, as literary landscapes, do the same for story itself. Lewis's conscious choice of an old form of storytelling more commonly associated with nurseries than universities gives his stories a certain shape and a certain porousness. Lewis writes that the images in his mind seemed to demand a form that excluded "close psychology." Fairy story, he says, does this. The form of fairy story, explains Lewis, is characterized by "its brevity, its severe restraints on description, its flexible traditionalism, its inflexible hostility to all analysis, digression, reflections and 'gas.'"[74] At its best, continues Lewis, the fantastic mode "can do more; it can give us experiences we have never had and thus, instead of 'commenting on life,' can add to it."[75] Unlike other literary modes, fairy story, or fantasy, can add to life by presenting "in palpable form not concepts or even experiences, but whole classes of experience."[76] By nature, therefore, fantasy is porous, open to the transcendent as a function of its reserve. By reserving commentary,

---

73. Ignatius of Loyola, *Spiritual Exercises*, 121.
74. Lewis, "Sometimes Fairy Stories," 36–37.
75. Lewis, "Sometimes Fairy Stories," 38.
76. Lewis, "Sometimes Fairy Stories," 38.

description, reflection, and psychology, the form contains deliberate gaps through which the transcendent can filter or, as in the Christian narrative, bodily enter. The very form and nature of fairy story embodies the love and desire at the heart of the incarnation of Christ, communicating to willing readers the "intolerable compliment" God has paid us "of loving us, in the deepest, most tragic, most inexorable sense."[77]

## BIBLIOGRAPHY

Carnell, Corbin Scott. *Bright Shadow of Reality: Spiritual Longing in C. S. Lewis*. Grand Rapids: Eerdmans, 1999.

*Catechism of the Catholic Church*. San Francisco: Ignatius, 1994.

Como, James. *Branches to Heaven: The Geniuses of C. S. Lewis*. Dallas: Spence, 1998.

Daigle-Williamson, Marsha. *Reflecting the Eternal: Dante's Divine Comedy in the Novels of C. S. Lewis*. Peabody: Hendrickson, 2015.

Herbert, George. "The Bag." In *George Herbert: The Complete English Works*, edited by Ann Pasternak Slater, 147. New York: Knopf, 1995.

Ignatius of Loyola. *The Spiritual Exercises*. In *Ignatius of Loyola: The Spiritual Exercises and Selected Works*, edited by George E. Ganss, 113–214. New York: Paulist, 1991.

Jacobs, Alan. "The Chronicles of Narnia." In *The Cambridge Companion to C. S. Lewis*, edited by Robert MacSwain and Michael Ward, 265–80. Cambridge: Cambridge University Press, 2010.

Lewis, C. S. *The Last Battle*. New York: Macmillan, 1970.

———. *The Lion, the Witch and the Wardrobe*. New York: Macmillan, 1970.

———. *Miracles: A Preliminary Study*. New York: Macmillan, 1947.

———. "On Stories." In *Of Other Worlds: Essays and Stories*, edited by Walter Hooper, 3–21. New York: Harcourt, 1994.

———. "On Three Ways of Writing for Children." In *Of Other Worlds: Essays and Stories*, edited by Walter Hooper, 22–34. New York: Harcourt, 1994.

———. *Prince Caspian*. New York: Macmillan, 1970.

———. *The Problem of Pain*. San Francisco: HarperCollins, 1996.

———. *Reflections on the Psalms*. New York: Harcourt Brace, 1958.

———. *The Silver Chair*. New York: Macmillan, 1970.

———. "Sometimes Fairy Stories May Say Best What's to Be Said." In *Of Other Worlds: Essays and Stories*, edited by Walter Hooper, 35–38. New York: Harcourt, 1994.

———. *Surprised by Joy: The Shape of My Early Life*. New York: Harcourt, 1955.

———. *Till We Have Faces: A Myth Retold*. New York: Harcourt, 1956.

———. *The Voyage of the Dawn Treader*. New York: Macmillan, 1970.

———. *The Weight of Glory and Other Addresses*. New York: HarperCollins, 2001.

McGrath, Alister E. *The Intellectual World of C. S. Lewis*. Malden: Wiley-Blackwell, 2014.

Payne, Leanne. *Real Presence: The Christian Worldview of C. S. Lewis as Incarnational Reality*. Westchester, IL: Crossway, 1988.

Schakel, Peter. *Imagination and the Arts in C. S. Lewis: Journeying to Narnia and Other Worlds*. Columbia, MO: University of Missouri Press, 2002.

---

77. Lewis, *Problem of Pain*, 35.

Simon, Caroline J. "On Love." In *The Cambridge Companion to C. S. Lewis*, edited by Robert MacSwain and Michael Ward, 146–159. Cambridge: Cambridge University Press, 2010.

Ward, Michael. *Planet Narnia: The Seven Heavens in the Imagination of C. S. Lewis*. Oxford: Oxford University Press, 2008.

Werge, Thomas. "Sanctifying the Literal: Images and Incarnation in *Miracles*." In *Word and Story in C. S. Lewis: Language and Narrative in Theory and Practice*, edited by Peter J. Schakel and Charles A. Huttar, 76–85. Eugene, OR: Wipf & Stock, 1991.

Wolfe, Gregory. "Language and Myth in the Ransom Trilogy." In *Word and Story in C. S. Lewis: Language and Narrative in Theory and Practice*, edited by Peter J. Schakel and Charles A. Huttar, 58–75. Eugene, OR: Wipf & Stock, 1991.

Wordsworth, William. *The Prelude*. In *Wordsworth: Selected Poetry*, edited by Mark Van Doren, 178–394. New York: Modern Library, 1950.

# 4

# C. S. Lewis, *Architecton*

Revisiting the Rhetorical Man

*James Como*

OF COURSE, WORDS AND teachers go together. The best teachers are those whose lives reveal the flames of truth that their words seek to kindle in others. The worst are those who lead people away from truth through their words and examples, even as they cause passions to burn like a wildfire. As James 3:1–6 (NABRE) reminds us, "Not many of you should become teachers, my brothers, for you realize that we will be judged more strictly. . . . the tongue is a small member and yet has great pretensions. Consider how small a fire can set a huge forest ablaze. The tongue is also a fire." To be a teacher is dangerous, especially for those who teach about the most important truths. As he demonstrated the Christian mind and showed others how to live as Christians, Lewis revealed himself both as a powerful teacher and a master of rhetoric, setting hearts and minds ablaze for Christ.

From word choice, sentence structure, paragraph organization, and the construction of whole works and series of works; apologetic arguments and explanations, penetrating scholarship, startling literary judgments, and countercultural social criticism; poetry, mythopoeic visions, and pastoral pen friendships; unto his writing career as a whole—for all of these C. S. Lewis's intellect, imagination, spirit, and will worked rhetorically as one. Moreover, that wholeness is the very strength of the edifice that this *architecton* built: nothing less than a single, yet variegated, palace of reason, inspiration, and hope, of sound judgment, awe, and the mitigation of doubt—and a trustworthy self as a guide to it all. Lewis is an embodiment of this *architectonic* art.

According to philosopher Richard McKeon, rhetoric is an *architectonic* art, "an art of structuring all principles and products of knowing, doing, and making."[1] It is a productive art that generates rather than simply reproduces. Lewis is an *architecton* or "master builder" because he uses rhetoric not merely to delight and instruct, but to help shape the modern world and to "function productively in the resolution of new problems and architectonically in the formation of new inclusive communities."[2] To a degree this is seen in Lewis's apologetic nonfiction, where he uses the rhetorical tool of analogy to make plain the metaphysical truths of mere Christianity. To a greater degree, Lewis's craftsmanship is witnessed in his fiction, where he creates other worlds that give readers a glimpse of alternate realities that help make our reality clearer, as in *Perelandra* where he masterfully portrays the nearly unimaginable—an unfallen world. Most significant for Lewis's readers is the application of the truths revealed within his rhetoric by the pattern of his own life. The *architecton* opens up greater truths by creating new frameworks for others to work within. Lewis creates a framework for the Christian mind that has enabled space in the jumbled modern world for ordinary Christians to work.

## LEWIS AS RHETORICIAN

When a person has written a good deal on a topic over a long period of time, it is hard to avoid repeating oneself.[3] But as Dr. Johnson has taught, people need to be reminded more often than instructed, which is what I propose to do, by attempting to provide and review answers to the following question: How did Lewis manage his marvel? Over the past two decades a small body of scholarship has shown C. S. Lewis's work to be infused with the methods of rhetoric;[4] that is, with rhetorical thinking and with heavy dependence

---

1. McKeon, "Use of Rhetoric," 2.

2. McKeon, "Use of Rhetoric," 2.

3. In a master's thesis, "The Rhetoric of Theme and Illusion," a rhetorical study of *Perelandra*; then my doctoral dissertation, *The Militant Intellect: The Conditions and Elements of the Rhetoric of C. S. Lewis*; thereafter in "The Centrality of Rhetoric to an Understanding of C. S. Lewis"; as well as in "Rhetorica Religii"; and finally and much more expansively in *Branches to Heaven: The Geniuses of C. S. Lewis* where I argue that rhetoric is the "chairman of the board" of Lewis's many geniuses.

4. Most insightful, in my opinion, are Anderson, "Most Potent Rhetoric," 195–221, along with his "C. S. Lewis's Sermons," 75–106; Coley, "Weight of Glory," 89–117; and

upon rhetorical instruments. Just so has a new picture of Lewis formed: the knowing practitioner of the art. As I suggested in *Branches to Heaven*, we cannot view Lewis especially "as a theologian, a philosopher or even a literary practitioner but as he was essentially: the wary yet energetic, ambivalent yet committed *homo rhetoricus*."[5] After all, he called himself a "rhetor" and, indeed, "a congenital rhetorician."

Lewis certainly knew the art of rhetoric, as he demonstrates with incomparable concision in *The Discarded Image*.[6] (That concision being the reason, no doubt, for Donatus and Priscian having to share a short paragraph, or for John of Salisbury being absent altogether.) He shows keen insight into the purpose of rhetoric in a famous passage from *A Preface to Paradise Lost* that ends, "Very roughly, we might almost say that in Rhetoric imagination is present for the sake of passion (and, therefore, in the long run, for the sake of action), while in poetry passion is present for the sake of imagination, and therefore, in the long run, for the sake of wisdom or spiritual health."[7] That cannot be improved upon, I think. And in his *Oxford History of English Literature in the Sixteenth Century Excluding Drama*, he shows he has done his due diligence with his discussion of Fraunce, Puttenham, Wilson and Peacham (rhetoricians), and with Lyly's *Euphues, The Anatomy of Wit*. Despite Lewis's expertise in rhetoric, with this paragraph I have referenced virtually all Lewis had to say about the art that was, in the period of his specialty, the *Queen* of the Arts. This thrift is at least puzzling.[8]

---

Tandy, *Rhetoric of Certitude*; and other ancillary works by Bruce Edwards and Jerry Root. The first scholar explicitly to apply methods of rhetorical criticism to Lewis's work, however, was Cunningham, *C. S. Lewis: Defender of the Faith*.

5. Como, *Branches to Heaven*, 180.

6. Although scholarship over the last twenty years has greatly clarified the influence of rhetoric in the Middle Ages. For example, Camargo, "Chaucer and the Oxford Renaissance," shows dispositively that Geoffrey of Vinsauf's *Poetria Nova* was probably unknown by the pre-*Canterbury Tales* Chaucer (rather, argues James Murphy, Evrard of Bethune was the more likely great influence, one not named by Lewis); Copeland, "Chaucer and Rhetoric," in *The Yale Companion to Chaucer*, rehearses a panoply of rhetorical influence—far beyond figures of speech and formulaic prescriptions—in Chaucer and others. Finally, there is Miller, *Chaucer: Sources and Backgrounds*, who shows us that certainly the classical, transitional, and medieval theorists knew narrative and dramatic art, structure and tone, and voice and its varying distances from subject matter, and that they knew the play of their work within social norms and literary conventions. In short, these writers of what we refer to as "handbooks" (not entirely without reason: having one at hand would be helpful, then *and* now) were not naïve. Rather they were learned, having gone to school themselves on the classical authors and the transitional giants, some of whom encompassed most of the learning there was both to teach and to know.

7. Lewis, *Preface to Paradise Lost*, 51.

8. I distinguish his description of rhetoric from his own advice. That we find in

Like Socrates delivering superb speeches in dialogues that complain against rhetoric, Lewis presents a similarly discomfiting paradox: a Christian renouncing his will who marshals an art that requires it. That latter contention seems self-evident, and, I believe, so it is; and it also comes from Lewis himself.

In his Oxford history he tells us, "Rhetoric is the greatest barrier between us and our ancestors. If the Middle Ages had erred in the devotion to that art, the *renascentia*, far from curing, confirmed the error." Lewis concludes, "This change of taste makes an invisible wall between us and them. Probably all our literary histories, *certainly that on which I am engaged*, are vitiated by our lack of sympathy on this point."[9] So though Lewis knew the art, he did not like the art. Happily must he have welcomed Richard Whately's declaration in his *Elements of Rhetoric* (1828): "That what is strictly and properly called Rhetoric, is much less studied, at least systematically studied, now, than formerly. . . . [S]uch is the distrust excited by any suspicion of Rhetorical artifice."[10]

Lewis's reservations, however, went beyond the academic. This is evidenced clearly in some of his poetry. For example, in "As the Ruin Falls" he writes, "All this is flashy rhetoric about loving you. / I never had a selfless thought since I was born."[11] Or this second example, from "The Apologist's Evening Prayer," not published during his lifetime: "From all my proofs of Thy divinity, / Thou, who wouldst give no sign, deliver me. . . . Take from me all my trumpery [i.e. his nearly his entire apologetic project!] lest I die."[12] Mere rhetoric could become a distraction from reality.

Within Lewis's corpus, a few other references to rhetoric are negative, even sneering, but no dismissal comes close to the alarm that Lewis expresses to his Latin correspondent, Father Giovanni Calabria. His despair in the late forties was such that he confesses, not only to accidia (sloth) but to creeping pride: such is the praise he has received that he would prefer never

---

essays and letters—and in *An Experiment in Criticism*, in which, for example, he emphasizes the need for "realism of presentation" to arouse the reader's credulity and variations of pattern to sustain the reader's attention.

9. Lewis, *English Literature in the Sixteenth Century*, 61.

10. Whately, *Elements of Rhetoric*, 28. Whately's comment was originally published in 1828, which is some eighty years before Lewis would begin his rhetorical schooling, just in time for the decline of rhetoric to be in full swing. See Heinrichs, "How Harvard Destroyed Rhetoric," 37–43: during his tenure as Boyleston Professor of Rhetoric and Poetry, Charles Copeland effectively transformed the chair into one of poetry. I think Lewis would have approved, and so it has remained; before his death in 2013 the occupant was Seamus Heaney.

11. Lewis, "As the Ruin Falls," 170.

12. Lewis, "Apologist's Evening Prayer," 198.

to write another word than to experience the temptation. Is it surprising, then, that so often—Orual dying in mid-word, Puddleglum stamping out the fire, Ransom punching the Un-man in the mouth—it is the cessation of rhetoric that moves the action and saves the day?

## THE NATURE OF RHETORIC

For a definition of *rhetoric* there is no need to go beyond Aristotle's, from the beginning of the second chapter of Book One of his *Rhetoric*: "The faculty of observing in the particular case the available means of persuasion." Central to this conception are three ideas: (1) Persuasion, the objective of rhetoric, is *change* (no matter how construed); (2) the "particular case," implying the need for a near-infinite number of tactical adjustments as functions of the *particularities*—of audience (or "judges," as Aristotle would have it), occasion, intermediate purpose (to instruct, to move to action, to stir the emotions), and the character of the speaker both implicit and as displayed by him or her; and (3) "faculty." We notice that, for Aristotle, the *discernment* of a situation (some exigency) requiring a response, along with the means of that response in order to effect the right change, is the fundamental rhetorical action. The response itself (also called "rhetoric") comes later.

Lewis would have read his Aristotle, of course, though he (uncharacteristically: I simply don't buy Anderson's "lost *Rhetoric*" suggestion) failed to annotate it; and he would have known, too, the "great bore" Cicero (*On Invention, De oratore, Brutus, Orator, Topics*), the *Rhetorica ad Herennium*, Quintilian's *Institutes of Oratory*, and Saint Augustine's *de Doctrina*, particularly its Book IV. Aristotle's *Rhetoric* notwithstanding, he annotated many other rhetoric books (for example, his Quintilian and Blair's *Lectures on Rhetoric and Belles Lettres*), probably for professional purposes. In short, he knew his art in all its definitions, categories, tools, requirements, and ethical landmines. Lewis knew that all choices, from the larger ones of genre, character depiction, scenery, venue for publication, and the like to the smaller ones of, say word choice, matter rhetorically, since all have some suasory impact on the audience, and Lewis knew it.

For him this must have meant, for example, considering the sort of airmen who would attend his Christian lectures when, during WWII, he toured their bases: what they most needed to hear, the circumstances surrounding his talks (e.g., Had they already returned from combat? Would they soon be returning *to* it?), his prior reputation with them, time limits, any opportunity to take questions, and the like. He did not think those talks a success, though *he* learned *from* them.[13] The same sorts of concerns would precede his BBC broadcasts, though in that case the choice, division, and sequence of material would matter greatly, as would linguistic style. (Cicero would say that the low, or simplest, would be best, and Lewis complies—until the end, a recurring pattern that routinely shows a rise in style, and of emotion, during his perorations.) We do find Lewis's primary reader or listener ever present to his mind when composing, otherwise why the many shifts of structure and style (of which there are many)?[14]

And to Lewis the combination of rhetorical inclination and knowledge, providential talent, the discernment of vocation, and unrelenting will mean one more thing: a radical reconceptualizing of "the particular case." That became nothing less than the entire zeitgeist, all of it, the whole of our "enemy-occupied" post-Christian age, with all its abandoned beliefs, twisted values, doctrinal ignorance, and linguistic fraudulence; and in it he would become a counter-cultural resister who, according to his friend Austin Farrer, fought as though "every dyke is his last ditch."[15] In that light, this *architecton* constructed a variegated but unified garden (to shift metaphors) within which the trustworthy self offers conviction, sound judgment, plausibility, awe, the mitigation of doubt, and above all Hope, all built by way of the queen of the arts, "an *architectonic* art" as McKeon puts it, "structuring all principles and products of knowing, doing, and making." He continues, "what rhetoric should be and to what conditions it is adapted are not separate theoretic questions but the single practical question of producing a schemata to guide the uses . . . in transforming circumstances."[16] He allows (as does Aristotle) that rhetoric, having no subject-matter of its own, organizes "thought concerning any *subject-matter*," thus joining "reason and

---

13. See Gilmore, "To the RAF," 309–16.

14. Lewis may well have known this, an incisive summary, from Petrarch's *Letters* (19–20): "The first thought of a letter writer must be the person he is writing to; then he will know what to say, how to say it, and all the rest. We should write one way to a strong man, another to a sluggard; one way to a green youth, another to an elder who has fulfilled his life. . . . There is no more similitude of minds than of faces . . . [and even] one mind is not to be fed on the same literary style. So the writer has a double task: to envision the person he is writing to, and then the state of mind in which the recipient will read what he proposes to write."

15. Cited in Como, "Introduction," 43. Not all his colleagues found this inclination as palatable as did Farrer. Anderson, "Most Potent Rhetoric," 211 reminds us of Dorothy L. Sayers's reservations: "One trouble . . . is his fervent missionary zeal . . . He is apt to think that one should rush into every fray and strike a blow for Christendom, whether or not one is equipped by training and temperament for that particular conflict." Sayers's complaint is personal, to some degree, having resisted a Lewis imprecation. But, too, she seems not to view the "particular case" as broadly or as urgently as did Lewis.

16. McKeon, "Rhetoric in the Middle Ages," 2.

sense, cognition and emotion, universal law and concrete occurrence."[17] Furthermore, in his introduction to McKeon's essays, Backman reminds us that "rhetoric can be fruitfully examined as the complex interplay of theory and practice."[18] Thereafter, Backman (echoing McKeon) gets to the nub: "In Aristotelian terms [the rhetor] commands the four causes: the formal, efficient, material, and final."[19]

Surely Lewis would view McKeon's conception as hyper-exalted, which is too bad, since Lewis practices what McKeon teaches, as he does Richard Weaver's encomium:

> Rhetoric speaks to man in his whole being and out of his whole past and with reference to values which only a human being can intuit. . . . In the restored man dialectic and rhetoric will go along hand in hand as the regime of the human faculties intended that they should.[20]

Near or far, the faculty, its functions, and its expression are ordained, inherent to our providentially provided *Logos*.

## RHETORIC AND THE CHRISTIAN MIND

Saint Augustine—another man with a Christian mind that recognized the unity of all reality—surely would have understood McKeon (as McKeon did him!). Backman tells us that "*On Christian Doctrine* develops a rhetorical method by which unchanging truth can be isolated and employed according to the needs of an ever changing and specifically determined Christian community," especially by dealing (now quoting Peter Brown on Augustine) "explicitly with the ties that had bound educated Christians to the culture of their age."[21]

Augustine devotes the first three books of his treatise to discovering arguments, what other rhetoricians call invention, which Augustine does not consider to be part of rhetoric. Moreover, at the outset of Book Four he tells us that his work is not intended as a treatise on rhetoric, by which

---

17. McKeon, "Rhetoric in the Middle Ages," 13. For a very different view of medieval and Renaissance rhetoric than Lewis's, see (still in Backman) McKeon's "Rhetoric in the Middle Ages" (121–66), nuanced and learned beyond any brief history of rhetoric of the period that I have read, and McKeon, "Poetry and Philosophy in the Twelfth Century," 167–93.

18. Backman, "Introduction," xiv.

19. Backman, "Introduction," xxii.

20. Weaver, "Cultural Role of Rhetoric," 183–84.

21. Backman, "Introduction," xxix–xxx.

he means a book of precepts, which matter but are "to be learnt elsewhere." What, then, does he instruct? He tells us that the Christian teacher must use different styles on different occasions, but that the teacher not be so "anxious about the eloquence as about the cleanness of his teaching." The heart must be moved as well as instructed: "the eloquent divine . . . must . . . not only give instruction [and] please so as to keep attention, but he must also sway the mind so as to subdue the will." Augustine's examples come from both Scripture and the fathers, and they illustrate one of his major points: the necessity of variety in style, "to prevent the hearer's attention from cooling or becoming languid." Near the end, just before telling us that "a teacher should govern his words, not let the words govern him," Augustine teaches that "the man whose life is in harmony with his teaching will teach with greater effect." He ends the chapter by quoting 1 Timothy 4:12 (KJV): "Be thou an example of the believers, in word, in conversation, in charity, in spirit, in faith, in purity."[22]

While reading "Sinners in the Hands of an Angry God," I have often thought that Edwards must have had Aristotle's *Rhetoric* open at his elbow. With Lewis it is Augustine who must be nearby. Surely it is the *architecton*'s blueprint; of course, not the only one—Thomas Hooker comes first, I think, as a model—but Saint Augustine is right there with him.

On the other hand, if Lewis had been around in their day, he might have been their model. Of the more than forty books he published, all but some poetry and the works of literary scholarship and criticism are either argumentative defenses of the plausibility of Christian doctrine, explanations of it for the purpose of persuading in its favor, or manifestly didactic fictions with Christian intent; six have a veiled intent with the Christian content submerged, but they fulfill precisely the same functions. This assessment applies even to *Till We Have Faces*, though as Lewis's one real novel (as opposed to allegory, fairy tale or romance) it differs considerably from its predecessors.[23] The same is largely true of the books published posthumously. All of his works give evidence of a Christian mind at work: seeing the unity of the world and using the best rhetorical techniques to point others toward it.

## LEWIS'S PERSUASIVENESS

In many modes, and at varying levels of intensity and directness, Lewis was relentlessly persuasive. He delivered only a handful of sermons, for example,

---

22. Augustine, *On Christian Doctrine*, xxvii–xxxviii.

23. Though different from his other fiction, as Gene Fant argues in chapter 6 of this volume, even Lewis's novel fulfills a similar purpose.

but they made history. "Transposition" was delivered from the pulpit of Mansfield College, close to the house in which Lewis stayed on his very first night in Oxford. "The Weight of Glory" and "Learning in War-Time" were preached to multitudes from the pulpit of the University Church of St. Mary the Virgin: Lattimer, Cranmer, and Ridley had been tried there, and Wesley, Keble, and Newman had preached from the same pulpit. These are impressive venues. But as impressive in their variety and modesty are the venues of some of his greatest essays.[24] No venue was too large for his idiomatic voice, nor audience too small for his concentrated attention; thus Lewis, in setting many forests ablaze with the fire of his rhetoric, exercised Saint James's command not to show partiality (Jas 2:1–13).

The subjects he treated were often the most difficult: if Jesus was God, why did he not return, as he seems to have promised, during the lifetime of those who actually heard him? If we are promised that prayers made faithfully will be answered, why are they so frequently not? If God is loving, why does he permit so much suffering, especially of the innocent—even of the beasts, who were not morally complicit in the fall? What explanation other than psychosis could explain "speaking in tongues"? In the absence of evidence why should we be "obstinate" in belief? How can we possibly reconcile *dogmatic* belief with the need to freely exercise our reason, presumably God-given? The range of work—in its content, mode, scope, style, and persistence—is unremitting. In its great array, the whole of the work speaks to a sufficient variety of tastes, intellectual ability, religious doubt, spiritual need, imaginative longing, levels of curiosity, and sheer patience with the written word to satisfy the preponderance of readers, no matter where they break in upon it. In believing that Christ intends for us to be persons (members of his person), Lewis uses an occasion to offer his audience recognizable facets of personality and to show them what they might become. Having taken seriously the claim that the universe is possessed of meaning, he then provides an image of reality sufficiently coherent and authoritative to make the claim credible. In other words, the function of Lewis's Christian mind is to help others perceive the unity and rationality of the world, thus pointing people from the distracted errors of modern culture to the solid truth of Christianity (cf. Jas 5:19–20).

In the conclusion to an essay on Lewis as rhetorician, Greg M. Anderson quotes Lewis's friend and fellow scholar Neville Coghill on Lewis's true

---

24. A representative sample includes such organs as *St. Jude's Gazette, World Dominion, Electrical and Musical Industries Christian Fellowship, Coventry Evening Telegraph, Bristol Diocesan Gazette, The Month, Breakthrough,* and *St. James's Magazine*; of course, there were also *The Saturday Evening Post, The Guardian* (small, but prominent in its day), *Time & Tide, Twentieth Century,* and *Spectator*.

genius: "the power to make ... generalizations that lead the reader into new territory. ... His sentences are homely English and yet there is something Roman in the easy handling of clauses, and something Greek in the ascent from analogy to idea."[25] It is this rhetorical ability that is on display, even in Lewis's academic work, which reveals the authenticity of his genius. For example, in *The Allegory of Love*, Lewis begins a paragraph: "Thus *Troilus* is what Chaucer meant it to be—a great poem in praise of love. Here also, despite the comic and tragic elements, Chaucer shows himself, as in the *Book of the Duchesse*, the *Parlement*, and the *Canterbury Tales*, our supreme poet of happiness." The periodic structure of the second sentence, coming after the alliterative punch of the first, is hard to resist. There is a generalization for the ages. But the paragraph goes on for another twenty-seven lines: it is almost the whole of the page. Here is how it ends: "the wild Provencal vine has begun to bear such good fruit that it is now worth taming"—such a metaphor that not only appeals to more than one sense but is exactly right for the period of interest.

That paragraph is typical in its length; some go on for two pages—virtual treatises—and the content they convey would, in the hands of other authors, be monographs. But that is not to gainsay the pithiness of Lewis's writing. His readiness of quotation, the perfectly sequenced references, and, especially, the irresistibly compelling rhythm of his sentences—we are discovering an idea here, it is close at hand, so come along and keep up, my variations of length and a sound device or two helping, I trust—these make his writing at once both substantial and light. Of course, Lewis the scholar will be Lewis the cultural critic, too. When discussing "inner conflict" (those are Lewis's own sneer quotation marks) he reminds us that "every metaphor is an allegory in little"; then, at the end of a paragraph only a page long (after contrasting the allegorist with the novelist, to the disfavor of the novelist), "if we could be free, for a little, of our own *Zeitgeist*, we might confess that it [an allegorical figure] is not very much more abstract than that 'self' or 'personality'[26] on whose rock-bottom unity we rest so secure and of which we would so much rather hear [the novelist] talk."[27] That sentence concludes the paragraph; like most final sentences it packs a punch. Or, consider just one more example that wraps up a two-and-a-half page paragraph on Spenser: "When he wishes to paint disease, the exquisite health of his own imagination shows him what images to exclude."[28]

25. Anderson, "Most Potent Rhetoric," 217.
26. Lewis readers will recall him calling that a "pestilent notion."
27. Lewis, *Allegory of Love*, 77.
28. Lewis, *Allegory of Love*, 416.

That is the *architecton* working at a high pitch: the writer demonstrating such command as to inspire great confidence, matter ordered incrementally so that the point comes with a spark and seems inevitable, and the audience conveyed along briskly and cogently. We see these qualities in a book generally regarded as his most difficult, *Miracles*, about which, Anderson reminds us, Flannery O'Connor said, "I also just read . . . *Miracles*, which is very fine. Deceptively simple. You really need to read every sentence twice."[29] Certainly it is severe in its logic; until the end—"Do not, I earnestly advise you, demand an ocular proof unless you are already perfectly certain that it is not forthcoming"—there is no rhetorical slack, scarcely any emotional proof (as seen in "The Weight of Glory"), nothing to keep the reader moving—except for Lewis's logic, which is inexorable. Here Lewis's building skills are arrayed adroitly at the book-level. His emphasis is on organization, the second canon of rhetoric. Its seven parts are necessary, sufficient, and almost geometrically ordered: (1) Frame the problem; (2) define terms; (3) address psychological reservations; (4) address logical objections; (5) hypothesize an explanation for the phenomena; (6) demonstrate the greater rationality of the new hypothesis; and as a peroration (7) make the new alternative to disbelief imaginatively appealing. This is almost always Lewis's *modus operandus*.

## LEWIS THE MASTER BUILDER

The expertise on display in Lewis the master builder is present at all levels of his written work. He builds his books and paragraphs no more carefully than he does his sentences, which, of course, makes him so quotable. "Time is to the universe as the metre is to a poem or the key is to music;"[30] the sort that make the reader say (usually, if I am that reader, saying aloud), "*Of course* that's what time is!" as though the reader had seen it—whatever the "it"—for himself. Gary Tandy, whose analysis of Lewis's style (the third canon of rhetoric) is the surest we have by far, has done us the yeoman service of going medieval on Lewis by doing the sort of thing that drove him crazy, that is, identifying figures of speech: polyptoton, anadiplosis, antimetabole, epistrophe, epanalepsis, parallelism, antithesis, and (to be sure) analogy, simile and metaphor. Tandy shows us the *architecton* working in microcosm.

From sentences, paragraphs, and books we move to a concept; and so we proceed from disposition and style back to invention (the first canon),

---

29. Anderson, "Most Potent Rhetoric," 216.
30. Lewis, "Seeing Eye," 59.

by looking at proof. *Pathos*—the arousal of an emotional state receptive to the proposition at hand—is a Lewisian specialty. It is everywhere and always, though sometimes muted or disguised (as humor, for example when he compares himself to a dinosaur in "De Descriptione Temporum"). But most frequently it manifests as spiritual inspiration, especially as hope. In one sense, Lewis's entire apologetic was an attempt to point people toward the hope revealed in the pages of Christian Scripture.

Based on my own reading, the whole of Lewis's apologetic work can be summarized with direct references, or even allusions, to special revelation. With Paul, Lewis urges his readers to "put on faith and love for a breastplate and the hope of salvation for a helmet" (1 Thess 5:8, NJB). As in Matthew's Gospel, we are reminded, "Everyone will hate you because of me, but the one who stands firm to the end will be saved" (Matt 10:22, NIV). With the author of Hebrews, Lewis tells us to "keep firm in the hope we profess, because the one who made the promise is trustworthy" (Heb 10:23, NJB). The list could well go on, to include finding purpose in suffering (Rom 5:5), receiving joy and peace through the Holy Spirit (Rom 15:13), an anchor for our soul from beyond the veil (Heb 6:19–20). Ultimately, Lewis's rhetoric, built on Scripture, is effective in providing us that great comfort, "the assurance of what is hoped for, the conviction of things unseen" (Heb 11:1–2, NASB). It is possible to argue that all of Lewis's work is an apologetic for the Christian mind, in which he imaginatively shows his readers what it would look like to live with a truly Christian mind. We see this at the very end of *The Chronicles*, the ante- and penultimate paragraphs of *Letters to Malcolm*, the second half of the final paragraph of *The Problem of Pain*, even the end of *An Experiment in Criticism*—there is the Oil of Gladness, with which Lewis, more than any other writer in English, anoints us. Here is hope. The evocation of this cardinal virtue seems ubiquitous in Lewis.

One thinks also of the chapter on hope in *Mere Christianity* (on which construction we know he labored mightily). There he discusses heaven and how belief in it has inspired earthly accomplishments; he discusses longing (what he calls Joy), though very briefly; and then he provides a tri-partite division of ways for dealing with the phenomenon, the correct way being the third, the Christian way. He ends with a *refutatio*, concluding with the genuinely punchy, "people who take these symbols literally might as well think that when Christ told us to be like doves, He meant that we were to lay eggs."[31] Altogether a tight, cogent performance, securely suited to the constraints of what was a BBC broadcast talk: as Cicero would say, the low style appropriate for instruction. "Tidy" is the word that comes to my mind.

---

31. Lewis, *Mere Christianity*, 137.

Then there is "The Weight of Glory," a sermon at the very heart of Lewis's theology and the center of his apologetic. "You have never met an ordinary mortal" is as much as I will quote, because . . . why stop? Instead I recommend Toby F. Coley's "'The Weight of Glory': C. S. Lewis's Most Pathetic Sermon."[32] Coley's command of rhetorical theory and its devices is impressive, but more impressive is his incisive application of them, along with his contextualizing ability. Coley is a supple critic, turning from Lewis's arguments to figures of speech to Lewis's use of emotional proof and to the structure of the sermon, fully appreciating Lewis's gift for peroration. In short, Coley shows us how Lewis makes this grand room for the many in his mansion.

Yet another great work where this is present is the second novel in Lewis's space trilogy. Nearly fifty years ago, in my Master of Arts thesis, I examined *Perelandra* with a paradigm not quite classical. Wayne Booth's landmark *The Rhetoric of Fiction*,[33] Lewis's own *An Experiment in Criticism*, and the work of I. A. Richards form a critical calculus by which to examine Lewis's control of both his reader and his material.[34] I suspect the approach still holds enough water to merit revisiting—someday. I also suggested that a combination of Frazer's *The Golden Bough* and C. G. Jung's theory of archetypes, if not a key or a code (I have small trust of the latter), was certainly an explanation of the power of the imagery and events of *Perelandra*. Richard Cunningham's *C. S. Lewis: Defender of the Faith* had just come out, so I could not profit from it, as surely I would have—perhaps excessively. If one cares to examine Lewis's rhetoric, best to begin with Cunningham, whose traditionally systematic examination of Lewis the apologist is admirably contextualized, detailed, and thorough.[35] The work is one of Lewis's most helpful theological works, though a work of fiction, and the power of his

---

32. Coley, "Weight of Glory," 89–120.

33. Booth, *Rhetoric of Fiction*.

34. For some time I have owned Lewis's copy of Richards's *Principles of Literary Criticism*, a gift to me from Walter Hooper, who had selected it as one of the books he was allowed to take from Lewis's library. Lewis not only has summarized each chapter and provided a running headline for each page, but along the way questions and argues with Richards in his marginalia. Lewis has noted that Richards claims (this in tiny handwriting) "all that matters is the development of the response." (There is *very* much about stimulus response.) My favorite Lewisian note is his summary of Richards's last chapter: "XXXIV Fictions are often necessary to produce desirable attitudes."

35. My hope is that there is a scholar now at work on *How He Did It, What He Was: The Rhetoric of C. S. Lewis: Its Foundations, Premises, Practices and Pervasiveness*; nothing less than such a robust eighteenth-century sort of title will do. If not, then *Hiding in Plain Sight: The Secret Behind the Success of C. S. Lewis*. Or *Rhetoric Incarnate: C. S. Lewis's Magic Elixir*. Or . . . well, fingers crossed.

vision of an unfallen world and sin resisted is masterfully enhanced through his expert rhetoric. Without the creative expertise of the *architecton* Lewis's fiction would have been a mere artifact of early-twentieth-century Christianity rather than an enduring work that continues to ignite the minds of new generations of Christians.

## CONCLUSION

At the end of the day, and looking at the whole corpus (including the scholarship and criticism), the rhetorical pattern I discern is a movement from the possible to the plausible to the intensely pleasurable (intellectual or emotional); in the religious writing that continues to the promising and thence, of course, to hope. Debra Winger, the actress who played Joy Davidman in *Shadowlands*, told me in an interview how she saw Lewis:

> He [makes] difficult questions accessible. I don't think he makes the answers "easy." I don't think he answers questions. I think he discusses them. He's in that school of discourse where his statements are not like books that are written by experts. He's saying "think about this." That's why I think he opened Christianity to so many people.

Certainly, the attainment of plausibility was a strength, but equally as consequential was his use of himself as a datum, whether it be his experience of Joy, his atheism, his response to weather and landscape, his doubt about a doctrine, or even his amateur standing. He was not far from the reader and in many respects had been "there and back again." That, I think, is the reason we might judge him by his own literary standard from *An Experiment in Criticism*: What sort of a response does he elicit?

Many responses to Lewis have been collected in two books: *The Lion and the Land of Narnia: Our Adventures in Aslan's World*,[36] illustrated and compiled by Robert Cording, and *Mere Christians: Inspiring Stories of Encounters with C. S. Lewis*, edited by Mary Anne Phemister and Andrew Lazo.[37] The accounts are terrifically poignant, very concrete, and highly personal. Beyond sales figures and numbers of translations, the outpouring of secondary sources or trans-media versions of his work, the increasing number of venues in which he is quoted in all his personae, it is the personal impact—one by one by one into the millions—that measures the power of Lewis's rhetoric, which is a personal power. Nearly forty years ago, in *Remembering C. S. Lewis*, Eugene McGovern (a founding member of The New

---

36. Cording, *Lion and the Land of Narnia*.
37. Phemister and Lazo, *Mere Christians*.

York C. S. Lewis Society) wrote of this truth in his "Our Need for Such a Guide":

> By learning about the man himself we find that, for this most reliable guide on the subjects that matter most, the center remained unchanged; he really did believe what he wrote, and he practiced what he preached.

McGovern concludes, "Our need for such a guide will not diminish in the years ahead," surely as prescient a prognosis as we are likely to encounter.[38]

In an age of artistic mediocrity among Christians, Lewis is an *architecton*. In a time when scandals threaten the moral witness of the church on both sides of the Tiber, Lewis shows the power of imagination to make what ought to be appear possible and even plausible. His rhetoric is consistent with the standards of the revered classical authors. But it is the consistency (as much a human can be consistent) with his presentation of the ideals of the Christian mind that gives Lewis staying power and ensures he will continues to have influence for generations to come.

Augustine teaches the Christian rhetorician to instruct, to sway, and, by variations of style, to "subdue the will" of the reader or listener. Above all, however, he insists that "the man whose life is in harmony with his teaching will teach with greater effect." Just so does Cunningham end his book: "When the idea of not-God and the idea of Lewis meet in a sympathetic mind, it is the idea of not-God that must change. Lewis himself is his finest Christian apology"[39]—with a tongue that is also a fire.

## BIBLIOGRAPHY

Anderson, Greg M. "C. S. Lewis's Sermons: The Oxford Don as Preacher." In *C. S. Lewis: Life, Work and Legacy*, edited by Bruce Edwards, 3:75–106. Santa Barbara: Praeger Perspectives, 2007.

———. "A Most Potent Rhetoric: C. S. Lewis's 'Congenital Rhetorician.'" In *C. S. Lewis: Life, Work and Legacy*, edited by Bruce Edwards, 4:195–221. Santa Barbara: Praeger Perspectives, 2007.

Augustine. *On Christian Doctrine*. Translated by J. F. Shaw. Mineola, NY: Dover, 2009.

Backman, Mark. "Introduction: McKeon and the Renaissance of Rhetoric." In *Rhetoric: Essays in Invention and Discovery*, by Richard McKeon, edited by Mark Backman, vii–xxxii. Woodbridge, CT: Ox Bow, 1987.

Booth, Wayne. *The Rhetoric of Fiction*. Chicago: University of Chicago Press, 1983.

Camargo, Martin. "Chaucer and the Oxford Renaissance of Anglo-Latin Rhetoric." In *Studies in the Age of Chaucer*, edited by David Matthews, 33:173–207. St. Louis: New Chaucer Society, 2012.

---

38. McGovern, "Our Need for Such a Guide," 238.
39. Cunningham, *C. S. Lewis*, 205.

Coley, Toby F. "'The Weight of Glory': C. S. Lewis's Most Pathetic Sermon." *Sehnsucht: The C. S. Lewis Journal* 9 (2015) 89–120.
Como, James T. *Branches to Heaven: The Geniuses of C. S. Lewis.* Dallas: Spence, 1998.
———. "The Centrality of Rhetoric to an Understanding of C. S. Lewis." *Bulletin of the New York C. S. Lewis Society* 25.1 (1993) 1–7.
———. "Introduction." In *Remembering C. S. Lewis*, edited by James Como, 33–51. San Francisco: Ignatius, 2005.
———. *The Militant Intellect: The Conditions and Elements of the Rhetoric of C. S. Lewis.* PhD diss., Columbia University, 1979.
———. "The Rhetoric of Theme and Illusion: *Belief in C. S. Lewis's* Perelandra." MA thesis, Queens College, City University of New York, 1970.
———. "Rhetorica Religii." *Renascence* 51.1 (1998) 3–19.
Copeland, Rita. "Chaucer and Rhetoric." In *The Yale Companion to Chaucer*, edited by Seth Lerer, 122–43. New Haven: Yale University Press, 2006.
Cording, Robert, ed. *The Lion and the Land of Narnia: Our Adventures in Aslan's World.* Eugene, OR: Harvest House, 2008.
Cunningham, Richard B. *C. S. Lewis: Defender of the Faith.* Philadelphia: Westminster, 1967.
Gilmore, Charles. "To the RAF." In *Remembering C. S. Lewis*, edited by James Como, 309–16. San Francisco: Ignatius, 2005.
Heinrichs, Jay. "How Harvard Destroyed Rhetoric." *Harvard Magazine*, July–August, 1995.
Lewis, C. S. *The Allegory of Love.* Cambridge: Cambridge University Press, 2013.
———. "The Apologist's Evening Prayer." In *Poems*, 198. New York: HarperCollins, 1964.
———. "As the Ruin Falls." In *Poems*, 170. New York: HarperCollins, 1964.
———. *English Literature in the Sixteenth Century Excluding Drama.* Oxford: Oxford University Press, 1954.
———. *An Experiment in Criticism.* Cambridge: Cambridge University Press, 2013.
———. *Mere Christianity.* New York: HarperCollins, 1952.
———. *Preface to Paradise Lost.* London: Oxford University Press, 1961.
———. "The Seeing Eye." In *C. S. Lewis: Essay Collection and Other Short Pieces*, edited by Lesley Walmsley, 58–65. London: HarperCollins, 2000.
McGovern, Eugene. "Our Need for Such a Guide." In *Remembering C. S. Lewis: Recollections of Those Who Knew Him*, edited by James T. Como, 227–40. San Francisco: Ignatius, 2005.
McKeon, Richard. *Rhetoric: Essays in Invention and Discovery.* Edited by Mark Backman. Woodbridge, CT: Ox Bow, 1987.
Miller, Robert P. *Chaucer: Sources and Backgrounds.* New York: Oxford University Press, 1977.
Phemister, Mary Anne, and Andrew Lazo, eds. *Mere Christians.* Grand Rapids: Baker, 2009.
Tandy, Gary L. *The Rhetoric of Certitude: C. S. Lewis's Nonfiction Prose.* Kent, OH: Kent State University Press, 2009.
Weaver, Richard. "The Cultural Role of Rhetoric." In *Language Is Sermonic: Richard M. Weaver on the Nature of Rhetoric*, edited by Richard Johannesen et al., 161–86. Baton Rouge: Louisiana State University, 1970.
Whately, Richard. *Elements of Rhetoric.* New York: Sheldon, 1872.

# 5

# Psalm 19, Revelation, and the Integration of Faith, Learning, and Life

*Daniel J. Estes*

C. S. LEWIS EXCLAIMED of Psalm 19: "I take this to be the greatest poem in the Psalter and one of the greatest lyrics in the world."[1] This familiar psalm begins with the thundering declaration, "The heavens declare the glory of God," as it portrays God as speaking through his world (vv. 1–6), the Lord as speaking through his word (vv. 7–11), and the psalmist responding to the divine revelation he has received (vv. 12–14). In the New Testament, its theme in vv. 1–6 is picked up by Paul in Acts 17 and Romans 1 as the apostle argues that all humans without exception deserve divine judgment because they have suppressed the truth that God has revealed to them in his creation.

Scholars have assessed the various emphases in Psalm 19 in diverse ways. Many have treated the psalm as though it were two independent and unrelated poems that were combined later by an editor.[2] Others have elevated verses 7–14 to the relative exclusion of verses 1–6. Lewis, however, rightly argued that Psalm 19 is a skillfully unified poem, and that it must be read as such.[3] Rather than hypothesizing about prior sources that may

---

1. Lewis, *Reflections on the Psalms*, 63.
2. For example, Weiser, *Psalms*, 197.
3. Lewis, *Reflections on the Psalms*, 63–64. Craigie, *Psalms 1–50*, 179, argues that

have been used by the psalmist, the reader should interpret the psalm in the form in which it has actually been transmitted. As Wagner has demonstrated convincingly, in its canonical form Psalm 19 has clear textual and thematic unity and logic, which he summarizes in these terms: "The psalmist's contemplation of the heavens' unceasing praise of El and his reflection on the beauty and perfection of Yhwh's Torah, lead to a heartfelt request for forgiveness and wholeness, a petition grounded in the trustworthy and gracious character of Yhwh himself."[4]

Psalm 19 is a central passage of Scripture for understanding the Christian mind, particularly sources for the knowledge of God and the relation of God to knowledge in general. This essay written in honor of Michael Travers brings together his interests in C. S. Lewis, the book of Psalms,[5] and integrative thinking. It will present a brief exposition of Psalm 19, which will serve as the basis for a theological summary of how Psalm 19 contributes to the Christian doctrine of revelation. The paper will culminate with a discussion on how Psalm 19 informs three topics related to the integration of faith, learning, and life.

## EXPOSITION OF PSALM 19

Psalm 19 ends with a prayer by the psalmist in verses 12–14, but the psalm does not manifest the standard lament form typically used in petitions. Taken as a whole, Psalm 19 is more a meditation on creation (vv. 1–6) and the *tôrâ* (vv. 7–11) that culminates in a prayer for forgiveness and acceptance by the Lord in verses 12–14.[6] The spirit of contemplation that pervades the psalm is similar to the tone evidenced in Psalm 8.

---

either the present psalm was composed as a unity, or that an older hymn (vv. 1–6) was extended by a later author into its present form, but Goldingay, *Psalms 1–41*, 285, questions this supplementary approach on textual grounds. The only form of Psalm 19 that is attested in the manuscripts is the unified form found in the MT. After a careful literary analysis of Psalm 19, Vos, "Theopoetical and Liturgical Patterns," 269, concludes, "The text, which is woven into a unit, is made up of many different threads. The poet's mastery is to be seen in the way in which he has used rhythm and imagery to create segments and then larger blocks of text. The result is a melodic and apparently effortless poem that fills us with delight. The psalm is woven like a many-coloured tapestry." For additional bibliography supporting the unity of Psalm 19, see Cooley, "Psalm 19: A Sabbath Song," 178.

4. Wagner, "From the Heavens to the Heart," 249.

5. In his book on the Psalms (Travers, *Encountering God in the Psalms*, 87–104), Michael presented a fine literary and theological discussion of Psalm 19.

6. Ross, *Commentary on the Psalms*, 467, notes well: "Psalm 19 is a classic presentation of divine revelation and its intended effects. The psalm falls into three distinct parts, the contemplation of divine revelation in nature, the reflection on the value and

The psalm begins in verses 1–6 by reflecting on the praise of God by the creation. The world created by God testifies to the glory of its Maker by means of its continuous declaration of his greatness (v. 1). The verb *sāpar* ("declare") is a term of worship, which in texts such as Psalm 97:6 proclaims the deeds and character of the Lord. In Psalm 19, the heavens, which represent the whole physical universe, declare the glory or transcendence of God. In the ancient world, features of nature were often worshiped as deities (see Deut 4:19; 17:3), but by contrast in Psalm 19 the heavens point beyond themselves to the Creator who made them.[7] This is a clear proclamation to all, not a whisper limited for only a select few. Because the heavens cover the entire planet, their testimony about God is available to all humans without exception.

The witness in creation is not only extensive, but it is also perpetual, because during both the day and the night creation reveals knowledge of the glory of God (v. 2). During the daytime, the warmth of the sun that prompts growth especially speaks of God's goodness, and during the nighttime the vast collection of stars and galaxies attests to his greatness. This *'ōmer* ("speech") is not meager, but it bubbles forth[8] in lavish testimony to the Creator. What the creation declares is knowledge (*da'at*), not a false claim but a true message about the glory of God proclaimed by his world. Therefore, as Paul concludes by alluding to this verse in Romans 1:19–20, humans are without excuse before God, because they have suppressed the truth that they have received in the creation about his existence and greatness.

Verse 3 indicates that although creation continually gushes forth *'ōmer* ("speech") in verse 2, that communication has no *'ōmer* ("speech") or *děbārîm* ("words"). The King James Version follows the Septuagint and Vulgate renderings in making line b subordinate to line a ("where their voice is not heard"), which fits well with verses 4–6, but it reverses the sense of the Hebrew text in verse 3.[9] What verse 3 asserts is that the creation communi-

---

benefits of written revelation in the word of the LORD, and a prayer for cleansing and preservation from sin—the designed effect of all revelation."

7. Weiser, *Psalms*, 198, observes, "The whole of Nature is in the service of a Supreme Being; its duty is to sing the praise of God and to be a vehicle of his revelation. The poet's vision vivifies the inanimate things in Nature; to him heaven, the firmament, day and night, are witnesses who have the gift of speech; by their words they testify to the divine majesty and to the grandeur of the work of creation. A master is known by his work."

8. Beyer, *NIDOTTE*, 3:15, notes that figurative examples of the verb *nbʿ* refer to bubbling forth with folly (Ps 94:4; Prov 15:2), God's praise (Pss 78:2; 119:171), and God's wisdom (Prov 1:23), and "bubbling forth" is the nuance in Psalm 19:2 as well.

9. Knierim, *Task of Old Testament Theology*, 328, in arguing against the assertion by Weiser, states, "בלי is in itself nothing more than a particle of negation, in our case

cates knowledge about God in pictures, but verse 4 states that it provides no captions to explain what the pictures mean. What is revealed about God in nature, then, is inherently limited, for the truth that creation reveals must be supplemented and explained. In verses 7–11, it is the *tôrâ* ("law") of Yahweh that interprets the pictorial language of the creation. To grasp the Lord's full message, therefore, humans need to consider both what his world and what his word reveal.

In verses 4–6, the expansiveness of the revelation in the creation that was hinted implicitly in verse 1 is developed explicitly. Verse 4 states that the *qaw* of the words of creation has gone out through all the earth.[10] This Hebrew term is used in Isaiah 28:10, 13, for unintelligible speech, but the Septuagint rendering *phthonggos* ("voice [of a herald]") is cited by Paul in Romans 10:18. The references to all the earth and to the end of the world indicate that everyone has received this word of God's glory through the heavens (cf. Pss 48:10; 59:13; Isa 42:10).

Beginning in the final line of verse 4 and extending through verse 6, the psalmist uses the analogy of the sun to state that this voiceless witness by creation is as extensive as the shining of the sun. Employing two images of the eager emergence of the sun each morning in verse 5, this revelation is pictured as a bridegroom the morning after the consummation of his marriage in the bridal chamber (cf. Joel 2:16) and as a warrior confidently anticipating the running of a race. The creation, then, is not a reluctant witness, but it delights in declaring the glory of God. As the sun traverses the entire earth, it declares God's glory to all humans on the planet (v. 6). Even the most remote areas on earth receive God's general revelation in creation, because wherever and whenever the sun shines, it proclaims the glory of God.

A transition occurs in verse 7: the reference to God (El) in verse 1 is replaced by LORD (Yahweh, the personal name of the Lord) in verses 7–9, and 14. In place of the silent witness of the created world in verses 1–6, in

---

negating עמשי. Its additional understanding as a relative clause particle, or the implication of a missing but assumable relative particle, is highly problematic."

10. Brown, "Night to Night," 68, explains, "The basic meaning of *qaw* is 'measuring line,' used for construction or demarcation. Good sense can be made of this literal meaning by recognizing that the psalmist is couching an essentially *visual* image in the language of verbal discourse. This curious term could refer either to the designated 'paths' or circuits that the celestial bodies follow, such as the sun's 'course' ('ōrah) referenced in v. 6, or, more likely, to beams or rays emanating from the astral bodies themselves, particularly the sun—a widespread motif in ancient Near Eastern iconography. Either way, it is clear that the cosmos is given a distinctly declarative voice, a 'voice' that communicates visually."

verses 7–9 the written word of the Lord is featured by six synonyms.[11] What is emphasized in verse 7 are the transforming effects of the Scriptures, as the Lord's law (*tôrâ*) enhances the soul, or life. The Lord's word is totally reliable as it teaches the simple youth (*petî*, cf. Prov 1:4) to be wise. For those who are teachable (cf. Ps 119:130), the word of the Lord is truly life-changing as he teaches them (cf. Pss 27:11; 71:17; 86:11; 94:10, 12).

What the Lord commands in his word is right, and obedience to it brings true joy to one's heart (v. 8). Sin may claim to lead to pleasure (cf. Prov 1:10–14), but only the word of the Lord enables one to see through the deceptions of sin and brings true rejoicing to the heart.[12] Obeying God's word leads to joy (Ps 119:111) and understanding (Ps 119:130), but disobeying it produces sadness and confusion.

In verse 9, "the fear of the LORD" is used to refer to the word of the Lord (cf. Ps 34:11), and not in the same sense as the expression is employed in the OT wisdom literature, where it speaks of reverence for the Lord that is at the heart of true skill in living. Goldingay, however, rightly notes that even though *yir'at yhwh* ("fear of the LORD") in Psalm 19:9 has a somewhat different nuance than in Proverbs, yet there is a general correspondence in meaning, in that here it refers to "teaching that indicates what reverence for Yhwh looks like."[13] In the second line, *mišpāṭîm* ("decrees") is the same term used twenty-two times in Psalm 119 as a synonym of *tôrâ*, with the nuance of instructions for living. God's word is described as pure and reliable. What the Lord says is as righteous as he is, so his word is his bond.

The blessing of God's word exceeds the value of the best material treasures (cf. Ps 119:72, 127; Job 28:17; Prov 8:19), and even the freshest honey cannot compare to the delight that God's word provides (cf. Ps 119:103), because it produces deep and lasting satisfaction, not just superficial and temporary pleasure. As God's word surpasses the best that his world can offer, analogously special revelation in the Bible (vv. 7–11) exceeds what he reveals through his creation (vv. 1–6).

Verse 11 functions as a hinge from the description of God's word in verses 7–10 to the personal application by the psalmist in verses 12–14. Using the term *'ebed* ("servant"), which implies a humble stance before one's

---

11. For a succinct discussion of the terms used in verses 7–9 for the word of the Lord, see VanGemeren, "Psalms," 5:184–87. For a more extensive discussion of these terms and of others found in Psalm 119, see Firth, "More than Just Torah," 68–75.

12. Clines, "Tree of Knowledge," 11, notes the echo of Genesis 3, when Adam and Eve ate the forbidden fruit, and their eyes were opened. In contrast to that damaging effect, Psalm 19:8, like Psalm 119:18, speaks of how the *tôrâ* opens one's eyes to see the wondrous things of Yahweh's law.

13. Goldingay, *Psalms 1–41*, 291.

master, the psalmist states that he is warned by the words of God. By carefully attending to God's instructions by his obedience, the psalmist receives great reward.

The psalm concludes with the psalmist's prayer for forgiveness and acceptance by the Lord in verses 12–14.[14] In the light of God's word, he realizes his unworthiness before the holy Lord. He acknowledges that he has hidden faults, because sin deceives and blinds humans to their wrongs. Even though these faults may be unintentional or involuntary, they are still sins that need to be dragged out into the light and exposed, and the psalmist calls on the Lord to do that for him (cf. Ps 139:23–24). Just as nothing escapes the sun's warmth (v. 6), so no human sins evade the knowledge and justice of the Lord (cf. Job 34:22; Jer 16:17; 23:24). As Schaefer notes, "The sun's heat penetrates invisible depths; likewise the divine law reaches the innermost regions of the conscience."[15]

As the Lord's servant, the psalmist wants to live under the Lord's rule, and not under the rule of sin. He realizes that just as he can fall into unintentional sins (v. 12), so he is prone to commit intentional sins as he arrogantly defies the Lord. His sin cannot be managed by his own personal resolution alone, but it must be defeated by divine power. Only by God's strength will he be able to live a blameless life, innocent of deliberate rebellion against the Lord.[16]

In the final verse, the psalmist expresses the proper human response to the Lord's revelation in his world and in his word. Just as the heavens perpetually glorify God, so he wants his life perpetually to glorify the Lord as well. He opens both the audible words of his mouth and the inner meditation in his heart to the Lord's scrutiny, because he desires to be acceptable[17] to the Lord in all of his behavior. In addressing the Lord as his Rock, he may

---

14. By discussing the textual links between verses 12–14 and verses 1–11, Wagner, "From the Heavens to the Heart," 257, demonstrates that the final section of Psalm 19 synthesizes the entire song. He says, "In the petition the psalmist draws on motifs and vocabulary from the preceding sections of the psalm; like a parabolic antenna, the petition collects the diverse waves of thought that resound throughout the poem and directs them toward the focal point of the psalm—the intense, intimate encounter of the psalmist with Yhwh."

15. Schaefer, *Psalms*, 47.

16. Carpenter and Grisanti, *NIDOTTE* 3:707, note that the Hebrew term used here (*pešaʿ*) "does not simply involve external disobedience or breaking a law, but entails the violation of a sacred covenant, i.e., revolt (a deliberate act of disloyalty and disobedience)."

17. Ross, *Commentary on the Psalms*, 484, observes that the verb *rāṣâ* "is another word that is used in the Levitical ritual with reference to the pleasing nature of acceptable sacrifices. The psalmist was well aware of the unacceptability of sinful people to God. His prayer to be acceptable would assume forgiveness and preservation from sin."

well be using the image to speak of refuge and protection from the threat of his bent to sin, and Redeemer perhaps speaks of deliverance from bondage to sin.[18]

## PSALM 19 AND REVELATION

When theologians speak of revelation, they most often refer to what God has made known *about himself*.[19] This divine revelation consists of both general revelation available to all humans, and special revelation, which is more limited in its recipients. Grudem contends, "People can obtain a knowledge that God exists, and a knowledge of some of his attributes, simply from observation of themselves and the world around.... To look at the sky is to see evidence of the infinite power, wisdom and even beauty of God; it is to observe a majestic witness to the glory of God."[20] In his argument demonstrating that all humans stand condemned before the holy God, Paul states in Romans 1:19 that what is known through general revelation in nature is genuine knowledge, or truth, about God. As Demarest notes, "That which has been disclosed to their minds apart from supernatural revelation is properly knowledge of God (*to gnoston theou*)."[21]

Psalm 19 begins in verses 1–6 by stating that the heavens declare the glory of God, and that this revelation is as extensive as the shining of the sun. Lewis notes, "The key phrase on which the whole poem depends is 'there is nothing hid from the heat thereof.' It pierces everywhere with its strong, clean ardour."[22] Through nature all humans know that God exists and that they should give thanks to him, but by their unrighteousness humans have suppressed the truth they know about God through nature (Rom 1:18–21). From these texts, Calvin concluded that "while there is a universal revelation that renders all people responsible, the habit of sinful human beings is to turn this general knowledge of God into idolatry."[23] General revelation

---

18. For a lucid discussion of the epithets applied to Yahweh in v. 14, see Klouda, "Dialectical Interplay of Seeing and Hearing," 189–90.

19. Lewis and Demarest, *Integrative Theology*, 1:61. They go on to provide a useful summary of the various facets of God's self-revelation through the created world (1:72).

20. Grudem, *Systematic Theology*, 121. Similarly, Erickson, *Introducing Christian Doctrine*, 34, cites Psalm 19:1 and Romans 1:20 as key biblical texts on general revelation, and then concludes, "These and numerous other passages, such as the 'nature psalms,' suggest that God has left evidence of himself in the world he has created. The person who views the beauty of a sunset and the biology student dissecting a complex organism are exposed to indications of the greatness of God."

21. Demarest, *General Revelation*, 230.

22. Lewis, *Reflections on the Psalms*, 74.

23. Migliore, *Faith Seeking Understanding*, 31.

in nature, then, is sufficient to condemn all humans, but by itself it does not provide a clear account of the good news of salvation through Christ. As Lewis notes in *The Four Loves*, "We have seen an image of the glory. We must not try to find a direct path through it [nature] and beyond it to an increasing knowledge of God. The path peters out almost at once. . . . We can't get through; not that way. We must make a *detour*—leave the hills and woods and go back to our studies, to church, to our Bibles, to our knees."[24]

The biblical testimony about general revelation in Psalm 19:1–6, Romans 1–2, and related passages has been misconstrued in three ways. First, natural theology sometimes overvalues the witness of nature, when proponents argue that "it is possible, without a prior commitment of faith to the beliefs of Christianity, and without relying upon any special authority, such as an institution (the church) or a document (the Bible), to come to a genuine knowledge of God on the basis of reason alone."[25] Later this morphed into secular rationalism in the Enlightenment, in which certain truth could be attained by human reason alone apart from divine revelation.

Second, other theologians undervalue the witness of nature, denying "that natural man can know anything of God through the general revelation found in nature, but insist[ing] that knowledge of God can only come through a knowledge of God's grace in Christ."[26] This perspective tends to overestimate the impact of the fall, assuming too much damage to human reason and too great a distortion of the witness of creation as a result of Adam's sin.

Third, although Psalm 19:1–6 speaks of how the heavens declare the glory of God, it is evident that God has also made known information that is not specifically about himself both in the Bible and in the created world. Many times "general revelation" has been imprecisely applied to this broader knowledge that God has made known to humans, even though in its technical theological sense revelation pertains specifically to what God has made known about himself. When Psalm 19:1–6 is used to validate the discovery of truth in the created world that does not pertain to knowledge about God, and that knowledge is called general revelation, that description goes beyond what Psalm 19 actually states when it says that the heavens declare the

---

24. Lewis, *Four Loves*, 27.

25. Erickson, *Introducing Christian Doctrine*, 35. Hoffmeier, "Heavens Declare the Glory of God," 20, concludes that "the revelation of God that is apprehended by looking at the expanse of the heavens, or any part of God's creation, is limited to providing veiled information about God, but not what is necessary to know God in any intimate or salvific sense."

26. Grudem, *Systematic Theology*, 121–22. Grudem is here referring to Barth's understanding of natural revelation. See also Demarest, *General Revelation*, 128.

glory of God. It would be better to distinguish carefully between "general revelation," which refers specifically to what God has revealed about himself in the created world (as well as in the human conscience [Romans 2] and in the flow of history [Psalms 78, 105, 106]), and perhaps language such as "discovered truth," which refers generally to knowledge that relates to "the spiritual, moral, and material dimensions of the world he created."[27]

## PSALM 19 AND THE INTEGRATION OF FAITH, LEARNING, AND LIFE

As has been seen in the previous section, Psalm 19 is a key text relating to God's revelation of himself in the creation, but many have wrongly extrapolated from this to refer to all knowledge derived from the academic disciplines as general revelation. There are at least three ways that Psalm 19 has been used imprecisely, which should be more carefully evaluated.

Over the past fifty years, there has been extensive discussion in Christian colleges and universities about the integration of faith and learning, or how Christian theology can be studied in conversation with the various academic disciplines.[28] In these discussions, Psalm 19 has often played a featured role, but in many cases how the psalm has been used has been imprecise. Specifically, Psalm 19 has factored into discussions relating to the doctrine of *sola Scriptura*, or the related issue of the sufficiency of Scripture. Also, since the early church there has been a longstanding claim that "all truth is God's truth,"[29] and that underlies the conception of the Christian academic enterprise as pursuing God's truth wherever he has made it known, whether in the Bible (cf. Ps 19:7–11), or outside of the Bible (cf. Ps 19:1–6). Finally, although Christian colleges and universities have typically spoken of the integration of faith and learning, Psalm 19:12–14 suggests that the scope of the integration task should be widened to include life as well. In each of these cases, there is need for a precise and carefully nuanced statement of what a biblically-informed model for integration entails.

---

27. Litfin, *Conceiving the Christian College*, 173.

28. E.g., Dockery, *Faith and Learning*; Henry and Agee, *Faithful Learning*; Lawson, *Professor's Puzzle*.

29. This quote has been sourced to multiple figures within church history, but it is, at least, a consistent paraphrase of Augustine, *On Christian Teaching*, 2.72.

## *Sola Scriptura*

Already in the early church there is clear evidence that the Bible was regarded as the ultimate authority for sound doctrine and "the rule by which all things must be measured."[30] For example, Athanasius stated that the "divinely inspired Scriptures are sufficient for the exposition of the truth," and Augustine wrote that "among the things that are plainly laid down in Scriptures are to be found all matters that concern faith and the manner of life."[31]

During the Reformation a key point of controversy between the Roman Catholic Church and Protestants, such as Luther and Calvin, was the supreme authority for determining church doctrine. In striking contrast to the church hierarchy, the Reformers insisted that Christ alone is the head of the church and that his word alone is the supreme authority for church doctrine, so "they concluded that all other would-be authorities (including popes, councils, and church traditions) must be subjected to Christ and his Word."[32] It is important to note, however, that for the Reformers, *sola Scriptura*, while relegating the church's magisterial authority and tradition to secondary status, does not eliminate altogether the legitimacy of other extrabiblical resources for the development of Christian theology.[33]

It is evident that the Reformers, in agreement with the early church testimony, used the phrase *sola Scriptura* to affirm that the Bible is the supreme authority or norm for evaluating all knowledge of God, and it is in that sense the Scriptures are sufficient. Saying that the Scriptures are sufficient, however, leaves a question hanging: sufficient *for what*? Cole traces how the scope of the normativity of the Scriptures has been debated, and that the same language has been used to speak of rather different things. He concludes, "Three possibilities, as regards the sufficiency of Scripture today, have already been canvassed. The micro view delimits Scripture's sufficiency

---

30. Busenitz, "Ground and Pillar of the Faith," 132.

31. Cited in Ward, *Words of Life*, 107–8. He goes on to demonstrate that in the Middle Ages "the predominant view was that Scripture was sufficient on matters relating directly to salvation."

32. Busenitz, "Ground and Pillar of the Faith," 116.

33. Vanhoozer, *Biblical Authority after Babel*, 111. Similarly, George, *Theology of the Reformers*, 315, notes, "In the sixteenth century the inspiration and authority of Holy Scripture was not a matter of dispute between Catholics and Protestants. All of the reformers, including the radicals, accepted the divine origin and infallible character of the Bible. The issue which emerged at the Reformation was how the divinely attested authority of Holy Scripture was related to the authority of the church and ecclesiastical tradition (Roman Catholics) on the one hand and the power of personal experience (spiritualists) on the other. The *sola* in *sola Scriptura* was not intended to discount completely the value of church tradition, but rather to subordinate it to the primacy of Holy Scripture."

to its role as the source and norm of the church's gospel proclamation; the macro extends Scripture's sufficiency to include doctrine, and the mega subsumes both and adds a view of Scripture as the foundation of all human inquiry."[34] This third category deserves more careful analysis.

It is important to differentiate between the Scriptures as the supreme norm for knowledge and the Scriptures being the exclusive source for knowledge. Thus, one can hold to a view of *sola Scriptura* that regards the Bible as the necessary measure for evaluating the legitimacy of all truth claims without having to conclude that the Bible alone is the only source in which all knowledge is discovered. For instance, Frame asserts that *sola Scriptura* "does not require the exclusion of all extrabiblical data, even from theology. It simply requires that in theology and in all other disciplines, the highest authority, the supreme standard, must be Scripture and Scripture alone."[35]

In recent years, *sola Scriptura* has come to be used by some in a way that diverges considerably from what the Reformers meant by the expression. Ward explains, "It is often the case in the history of the church that a doctrine is explained with clarity and conviction in one period, and then is slowly transformed over time into something rather different, but with its descriptive label still attached. That is especially so with *sola Scriptura*. When it is described both by contemporary supporters and contemporary opponents, the doctrine in view often differs significantly from what we find in the writings of Luther, Calvin, and other Protestant writers of past centuries."[36] In this new version, *sola Scriptura* is presented in a way that approaches the *nuda Scriptura* that is described by Lane as a distortion of Reformation theology: "Again, *sola Scriptura* did not for the Reformers mean *nuda Scriptura*. It has been shown that neither for the Reformers, nor for Protestant theology does *sola Scriptura* imply that Scripture is either the sole source or the sole resource, although it is undoubtedly the supreme source. . . . But for the Reformation and for evangelical theology Scripture

---

34. Cole, "Sola Scriptura," 30.

35. Frame, *Apologetics*, 18.

36. Ward, *Words of Life*, 140. He goes on to conclude (p. 151), "Thus *sola Scriptura*, in its proper formulation as found in the thinking of the mainstream Protestant Reformers, is not what many of its modern critics or defenders imagine it is. It does not deny the necessity of traditions of biblical interpretation, creedal formulations of biblical faith, and inherited church practices that help to express and pass on that faith. Rather it ensures that those traditions serve Scripture, the supreme authority, rather than compete with it. *Sola Scriptura* means 'Scripture supreme.'" Lillback and Gaffin, *Thy Word is Still Truth*, in its 1348 pages of mainly primary sources, contains no mention of the sufficiency of Scripture or *sola Scriptura* being used to affirm that God's revealed truth is limited to the Bible alone.

remains the final authority, to which one can appeal against all ecclesiastical authority. This was and remains the heart of the meaning of *sola Scriptura*."[37]

John MacArthur is a leading advocate for this adapted version of *sola Scriptura*. He has written at least three articles on the topic, as well as editing two books that relate to it. In his study on the sufficiency of Scripture in Psalm 19, MacArthur barely touches on verses 1–6, but he focuses on verses 7–11, and concludes that the central point of the psalm is that "Scripture is not only true, inerrant, and authoritative; it is also *sufficient*. It gives us every truth that really matters. It shows us the way of salvation and then equips us for every good work (2 Tim. 3:15–17). . . . Scripture is eternally true, always applicable, and perfectly sufficient to meet all our spiritual needs."[38] However, he also qualifies the sufficiency of the Scriptures by saying, "Obviously, the Bible is not an encyclopedic source of information about every conceivable subject. But as God's instruction for man's life, it is perfect. It contains everything we need to know about God, his glory, faith, life, and the way of salvation."[39] This raises two questions that he does not address. First, if the Bible contains everything humans need to know about God's glory, then what does Psalm 19:1 mean when it says the heavens are declaring the glory of God, and how is it that Paul argues in Romans 1:18–21 that humans stand guilty before God because they have suppressed the truth about God that they have come to know *through the created world*? Second, if God's instruction for human life in the Bible is perfect, does that include all aspects of human life, or only some aspects of human life?

At its worst, some interpretations of *sola Scriptura* are reductionistic and effectively cut off Christians from potentially beneficial ideas that are not drawn directly from the pages of the Bible. This is particularly a concern among some circles of biblical counselors who reject the findings of psychology because they believe Scripture's sufficiency prevents needing

---

37. Lane, "Sola Scriptura," 327. Similarly, Barrett, *God's Word Alone*, 343–44, reasons, "If Scripture is sufficient, is it wrong for the believer to look to or utilize extrabiblical sources? No. Remember, *sola Scriptura* is not arguing that Scripture is the only authority or the only source from which we can draw (i.e., *nuda Scriptura*). It is arguing that while there may be other good sources, these are always fallible and inferior to Scripture, which alone is infallible and supreme, and unlike other sources it alone is divine revelation. When the Reformed confessions say Scripture is our 'sole' authority, they do not mean that there are no other authorities we should listen to or even submit to (creeds, councils, etc.), but rather that these authorities and sources are always subordinate to Scripture. Therefore, it is not a violation of *sola Scriptura* to recognize that extrabiblical sources, though never to be put on par with Scripture, can be helpful and advantageous."

38. MacArthur, "Sufficiency of Scripture," 39.

39. MacArthur, "Sufficiency of Scripture," 29–30.

additional sources beyond the canon.[40] Examples outside academic circles can be seen when people promote "biblical diets" and similar faddish ideas that claim to replace contemporary scientific understanding with questionable interpretations of Scripture. Psalm 19 helps point Christians away from presentations of *sola Scriptura* that cut off believers from extra-biblical sources of information, while pointing them toward the goodness and sufficiency of God's word.

## *All Truth is God's Truth*

In addition to the sufficiency of Scripture debate, Psalm 19 also factors into claims that all truth is God's truth. This expression, which has a long history of use from the early church to the present day, has a number of nuances, which have been capably summarized by Litfin.[41] Until the recent adaptation of the understanding of the sufficiency of Scripture, the idea that all truth is God's truth was regarded as fully compatible with *sola Scriptura*, for as Packer contends, "*Sola Scriptura* was never meant to imply that what is not mentioned in the Bible is not real, or is unimportant and not worth our attention, or that the history of biblical exegesis and exposition, and of theological construction and confession, over two millennia, need not concern us today, or that we should restrict our interest in God's world and in the arts, sciences, products, and dreams of our fellow-human beings to matters which at least one Bible writer directly discusses."[42] What "all truth is God's truth" indicates is that while the Bible is *sufficient* as the supreme authority and norm, it does not present *exhaustive* truth. Holmes contends, "The Christian regards the biblical revelation as the final rule of faith and conduct, but he does not think of it as an exhaustive source of all truth. The teaching authority of Scripture commits the believer at certain focal points and so provides an interpretive framework, an overall glimpse of how everything relates to God. . . . Moreover, if all truth is God's truth and truth

---

40. In an article on biblical counseling, MacArthur protégé Wayne Mack writes that Scripture "contains a God-ordained, sufficient, comprehensive system of theoretical commitments, principles, insights, goals, and appropriate methods for understanding and resolving the non-physical problems of people. It provides for us a model that needs no supplement. God, the expert on helping people, has given us in Scripture counseling perspectives and methodology that are wholly adequate for resolving our sin-related problems." Mack, "Sufficiency of Scripture in Counseling," 82. This is, essentially, a declaration that there is no value in discoveries about psychology outside of the Bible.

41. Litfin, *Conceiving the Christian College*, 86–95.

42. Packer, "Bible in Use," 77.

is one, then God does not contradict himself, and in the final analysis there will be no conflict between the truth taught in Scripture and truth available from other sources."[43]

When speaking of truth, it is crucial to define the term precisely, because it is used in many disparate ways. For example, a scientific truth is a claim that has been accepted as accurate at the present time, even though it is acknowledged that further research may well require it to be revised. There are many political, social, economic, and religious dogmas that are regarded by their proponents as truth to such an extent that they regard those who differ from their dogma to be in error. For many people, truth is their individual perspective or what has been constructed by their social group, so that the truth of one person or group is held alongside the truths of other people or groups. Some within the Christian community have insisted that truth is exclusively what God has revealed in the Bible, so that if it is in the Bible it is truth, but that there is no truth sourced outside of the Bible.

The Bible does indeed declare itself to be God's truth (cf. John 17:17), but it also points outside of itself to other aspects of God's truth. For example, Jesus states that he is the truth (John 14:6), and in Romans 1:18–25 Paul (alluding to Psalm 19:1–6) speaks of how the wrath of God is revealed from heaven against those who suppress the truth that they have come to know in the created world, not in the Bible. In addition, John 20:30–31 and 21:24–25 indicate that Jesus taught and did many things that are not included in the biblical text, and Deuteronomy 29:29 refers to the secret things that God has not chosen to reveal to his people.[44] Taking all of this biblical evidence into account, it seems best to define truth as the sum total of reality known fully by the omniscient God. Some of the truth that God alone knows fully he has made knowable in the Bible, some of it he has made knowable by means outside of the Bible, and some he has retained to himself, such that it is not knowable, at least at present, to the human mind. All of the truth, then, is God's truth, ultimately finding its source in God. As Dockery reasons, this divine source of all truth provides the beginning place for integrative Christian higher education: "All true knowledge flows from the one Creator to His one creation. Thus specific bodies of knowledge relate to one another not just because scholars work together in community, not just because

---

43. Holmes, *Idea of a Christian College*, 18.

44. Frame, *Doctrine of the Word of God*, 47, argues, "Scripture is God's sufficient revelation to us today, for all of life. But it would not be right to say that the Bible is the *only* word of God that has ever been spoken.... Further, it is evident that the prophets, apostles, and Jesus all uttered inspired spoken words that did not end up as part of the canon of Scripture. And God speaks also to angels (Ps. 103:20) and to the natural world (Pss 147:15–18; 148:8), words that we do not have in written form."

interdisciplinary work broadens our knowledge, but because all truth has its source in God, composing a single universe of knowledge."[45]

As humans endeavor to understand God's truth, whether that truth be accessible in the Bible or outside of the Bible, they are able to know, but only in part (cf. 1 Cor 13:12). This limitation is due in part to the fact that God has not revealed all that he knows, and in part to the reality that humans have only finite ability to perceive the truth that God has revealed. To complicate the problem, the noetic effect of the fall distorts human perceptions of the truth that God has made knowable, with the result that not all truth claims propounded by humans are valid. Litfin reasons well: "Because of their finiteness and sinfulness, humans do not always or even typically understand God's reality accurately.... Humans may misunderstand what God has said in his word, or they may misconstrue what they discover within the created order. In either case, to the extent their apprehensions, or their expressions of those apprehensions, accord with reality as God knows it to be, their apprehensions or expressions may be said to be truthful. To the extent they do not accord with that reality, they are in error."[46] To counteract this propensity to error, all truth claims must be viewed and evaluated through the lens of what God has made known in Scripture, because it is the supreme authority and norm for evaluating all knowledge. It is not necessary for the truth to be sourced specifically within the Bible for it to be regarded as belonging to the sum total of reality known to the omniscient God, but it must be compatible with what God has revealed in the Bible. As aspects of God's truth are validated in the light of the Bible, the ongoing goal of the integration of faith and learning is to bring these pieces of truth together in order to recreate more and more fully the picture of truth as God alone knows it perfectly. As Holmes envisions it, if all truth is God's truth, "then our task is to interpret it as such by developing Christian perspectives in the natural and social sciences and the humanities, so as to structure a Christian worldview that exhibits plainly the principle that truth is one and all truth is God's."[47]

It is just this perspective of the unification of truth that Lewis seemed to espouse as consistent with the Christian mind and effective for evangelism. Often it is the unity of truth that has apologetic power, as Lewis notes, "I believe that any Christian who is qualified to write a good popular book on any science may do much more than by any directly apologetic work.... What we want is not more little books about Christianity, but

---

45. Dockery, *Renewing Minds*, 63.
46. Litfin, *Conceiving the Christian College*, 92.
47. Holmes, *Idea of a Christian College*, 63.

more little books by Christians on other subjects—with their Christianity latent."[48] The ability to attest to legitimate truths outside of Scripture, showing them (without contortions) to be harmonious with the truth of Scripture, is a central attribute of the Christian mind. As Gene Fant argues in his essay in this volume, wisdom entails the ability to integrate knowledge from the world around into an orthodox, consistent Christian understanding of the cosmos.[49] The Christian mind can thus effectively resist various errors by an expansive vision of reality, uniting the aspects of truth that God, who is Truth, has made knowable through both his created world and his inspired word.

## *The Integration of Faith, Learning, and Life*

Finally, it must be mentioned briefly that Psalm 19 may point toward a broader notion of integration than what is usually conceived. The extensive literature on Christian higher education typically refers to the integration of faith and learning.[50] However, the personal response by the psalmist (vv. 12–14) to what the creation reveals about the glory of God (vv. 1–6) and to what the *tôrâ* reveals (vv. 7–11) suggests that the standard terminology should be expanded to speak also of the integration of faith, learning, *and life*. Viewed in this way, education that is thoroughly Christian is not merely an intellectual activity, but it must be applied to and appropriated in every area of life, ranging from the individual person to the largest issues confronting humanity. Although this expansive life context is not delineated explicitly in Psalm 19, the life response by the psalmist to what is revealed in God's world and in God's word suggests and is consistent with this broader agenda.

Lewis saw this expansion of Christianity into all of life as an essential attribute of faithful living. This is evident in his essay, "Good Work and Good Works," where he writes, "Let choirs sing well or not at all. Otherwise we merely confirm the majority in their conviction that the world of Business, which does with such efficiency so much that never really needed doing, is the real, the adult, and the practical world; and that all this 'culture' and all

48. Lewis, "Christian Apologetics," 150.

49. See Fant's essay in chapter 6.

50. For example, Litfin, *Conceiving the Christian College*, 173, observes, "The Christian's intellectual task therefore consists of glorifying God by, among other things, utilizing our God-given capacities to discover and correlate truth—truth about God and truth about the spiritual, moral, and material dimensions of the world he created. This process of apprehension and correlation is what we mean by the phrase 'the integration of faith and learning.'"

this 'religion' (horrid words both) are essentially marginal, amateurish, and rather effeminate activities."[51] No, if Christianity is true, then the Christian mind should see all truth in unity and integrate faith with all of life.

## CONCLUSION

Psalm 19 has often been adduced in discussions relating to various issues in theology and in Christian education. This article has endeavored to clarify more precisely how Psalm 19 relates to general revelation, to *sola Scriptura* and the sufficiency of Scripture, and to the claim that all truth is God's truth, and it concludes by suggesting that an expanded conception of the integration of faith and learning to include life response as well is warranted. Although it has not always been properly applied, Psalm 19 remains a central passage of Scripture for understanding the nature of truth and its relationship to the Christian mind.

## BIBLIOGRAPHY

Brown, William P. "'Night to Night,' 'Deep to Deep': The Discourse of Creation in the Psalms." In *"My Words are Lovely:" Studies in the Rhetoric of the Psalms*, edited by Robert L. Foster and Daiv M. Howard Jr., 63–74. New York: T. & T. Clark, 2008.

Busenitz, Nathan. "The Ground and Pillar of the Faith: The Witness of Pre-Reformation History to the Doctrine of Sola Scriptura." In *The Inerrant Word: Biblical, Historical, Theological, and Pastoral Perspectives*, edited by John MacArthur, 115–33. Wheaton: Crossway, 2016.

Clines, D. J. A. "The Tree of Knowledge and the Law of Yahweh (Psalm XIX)." *Vetus Testamentum* 24 (1974) 8–14.

Cole, Graham. "Sola Scriptura: Some Historical and Contemporary Perspectives." *The Churchman* 104 (1990) 20–34.

Cooley, Jeffrey L. "Psalm 19: A Sabbath Song." *Vetus Testamentum* 64 (2014) 177–95.

Craigie, Peter C. *Psalms 1-50*. Word Biblical Commentary 19. Waco: Word, 1983.

Demarest, Bruce A. *General Revelation: Historical Views and Contemporary Issues*. Grand Rapids: Zondervan, 1982.

Dockery, David S. *Renewing Minds: Serving Church and Society through Christian Higher Education*. Nashville: B & H Academic, 2007.

Dockery, David S., ed. *Faith and Learning: A Handbook for Christian Higher Education*. Nashville: B&H Academic, 2012.

Erickson, Millard. *Introducing Christian Doctrine*. Grand Rapids: Baker, 1992.

Firth, David G. "More than Just Torah: God's Instructions in the Psalms." *Southeastern Theological Review* 6 (2015) 68–75.

Frame, John M. *Apologetics: A Justification of Christian Belief*. Phillipsburg: P & R Publishing, 2015.

———. *The Doctrine of the Word of God*. Phillipsburg: P & R Publishing, 2010.

George, Timothy. *Theology of the Reformers*. Nashville: Broadman, 1988.

---

51. Lewis, "Good Work and Good Works," 383.

Goldingay, John. *Psalms, Vol. 1: Psalms 1–41*. Baker Commentary on the Old Testament Wisdom and Psalms. Grand Rapids: Baker Academic, 2006.

Grudem, Wayne. *Systematic Theology: An Introduction to Biblical Doctrine*. Grand Rapids: Zondervan, 1994.

Henry, Douglas V., and Bob R. Agee, eds. *Faithful Learning and the Christian Scholarly Vocation*. Grand Rapids: Eerdmans, 2003.

Hoffmeier, James K. "'The Heavens Declare the Glory of God': The Limits of General Revelation." *Trinity Journal* 21 (2000) 17–24.

Holmes, Arthur F. *The Idea of a Christian College*. Grand Rapids: Eerdmans, 1987.

Klouda, Sheri L. "The Dialectical Interplay of Seeing and Hearing in Psalm 19 and Its Connection to Wisdom." *Bulletin of Biblical Research* 10 (2000) 181–95.

Knierim, Rolf P. *The Task of Old Testament Theology: Substance, Method, and Cases*. Grand Rapids: Eerdmans, 1995.

Lane, Anthony N. S. "Sola Scriptura? Making Sense of a Post-Reformation Slogan." In *A Pathway into the Holy Scripture*, edited by Philip E. Satterthwaite and David F. Wright, 297–328. Grand Rapids: Eerdmans, 1994.

Lawson, Michael S. *The Professor's Puzzle: Teaching in Christian Academics*. Nashville: B&H Academic, 2016.

Lewis, C. S. "Christian Apologetics." In *C. S. Lewis: Essay Collection and Other Short Pieces*, edited by Lesley Walmsley, 379–83. London: HarperCollins, 2000.

———. *The Four Loves*. New York: HarperCollins, 1960.

———. "Good Work and Good Works." In *C. S. Lewis: Essay Collection and Other Short Pieces*, edited by Lesley Walmsley, 147–59. London: HarperCollins, 2000.

———. *Reflections on the Psalms*. New York: Harcourt, Brace, 1958.

Lewis, Gordon R., and Bruce A. Demarest. *Integrative Theology*. 3 vols. Grand Rapids: Zondervan Academic, 1987–94.

Lillback, Peter A., and Richard B. Gaffin, eds. *Thy Word is Still Truth: Essential Writings on the Doctrine of Scripture from the Reformation to Today*. Phillipsburg: P & R Publishing, 2013.

Litfin, Duane. *Conceiving the Christian College*. Grand Rapids: Eerdmans, 2004.

MacArthur, John. "The Sufficiency of Scripture: Psalm 19." In *The Inerrant Word: Biblical, Historical, Theological, and Pastoral Perspectives*, edited by John MacArthur, ##–##. Wheaton: Crossway, 2016.

Mack, Wayne A. "The Sufficiency of Scripture in Counseling." *The Master's Seminary Journal* 9 (1998) 63–84.

Migliore, Daniel L. *Faith Seeking Understanding: An Introduction to Christian Theology*. 2nd ed. Grand Rapids: Eerdmans, 2004.

Packer, J. I. "The Bible in Use: Evangelicals Seeking Truth from Holy Scripture." In *Your Word Is Truth*, edited by Charles Colson and Richard John Neuhaus, ##–##. Grand Rapids: Eerdmans, 2002.

Ross, Allen P. *A Commentary on the Psalms: Volume 1 (1–41)*. Kregel Exegetical Library. Grand Rapids: Kregel, 2011.

Schaefer, Konrad. *Psalms, Berit Olam: Studies in Hebrew Narrative & Poetry*. Collegeville: Liturgical, 2001.

Travers, Michael E. *Encountering God in the Psalms*. Grand Rapids: Kregel, 2003.

VanGemeren, William A. "Psalms." In *The Expositor's Bible Commentary: Psalms, Proverbs, Ecclesiastes, Song of Songs*, edited by NAME(S) HERE, 5:##–##. Grand Rapids: Zondervan, 1991.

VanGemeren, William A., ed. *New International Dictionary of Old Testament Theology and Exegesis.* 5 vols. Grand Rapids: Baker, 1997.

Vanhoozer, Kevin. *Biblical Authority after Babel: Retrieving the Solas in the Spirit of Mere Protestant Christianity.* Grand Rapids: Brazos, 2016.

Vos, Cas J. A. "Theopoetical and Liturgical Patterns of the Psalms with Reference to Psalm 19." In *Psalms and Liturgy*, edited by Dirk J. Human and Cas J. A. Vos. London: T. & T. Clark, 2004.

Wagner, J. Ross. "From the Heavens to the Heart: The Dynamics of Psalm 19 as Prayer." *CBQ* 61 (1999) 245–61.

Ward, Timothy. *Words of Life: Scripture as the Living and Active Word of God.* Downers Grove: IVP Academic, 2009.

Weiser, Artur. *The Psalms.* Translated by Herbert Hartwell. Philadelphia: Westminster, 1962.

# 6

## The Fox and the Fool

"Wisdom of the Greeks" and the Godly Fool
in *Till We Have Faces*

*Gene C. Fant, Jr.*

WHEN C. S. LEWIS sat down to rework the myth of Cupid and Psyche in *Till We Have Faces*, he was a storyteller at the peak of his powers. Additionally, he was a scholar whose compendious knowledge of literature and comparative myths provided him with a larder full of ideas that would fuel his work. Some critics, such as Sharon Jebb, have called his final novel his best, and there seems to be a love for *Faces* on the part of some critics that is not offered to some of Lewis's other works.[1]

For the educated reader, *Faces* is densely textured with allusions, literary devices, and sensibilities borrowed from Western masterpieces, from Dante to Milton to Shakespeare to the Middle English *Pearl*. The sheer mythic power of Lewis's version of the story manifests itself throughout the novel. The subtitle itself reveals just how self-consciously Lewis fashioned his version: "A Myth Retold."

Lewis often avoids overt references to Christianity in his fictional works, preferring to be allusive in his methodology, and *Faces* drips with Christian presumptions, including the strong sense of justice and the power

---

1. Jebb, "I Lived and Knew Myself," 111.

of the supernatural that dominate the text. Among these presumptions is that of godly wisdom and the contrast between the so-called wisdom of this world and the actual wisdom of the divine. This is the sort of perspectival divide that fills Job 38:2–4's declarations from God: "Who is this that darkens counsel by words without knowledge? Dress for action like a man; I will question you, and you make it known to me. Where were you when I laid the foundation of the earth? Tell me, if you have understanding."[2] Godly wisdom is a key attribute of the Christian mind as Lewis envisions it in *Faces*. Through Orual, Psyche, and the Fox, we may see how true wisdom is explored, even as we see how Lewis uses allusive inversions and paradoxes to weave a richly textured tale that brings the reader to the realization that true wisdom is not of our own construction.

## THE MYTH OF CUPID AND PSYCHE

The Roman poet Apuleius gave the West the tale of Cupid and Psyche in *The Golden Ass*, his second-century collection of tales. The lovers became prominent in popular culture almost immediately, retaining a place even in Christian culture until the Renaissance, when the story again captured the European imagination through poetry, sculpture, and paintings. The myth has continued to inspire creative works ever since, even as recently as the 1980s, when the New Wave band Scritti Politti released a successful CD titled "Cupid and Psyche 85."

In the basic myth, Cupid falls in love with the overwhelmingly beautiful Psyche and provides her with an invisible mansion in which she may live. He demands that his appearance must be hidden from her and that she cannot see him as he is. When Psyche's sisters trick her into revealing the god's face, Psyche is exiled as a punishment. Embedded within the myth were the larger truths related to love, justice, and family relationships.

Lewis's retelling focuses on one sister, Orual, who loved Istra/Psyche in a particularly maternal way, providing an alternative backstory posing as a first-person accusation against the gods. Lewis's version is not a demythologization but rather a pre-mythologization, asserting a fictionally historical background that grew into myth. This qualifies as a type of *mythopoesis* (the generation of a myth), which both Lewis and his associate J. R. R. Tolkien believed was a primary goal for writers.[3] In fact, the latter portions of

---

2. An argument could be made that *Faces* follows a similar structure to Job, with Orual parallel to Job, the Fox to Job's collection of scoffing friends, and the final vision being similar to God's speech from the whirlwind. All Scripture references are from the English Standard Version.

3. Tolkien coined the term "mythopoesis" circa 1931 in a poem of that title; his use

the story (when Orual writes her version of the story) are self-conscious assertions of the tension between the "true" story and the mythic version. Orual clings to the veracity of her version of the story (against that of the latter writers she imagined, such as Apuleius), bemoaning, "I saw all in a moment how the false story would grow and spread and be told all over the earth; and I wondered how many of the other sacred stories are just such twisted falsities as this."[4] As she ostensibly writes the document that becomes *Faces*, she complains, "All day, and often all night too, I was recalling every passage of the true story, dragging up terrors, humiliations, struggles, and anguish that I had not thought of for years, letting Orual wake and speak, digging her almost out of a grave, out of the walled well."[5]

The Christian framework of *Faces* is clear in a number of places, as Lewis follows the New Testament Passion narrative via the pivotal sacrifice of Psyche and its aftermath. While Lewis claims that as a writer he is not a fan of allegory, *Faces* is soundly allegorical, tapping the biblical Christ story for power and structure.[6] The plague and drought afflicting Glome symbolize the plague of sin in the post-fallen world. Only a blood sacrifice will overcome the death pall that saps the land, just as only a holy sacrifice can overcome humankind's sin guilt. In *Faces*, the sacrifice is found in the death of Glome's best, the beautiful princess Psyche, whom the king offers freely and pragmatically. Just as the mob precedes Christ's death march, Psyche is carried to her apparent death by a procession of Glomians. She appears after her supposed death and is translated to a new state afterwards.

For Lewis, mythic does not necessarily mean "false." Mythic means "powerful," a tale that reflects larger truths that speak to culture. Myth is better defined, perhaps, as a powerful story that provides meaning to a culture or set of cultures. The matter of Cupid and Psyche speaks about larger truths. It is these truths that, although inexact in their reflection of the full divine truth, the Christian mind can use to point toward the unity in diversity in all reality. Lewis, then, sees the tale as a means by which he can produce his own *magnum opus*.

---

of the term recast the formation of myth from a diachronic process over many generations or centuries to a deliberate act by an author or group of authors. Tolkien, *Tree and Leaf*, 97–101.

4. Lewis, *Till We Have Faces*, 244.

5. Lewis, *Till We Have Faces*, 247.

6. See, for example, Miller, "*Pearl* Maiden's Psyche," 43; and Arnell, "On Beauty, Justice, and the Sublime," 23–33.

## THE THEME OF WISDOM

Among the dominant themes of *Faces* is wisdom. Wisdom is a dear theme for Lewis; his corpus of works makes it clear that he values effective learning, meaning learning that effects more than factual mastery or intellectual callowness. He sums this up in his now famous pronouncement, "We make men without chests and expect of them virtue and enterprise. We laugh at honour and are shocked to find traitors in our midst. We castrate and bid the geldings to be fruitful."[7] He clearly worries about the future of education in the West, and in Christendom in particular. He worries about the loss of the vision of the wholeness of the *cosmos* as it reveals the nature and works of God.

Readers witness the intellectual growth and character development of Orual through the story's arc, watching the Fox mentor her through adolescence and into her own reign. As inheritors of the Enlightenment, most readers view the Fox as the epitome of wise counsel. His keen intellect makes him clearly the wisest man in Glome, though other men such as Bardia possess insight, too. The Fox, however, has brought the intellectual treasures of Greece (and the West more largely) to the outlands, depositing his hoard into the eager mind of Orual in particular. His role as a pedagogue for the royal household and counselor to King Trom positions him as an authority on matters that require discernment and subtlety.

The Fox taps into a significant tradition in English letters, that of the court advisor who provides a sounding board for the royal household. Shakespeare, for example, distills this tradition in two plays: *Hamlet* and *King Lear*, in the characters, respectively, of Polonius and the Fool. While Polonius is the epitome of the scrupulously politic counselor, *Lear*'s Fool is a remarkable counselor who speaks truth to power in ways similar to those of the Fox, who is as forceful as he is reliable. His voracious sense of curiosity causes Orual to note, "I never knew such a man for questions. He wanted to know everything about our country and language and ancestors and gods, and even our plants and flowers."[8] This curiosity leads naturally to questions about the worship of Ungit, the national deity of Glome. When Orual describes the occasional demand for a human sacrifice, the Fox winces and mumbles a vague grievance.[9] Throughout her education, Orual hears the Fox's cynical responses to the outlandish superstitions of the people, as he sneers cynically at the folk religion that has grown up around Ungit's followers. As the story unfolds, the Fox counters nearly every assumption of Ungit

---

7. Lewis, *Abolition of Man*, 26.
8. Lewis, *Till We Have Faces*, 7.
9. Lewis, *Till We Have Faces*, 7–8.

worship with a deflating assertion of physical reality. When, for example, Orual describes how Glomian women seek to conceive male children through the construction of beds from a certain type of eastern wood ("four of every five children begotten in such a bed would be male"[10]), he responds, "All folly, child, these things come about by natural causes."[11] To this man with a materialistic needle, everything religious looks like a balloon in need of bursting.

Readers face a dilemma regarding the Fox, however. He is the most nurturing father figure in the story, a contrast to the cool, abusive King Trom. In a brutal court filled with intrigue and heartbreak, the Fox is a strikingly modern character who naturally draws readers into his confidence and admiration. Even his skepticism strikes us as worthy of our admiration. Certainly we shudder along with him at the thought of a human sacrifice and find the irrationality of much of Glomian life repugnant, too. The educated reader is likely to find much to admire about the Fox.

The challenge of the Fox's character arises when Christian readers begin to analyze the beliefs that he actually espouses: namely, the thoroughgoing materialism that denies anything beyond his understanding of the natural order. As careful readers, we must therefore admit that his beliefs run contrary to those of the orthodox faith, which not only must acknowledge the possibility of the supernatural but also must affirm the necessity of it, particularly where matters of the gospel are concerned, including Christ's crucifixion and resurrection.[12]

## THE FOLLY OF GREEK WISDOM

Lewis pulls a bit of sneaky authorial nudging on his readers, confounding readers who wish to identify with the Fox through most of the novel. An extended exchange with the priest of Ungit highlights this issue. When the priest imposes on the court a demand for a human sacrifice in order to redeem the land from the grip of an oppressive plague and drought, contemporary readers cringe at the barbarism of such a demand. Readers tend to side automatically with the Fox, who howls at the suggestion that the Brute (Cupid as understood by the people of Glome) might be worthy of such sacrifice. The Fox shrugs off the reported sightings of the Brute as

---

10. Lewis, *Till We Have Faces*, 10.
11. Lewis, *Till We Have Faces*, 10.
12. See also, Kilby, *Christian World*, 63–64.

mere figments of someone's imagination, declaring, "The man was scared and new waked from sleep. He took a shadow for a monster."[13]

The priest, however, believes in the supernatural and in the contours between the spiritual and materialistic worlds. He does not feel shackled by rationalistic chains and turns the dismissal back on the Fox, glibly responding, "That is the wisdom of the Greeks."[14] Through this assertion that the Fox is a mere materialist, the scoffer is thus scoffed at by the recipient of the original scoffing. As the argument persists, the priest wearies of the Fox's viewpoint and protests, "We are hearing much Greek wisdom this morning, King. And I have heard most of it before. I did not need a slave to teach it to me. It is very subtle. But it brings no rain and grows no corn; sacrifice does both."[15]

After the sacrifice takes place, its apparent efficacy is established in the form of rain and a return of fertility. Almost immediately after Psyche is sent to the Holy Mountain for marriage to the Brute, the long-sought-after rains arrive. Even Orual is shocked by the seeming connection between the act and the aftermath, as evidenced by a conversation with the Fox:

> "Grandfather, do you still think that Ungit is only lies of poets and priests?"
> 
> "Why not, child?"
> 
> "If she were indeed a goddess what more could have followed my poor sister's death than has followed it? All the dangers and plagues that hung over us have been scattered. Why, the wind must have changed the very day after they had—"[16]

The Fox dismisses the coincidence, declaring it a "cursed chance.... It is these chances that nourish the beliefs of barbarians.... That southwest wind came over a thousand miles of sea and land. The weather of the whole world would have to have been different from the beginning if that wind was not to blow. It's all one web; you can't pick threads out nor put them in."[17] The Fox, thus, discounts the connection between the sacrifice and the coming of the rains, precluding any supernatural connection. Orual momentarily holds out hope that Psyche's death is not in vain; however, the Fox's declaration that there is no supernatural involvement in play hits its mark in her mind, and she finally laments, "She died to no purpose. If the King had waited a few days later, we could have saved her, for all would have

13. Lewis, *Till We Have Faces*, 48.
14. Lewis, *Till We Have Faces*, 48.
15. Lewis, *Till We Have Faces*, 50.
16. Lewis, *Till We Have Faces*, 84.
17. Lewis, *Till We Have Faces*, 85.

begun to go well of itself. And this you call comfort?"[18] Lewis thus reveals the ultimate end of materialism: a comfortless ennui.

## THE SOUL'S WISDOM

Psyche does not share this comfortlessness, however, for when she prepares to face her sacrificial role, she describes the hope that she possesses about even death. She ignores the grief that Orual already articulates, scolding,

> We have made little use of the Fox's teaching if we're to be scared by death. And you know, Sister, he has sometimes let out that there were other Greek masters than those he follows himself; masters who have taught that death opens a door out of a little, dark room (that's all the life we have known before it) into a great, real place where the true sun shines and we shall meet—[19]

Psyche's hope anticipates something beyond the present, which further anticipates Christian ideas about the resurrection that are facilitated by Christ's sacrifice.[20] In short, she provides the novel with a new perspective on the spiritual world, one that differs from those of the Fox and the priest. As she tells Orual, "We don't understand. There must be so much that neither the Priest nor the Fox knows."[21]

Psyche's declaration that the Fox's teaching should have prepared them for death (as well as life) is ironic since he apparently had been afraid to die and was thus captured and enslaved. While he is introduced as merely one of the "foreign slaves" in the household, we find out about how he became a slave in his exchange with the priest over the sacrifice.[22] The priest scolds the Fox harshly: "[Greek wisdom] does not even give them boldness to die. That Greek there is your slave because in some battle he threw down his arms and let them bind his hands and lead him away and sell him, rather than take a spear-thrust in his heart. Much less does it give them understanding of holy things."[23] The Fox's dominant materialism gave him thin comfort when faced with the reality of death.

---

18. Lewis, *Till We Have Faces*, 85.
19. Lewis, *Till We Have Faces*, 73.
20. Readers of English history will recognize the allusion to the Venerable Bede's account of the conversion of King Edwin of Northumberland at the hands of Paulinus. See Bede, *Ecclesiastical History*, 129–30.
21. Lewis, *Till We Have Faces*, 72.
22. Lewis, *Till We Have Faces*, 7.
23. Lewis, *Till We Have Faces*, 50.

Indeed, despite the Fox's protestations, the rest of the novel deals with the supernatural reality precipitated by and revealed through Psyche's sacrifice. As much as readers might identify with "the wisdom of the Greeks," the novel does not affirm mere materialism; it affirms instead the reality of a spiritual component to the world.[24]

## WISDOM RECONSIDERED

The phrase "the wisdom of the Greeks" should resound loudly in the minds of Christian readers, for the words are drawn directly from Paul's powerful discourse about wisdom in 1 Corinthians. Careful readers, then, will suddenly find the assertions of the priest of Ungit and Psyche about spiritual realities in consonance with their own beliefs.

In some ways, Orual's struggle with the loss of Psyche is an inverted crisis of faith: she has absorbed materialism from the Fox and this skepticism ends up ruining her relationship with Psyche and souring her own view of the world and of the divine. The second part of the novel asserts that supernatural things do, in fact, have a part in reality and that faith in the divine is not wholly absurd.[25]

Understanding what Lewis does here requires knowledge of the biblical foundations of godly wisdom. The Judeo-Christian tradition is practically obsessed with wisdom. Psalm 111:10 ("The fear of the LORD is the beginning of wisdom") and Proverbs 1:7 ("The fear of the LORD is the beginning of knowledge: but fools despise wisdom and instruction") are characteristic of Old Testament declarations that the nature of wisdom is rooted directly in the nature and person of God.

Paul ramps up this connection between God and wisdom by emphasizing the supernatural character of God as integral to true wisdom. Paul, perhaps, does this directly because of the conflict on the immediate horizon between Greek and Hebrew thought and the stark differences between the two worldviews. In Romans 1:14, Paul admits that he is "under obligation both to Greeks and to barbarians, both to the wise and to the foolish." Paul links "Greeks" and "wise" as a reference to the overriding stereotype (which was based in historical reality) of Greek learning as the gold standard for

---

24. Lewis faced constant criticism that "there was too much of the supernatural in his position, especially in the sense that the next world loomed so large." Harries, *Man and His God*, 81. Tolkien was dogged by similar criticisms, which he turned on literary critics in a particularly effective way in perhaps the most influential essay on *Beowulf* ever published (in 1936), "Monsters and the Critics," 14–44.

25. Interestingly, Lewis follows on the heels of many Greek dramatists, notably, Sophocles, who advocates a similar view in *Oedipus Rex*.

the Western world. Greek thought tended to be materialistic, especially by the first century AD. Epicureanism embraced atomic materialism, espousing pleasure (and later consumption) as the chief pursuit of humankind. They opposed the Stoics, material determinists who proposed that logic and virtue are the highest goods; in *Faces*, the Fox generally follows a Stoic path (emphasizing virtue and accord with the "nature" of things).[26] Another influential thread was Cynicism, which declared ascetic simplicity to be the chief end of humankind.

Paul's address at Mars Hill in Acts 17 specifically addresses Epicureans and Stoics (see v. 18). He ranges from the creative agency of God to the power of Christ's resurrection, which was met with sharp disagreement, as evidenced in verse 32: "Now when they heard of the resurrection of the dead, some mocked. But others said, 'We will hear you again about this.'"

Paul knows that the literal crucifixion and resurrection is critical to Christian faith, and that the literal nature of the supernatural reality of these facts is unnegotiable. In 1 Corinthians 15:12–19, he is dogmatic in these assertions:

> Now if Christ is proclaimed as raised from the dead, how can some of you say that there is no resurrection of the dead? But if there is no resurrection of the dead, then not even Christ has been raised. And if Christ has not been raised, then our preaching is in vain and your faith is in vain. We are even found to be misrepresenting God, because we testified about God that he raised Christ, whom he did not raise if it is true that the dead are not raised. For if the dead are not raised, not even Christ has been raised. And if Christ has not been raised, your faith is futile and you are still in your sins. Then those who have fallen asleep in Christ have perished. If in Christ we have hope in this life only, we are of all people most to be pitied.

For this reason, Paul recognizes the materialistic tendencies of contemporary Greek thought and warns the church in Corinth that the gospel defies purely materialistic thought by its nature. The sacrifice of Christ, along with the resurrection, defies human logic but reflects instead the reality of divine love. In 1 Corinthians 1:17–31, he declares,

---

26. *Faces* actually includes an excerpt from the master Stoic Marcus Aurelius. Psyche says, "I have learned the Fox's lessons. . . . 'Today I shall meet cruel men, cowards, and liars, the envious and the drunken. They will be like that because they do not know what is good from what is bad. This is an evil which has fallen upon them not upon me. They are to be pitied,'" which is almost verbatim a translation of the Latin in the opening of Book 2 of the *Meditations*.

> For Christ did not send me to baptize but to preach the gospel, and not with words of wisdom, lest the cross of Christ be emptied of its power. For the word of the cross is folly to those who are perishing, but to us who are being saved it is the power of God. For it is written, I will destroy the wisdom of the wise, and the discernment of the discerning I will thwart. Where is the one who is wise? Where is the scribe? Where is the debater of this age? Has not God made foolish the wisdom of this world? For since, in the wisdom of God, the world did not know God through wisdom, it pleased God through the folly of what we preach to save those who believe. For Jews demand signs, and Greeks seek wisdom, but we preach Christ crucified, a stumbling block to Jews and folly to Gentiles, but to those who are called, both Jews and Greeks, Christ the power of God and the wisdom of God. For the foolishness of God is wiser than men, and the weakness of God is stronger than men. For consider your calling, brothers: not many of you were wise according to worldly standards, not many were powerful, not many were of noble birth. But God chose what is foolish in the world to shame the wise; God chose what is weak in the world to shame the strong; God chose what is low and despised in the world, even things that are not, to bring to nothing things that are, so that no human being might boast in the presence of God. And because of him, you are in Christ Jesus, who became to us wisdom from God, righteousness and sanctification and redemption, so that, as it is written, "Let the one who boasts, boast in the Lord."

Paul continues this contrast in 1 Corinthians 3:18–19: "Let no one deceive himself. If anyone among you thinks that he is wise in this age, let him become a fool that he may become wise. For the wisdom of this world is folly with God. For it is written, 'He catches the wise in their craftiness.'" To this end, then, Paul summarizes, "We are fools for Christ's sake" (4:10). The Christian mind is, therefore, the embodiment of divine wisdom, which appears as foolishness to the world.

The notion of a transcendent sacrifice is, for Paul, a clear stumbling block that he understood Greek "wisdom" would reject as an irrational act. This is the exact sentiment that Lewis places in the mouth of the Fox; the words of the priest of Ungit are in the spirit of Paul, linking Greek thought with a failure to understand the meaning of sacrifice. *Faces* is explicit in the groundwork for this failure, when the priest of Ungit declares the need for "the Great Offering,"[27] which transcends the usual petty offerings. The

---

27. Lewis, *Till We Have Faces*, 47.

priest claims, "Bulls and rams and goats will not win Ungit's favour while the land is impure. . . . Her anger . . . never ceases without expiation."[28] He demands a human sacrifice, Istra, to atone for the unfaithfulness of the land and its leaders. Christians will recognize her as a Christ-type, even down to the location of the sacrifice: "The victim is led up the mountain to the Holy Tree."[29]

The priest emphasizes that sacrifice must not be just anyone, however; it must be the most perfect sacrifice available: Istra/Psyche. The priest prescribes, "In the Great Offering, the victim must be perfect."[30] Ironically, the victim will be called the Accursed, as she will take on herself the guilt of the entire land of Glome for misplaced worship. The Fox is incapable of responding to the demand by any means other than logic, first dismissing it, "a child of six would talk more sense,"[31] and then picking apart the priest's words, arguing that "a moment ago the victim of this abominable sacrifice was to be the Accursed, the wickedest person in the whole land, offered as a punishment. And now it is to be the best person in the whole land—the perfect victim—married to the god as a reward."[32] The priest again dismisses the rational analysis by the Greekling, countering that there are other ways of understanding the world's processes: "Holy places are dark places. It is life and strength, not knowledge and words, that we get in them. Holy wisdom is not clear and thin like water, but thick and dark like blood. Why should the Accursed not be both the best and the worst?"[33]

## LIMITATIONS OF HUMAN WISDOM

The priest carries forth his argument carefully, emphasizing that human discovery can only go so far. Materialism is limited to the physical realm and if a metaphysical realm exists, then materialism is ill-suited for explaining some of the occurrences of this world. Even Orual tries desperately to cling to a glimmer of hope that the Fox is wrong quite late in the novel, when she almost begs the Fox to admit the possibility of a spiritual realm: "You don't think—not possibly—not as a mere hundredth chance—there might be things that are real though we can't see them?"[34] The Fox's re-

---

28. Lewis, *Till We Have Faces*, 45.
29. Lewis, *Till We Have Faces*, 48.
30. Lewis, *Till We Have Faces*, 49.
31. Lewis, *Till We Have Faces*, 49.
32. Lewis, *Till We Have Faces*, 49–50.
33. Lewis, *Till We Have Faces*, 50.
34. Lewis, *Till We Have Faces*, 141.

sponse reveals that he is utterly incapable of conceiving of such truth, as he talks about conceits, abstractions, and even material objects in a state of physical darkness that prevents sight. Even earlier Psyche had anticipated this and had realized that the Fox was flawed in his thinking, stating, "The Priest . . . is not what the Fox thinks. Do you know, Sister, I have come to feel more and more that the Fox hasn't the whole truth. Oh, he has much of it. It'd be dark as a dungeon within me but for his teaching. And yet . . ."[35] Orual seems to agree slightly, but accounts, perhaps to the physical limitations of his human virtue: "It never entered his mind—he was too good—to believe that the gods are real, and viler than the vilest men," to which Psyche responds, "Or else, . . . they are real gods but don't really do these things. Or even—mightn't it be—they do these things and the things are not what they seem to be?"[36] The thought that the Fox might be rather more limited in his understandings, and perhaps even his wisdom, seems to have never crossed the mind of Orual in particular.

Because Orual had never questioned the actual basis of the Fox's teachings, she comes to understand that she has led an intellectual life that was filled with cognitive dissonance. As she moves to the latter part of the novel's first section, she begins to realize this, even as she is bitter toward her circumstances. She ponders,

> I now saw that I had, strangely, taken both Bardia's explanation and the Fox's (each while it lasted) for certain truth. Yet one must be false. And I could not find out which, for each was well-rooted in its own soil. If the things believed in Glome were true, then what Bardia said stood; if the Fox's philosophy were true, what the Fox said stood. But I could not find out whether the doctrines of Glome or the wisdom of Greece were right. I was the child of Glome and the pupil of the Fox; I saw that for years my life had been lived in two halves, never fitted together.[37]

This dissonance and the intellectual handicap that arises from a purely materialistic viewpoint are exactly what the Fox declares when he appears to Orual in the concluding dream. He confesses his guilt in faulty teaching, claiming, "I am to blame for most of this, and I should bear the punishment. I taught her . . . to say, 'Lies of poets,' and 'Ungit's a false image.' I made her think that ended the question. . . . I made her think that a prattle of maxims would do, all thin and clear as water. For of course water's good;

---

35. Lewis, *Till We Have Faces*, 70.
36. Lewis, *Till We Have Faces*, 71.
37. Lewis, *Till We Have Faces*, 151.

and it didn't cost much, not where I grew up. So I fed her on words."[38] He begs for Orual's forgiveness, kissing her as a child, "One thing that I told you was true. The poets are often wrong. But for all the rest—ah, you'll forgive me?"[39] Having admitted his errors, he even asserts an understanding from his new, supernatural perspective that "there must be sacrifices."[40]

## WISDOM IN CHRISTIAN PERSPECTIVE

Christian readers will recognize the priest's pronouncement that Psyche will carry an expiatory value for the entire land as a specific reference to the biblical underpinnings of Christ's sacrificial death. Multiple passages in the Old Testament begin to outline the ineffectiveness of the sacrificial system. In Psalm 51:16, for example, David observes, "For you will not delight in sacrifice, or I would give it: you will not be pleased with a burnt offering." The prophets extend this into specific warnings against a reliance on the sacrifice of animals. Isaiah 1:11 offers God's perspective on sacrifice: "'What to me is the multitude of your sacrifices?' says the LORD; 'I have had enough of the burnt offerings of rams and the fat of well-fed beasts; I do not delight in the blood of bulls, or of lambs, or of goats.'" Hosea 6:6 echoes these instructions, declaring that God "desire[s] steadfast love and not sacrifice, the knowledge of God rather than burnt offerings."

The New Testament authors view Christ as the ultimate fulfillment of the sacrificial system, positioning the Cross as the ultimate, for-all-time sacrifice on behalf of humanity. Likewise, the description of Psyche's sacrifice in *Faces* emphasizes the singular nature of the act. King Trom says, "Ungit must have her due. What's one girl—why, what would one man be—against the safety of us all? It's only sense that one should die for many. It happens in every battle."[41] Orual admits this, saying, "Father, . . . you are right. It is fit that one should die for the people."[42] While Psyche is a Christ-type to a certain extent as a "one-for-all" sacrifice, she is not wholly transcendent as a "once-for-all" sacrifice; she is merely an extension or intensification of the animal sacrificial system.[43] The author of Hebrews is very specific in

---

38. Lewis, *Till We Have Faces*, 295.
39. Lewis, *Till We Have Faces*, 296.
40. Lewis, *Till We Have Faces*, 295.
41. Lewis, *Till We Have Faces*, 61.
42. Lewis, *Till We Have Faces*, 61.

43. Psyche's sacrifice does possess an allusory transcendence rooted in an Old Testament concept. The priest notes, "Some say the loving and the devouring are all the same thing." Lewis, *Till We Have Faces*, 49. The notion of mixing devotion and consumption in a single act is found in the Hebrew verb "cherem," used in passages

contrasting the transcendent efficacy of Christ with the ultimate failure of animal sacrifices. In Hebrews 9:12, Christians are told that Christ sealed our eternity through his personal sacrifice: "not by means of the blood of goats or calves but by means of his own blood, thus securing an eternal redemption." The argument persists into Hebrews 10:1–6, 10–12, with explicit ramifications for *Faces*:

> For since the law has but a shadow of the good things to come instead of the true form of these realities, it can never, by the same sacrifices that are continually offered every year, make perfect those who draw near. Otherwise, would they not have ceased to be offered, since the worshipers, having once been cleansed, would no longer have any consciousness of sins? But in these sacrifices there is a reminder of sins every year. For it is impossible for the blood of bulls and goats to take away sins. Consequently, when Christ came into the world, he said, "Sacrifices and offerings you have not desired, but a body have you prepared for me; in burnt offerings and sin offerings you have taken no pleasure." . . . And by that will we have been sanctified through the offering of the body of Jesus Christ once for all. And every priest stands daily at his service, offering repeatedly the same sacrifices, which can never take away sins. But when Christ had offered for all time a single sacrifice for sins, he sat down at the right hand of God.

In Hebrews, Christ does not undergo deification but rather affirmation of his divine Personhood through the fulfillment of his purpose. In *Faces*, Istra/Psyche undergoes apotheosis (transformation into deific status), which affirms her sacrificial death as purposeful.

Psyche's apotheosis bears a striking set of comments from the text that are worth noting. When Bardia, one of Orual's closest advisors, hears of the sacrifice, he mourns for the impending loss of the beautiful Psyche and he laments, "I wonder do the gods know what it feels like to be a man."[44] He complains that the gods are, to some extent, inhuman, a complaint that echoes Orual's consistent perspective throughout the book. Psyche's sacrifice, however, is something of an antidote to this view, in that her apotheosis means that at least one god did know what it meant to be human. As the priest of Istra (that is, of Psyche) notes about his deity, "She is a very young goddess. She has only just begun to be a goddess. For you must know that,

---

such as Joshua's depiction of the destruction of Jericho and several other cities in the Israelite conquest of the Promised Land. "Cherem" means, simultaneously, "to devote wholly" and "to destroy utterly."

44. Lewis, *Till We Have Faces*, 66.

like many other gods, she began by being a mortal."[45] What they do not seem to understand, however, is that the problem is not that the gods do not think like humans but rather that humans do not think with a longer, more supernatural perspective such as that of the gods. Humankind is too limited by the physical world.

## THE SHADOW OF SACRIFICE

Hebrews also calls the sacrificial system a "shadow of things to come, and not the very image of things," which informs the interpretation of *Faces*. By emphasizing the importance of the need for a sacrifice, despite our post-Enlightenment sensibilities, Lewis confronts his readers with the possibility that Psyche's sacrifice might be an emulative shadow of Christ's sacrifice, that a blood sacrifice might defy our rationalistic view of piety and affirm the Christ story.

Paul affirms this shadow view in 1 Corinthians 13, the same epistle where he proposes the notion of Christ's sacrifice being a stumbling block to the Greeks. In verses 11–12, Paul notes the progression of understanding Christians have as their minds are transformed by the Holy Spirit: "When I was a child, I spoke like a child, I thought like a child, I reasoned like a child: but when I became a man, I gave up childish things. For now we see in a mirror dimly, but then face to face. Now I know in part; then I shall know fully, even as I have been fully known."

The Fox, in the novel's concluding heavenly vision, says that in the future, they will understand the gods, and divine things, more fully. He proposes, "In that far distant day when the gods become wholly beautiful, or we at last are shown how beautiful they always were. . . . Only this I know. This age of ours will one day be the distant past. And the Divine Nature can change the past. Nothing is yet in its true form."[46] The Fox here shows his personal transformation; no longer the materialist, his death has been accompanied (at least in the dream vision) by a new understanding that, as Shakespeare's Hamlet states, "There are more things in heaven and earth . . . than are dreamt of in . . . philosophy."[47] In fact, the entire final section of *Faces* is Orual's own realization that what she has been taught by the Fox is incomplete and limited by human understanding. The "true form" of the world could not be comprehended until a transformation had occurred. *Faces* recasts both Orual and the Fox as godly fools, at least in a pagan sense

---

45. Lewis, *Till We Have Faces*, 241.
46. Lewis, *Till We Have Faces*, 305.
47. Shakespeare, *Hamlet*, 1.5.166–67.

that anticipates a Christian understanding of transcendence. In the case of the Fox, he now takes on an even more resonant role as an advisor to Orual, even more in the vein of his literary antecedent, *King Lear*'s Fool.

Lewis's biography is helpful to us at this point. Readers familiar with his conversion experience can already anticipate the direction of this point. In 1931, Lewis has a momentous conversation with his friend J. R. R. Tolkien about myth.[48] As Lewis asserts that myths are ultimately lies and therefore unhelpful for anything other than good stories, Tolkien responds that Lewis was being shortsighted in his view. As Lewis parries with myths that parallel elements of Christianity, Tolkien proposes that Christianity is not a myth like any other because it is, after all, true: "The heart of Christianity is a myth which is also a fact. . . . By becoming fact it does not cease to be myth: that is the miracle. . . . God is more than a god, not less; Christ is more than Balder [a Norse god who parallels Christ's sacrifice], not less."[49] By that argument, Lewis recalibrates his view of myth: Christianity is not one myth among many but rather is the genuine reality that all other myths merely foreshadowed or approximated.

As Louis Markos observes in pondering this realization, "If Christianity is true, then the God who created both us and the universe chose to reveal himself through a sacred story that resembles more the imaginative works of epic poets and tragedians than the rational meditations of philosophers and theologians. . . . Is it so unbelievable that he should have used the greatest poets, storytellers and 'prophets' of antiquity to prepare the hearts of the pagans?"[50] *Faces* builds on the poetic story of Cupid and Psyche in ways that Lewis finds useful for identifying how hearts might be prepared for the Christian story.[51]

Certainly Lewis has a soft spot in his heart for the power of myth to confound the rationalist's objections to the gospel, for he himself once offered those same objections. The fact that he returns to a myth for his final masterpiece should not surprise us, nor should the fact that he revisits how we might read an ancient myth by the light of the gospel, penetrating the dark shadows with a brilliant illumination that allows the retelling of the

---

48. The idea of *mythopoeia* was instrumental in Lewis's conversion, which underscores the centrality of this idea in Lewis's later work. Carpenter's account of these 1931 conversations are instructive. Carpenter, *Inklings*, 33–45.

49. Lewis, "Myth Became Fact," 141.

50. Markos, *From Achilles to Christ*, 249.

51. Indeed, a recent volume on Christian apologetics makes the case throughout that *Till We Have Faces* functions as an apologetic volume similarly to some of Lewis's nonfiction works by imaginatively illustrating the moral argument for God. Baggett and Baggett, *Morals of the Story*.

myth, a mythopoetic act, to likewise become a matter of ultimate truth-telling. This, then, is the power of myth and the power of *Till We Have Faces*: myth transforms our understanding of the nature of the universe, even as the story transforms the understanding of Psyche's death. The Christian mind perceives patterns of truth wherever they arise.

## CONCLUSION

The depiction of wisdom in *Till We Have Faces* asserts something beyond a purely materialistic understanding of the world. The supernatural world of *Faces* is not real, of course, but it is a metaphor for what is real. Psyche's willingness to sacrifice her life for the salvation of her people reflects the myth that is true: Christ's sacrifice. Psyche's "resurrection" from that sacrifice echoes the myth that is true: Christ's resurrection. Psyche's apparent apotheosis taps the power of the myth that is true: the resurrected God-Man whose resurrected body defies physical laws and returns to the heavens to reign in power.

Readers are wise to ponder Lewis's motivation in writing *Faces*; it smacks of a literary farewell of sorts, as Lewis's age certainly reminds him that his opportunities for lengthy works will be limited. *Till We Have Faces* is not the postured affectation of a young intellectual trying to show off or build a reputation but rather is the fruit of a lifelong thinker who cannot help but produce a work of substance. The result is dazzling.

Lewis's myth retold thus carries with it the force of grounding abstract concepts in a story that allows mere mortals to wrap their minds around aspects of transcendent abstractions even as they cannot grasp the totality. The gravity of mythic stories such as *Faces* forces us to turn toward a future when we can approach the ideal itself. In works like this we are seeing it for the first time (as Paul states it) "face to face" or after waiting for our own spiritual translations (as Lewis terms it) "till we have faces."

## BIBLIOGRAPHY

Arnell, Carla A. "On Beauty, Justice, and the Sublime in C. S. Lewis's *Till We Have Faces*." *Christianity and Literature* 52.1 (Autumn 2002) 23–33.

Baggett, David, and Marybeth Baggett. *The Morals of the Story: Good News About a Good God*. Downers Grove: IVP Academic, 2018.

Bede. *Ecclesiastical History of the English People*. Translated by L. Sherley-Price. Rev. ed. New York: Penguin, 1968.

Carpenter, Humphrey. *The Inklings*. London: HarperCollins, 2006.

Harries, Richard. *C. S. Lewis: The Man and His God*. Wilton, CN: Morehouse-Barlow, 1987.

Jebb, Sharon. "'I Lived and Knew Myself': Self-Knowledge in *Till We Have Faces*." *Renascence: Essays on Values in Literature* 62.2 (Winter 2011) 111–29.

Kilby, Clyde. *The Christian World of C. S. Lewis*. Grand Rapids: Eerdmans, 1964.

Lewis, C. S. *The Abolition of Man*. New York: HarperCollins, 2001.

———. "Myth Became Fact." In *C. S. Lewis: Essay Collection and Other Short Pieces*, edited by Lesley Walmsley, 138–42. London: HarperCollins, 2000.

———. *Till We Have Faces: A Myth Retold*. Orlando: Harcourt, 1984.

Markos, Louis. *From Achilles to Christ: Why Christians Should Read the Classics*. Downers Grove: IVP Academic, 2007.

Miller, T. S. "The *Pearl* Maiden's Psyche: The Middle English *Pearl* and the Allegorical-Visionary Impulse in *Till We Have Faces*." *Mythlore* 30.1–2 (Fall–Winter 2011), 43–75.

Shakespeare, William. *Hamlet: The Riverside Shakespeare*. Boston: Houghton Mifflin, 1974.

Tolkien, J. R. R. "*Beowulf*: The Monsters and the Critics." In *Interpretations of Beowulf: A Critical Anthology*, edited by R. D. Fulk, 14–44. Bloomington: Indiana University Press, 1991.

———. *Tree and Leaf: Including the Poem Mythopoeia*. Boston: Houghton Mifflin, 1988.

# 7

# Reality and Pre-Evangelism in the Christian Minds of C. S. Lewis and Francis Schaeffer

*Bruce Little*

How often, in the course of one's lifetime, does a seemingly routine choice yield unexpected consequences—sometimes for good and sometimes for harm? Happy is the person for whom those consequences beget true good. Count me among this happy tribe. Several years ago, I agreed to teach a philosophy course with Michael Travers when we were both on faculty at Southeastern Baptist Theological Seminary—a seemingly routine decision. The course examined the philosophical thought of C. S. Lewis and Francis A. Schaeffer, with Michael teaching on Lewis and I, Schaeffer. The unexpected consequences came in two forms—both good. The first good was of a personal nature. During that time, I witnessed Michael's integrity as a person and his professionalism as a teacher. Both affected me deeply. From this, a friendship developed lasting until his untimely death. How often Michael would conclude some insight from Lewis with "Come further up, come further in." Now Michael can say with the Unicorn, "I have come home at last! This is my real country! I belong here."[1]

---

1. Lewis, *Last Battle*, 196.

The second good was of the intellectual kind. There was confirmation that the two great twentieth-century apologists (or evangelists), Lewis and Schaeffer, shared a common vision of reality. It was this vision of reality that shaped their approach to evangelism. Interestingly, to the best of my knowledge, there was never any correspondence between them nor is there any evidence they ever met.[2] What is known is that Schaeffer had read some of Lewis. In Schaeffer's book *Back to Freedom and Dignity*, when discussing the disturbing direction of science in the twentieth century, Schaeffer wrote, "Here is C. S. Lewis's *That Hideous Strength* with a vengeance. I strongly urge Christians to read carefully this prophetic piece of science fiction. What Lewis casts as a warning in the form of fantasy and science fiction is much closer today."[3] Notwithstanding, it appears they developed their ideas on apologetics quite independent of the other. And why should anyone care? The answer is that Lewis and Schaeffer are on a very short list of important apologists of the twentieth century and considered by many as important voices for Christianity in the twenty-first century. Both had a powerful vision of the Christian mind grounded in objective reality and used that image to lead people toward faithful Christian living.

Furthermore, it is more than a curiosity that they independently developed a similar approach to evangelism, an approach unique for their time. More to the point for contemporary concerns, I would argue this approach is uniquely fitted for the twenty-first century. Both shared a vision of reality known as metaphysical realism. Metaphysical realism affirms there is a real Reality above experience that supports and orders physical reality. It is often referred to as a Platonic vision of reality where the Real is grasped through the intellect and by which man's experience is understood. Metaphysical realism uses the language of universals and particulars, or Grace and Nature respectively, to speak of the two aspects of reality. Lewis spoke of this when pointing out that the idea of right and wrong rested on what he called the Law of Human Nature, which he said was in the "class of mathematics."[4] Lewis put this Law as a universal (in the transcendent realm). Man is made in the image of God, which explains why man has this idea of right and wrong. In the language of Plato, universals were *Forms*.

---

2. I have researched the Francis Schaeffer Collection in the library of Southeastern Baptist Theological Seminary and can find no correspondence between the two, although there is some evidence that Schaeffer was familiar with at least some of Lewis's writings. Of course, Lewis and Schaeffer traveled in different circles. One lived in England and the other in Switzerland. It is possible Lewis may have been aware of Schaeffer through the article on Schaeffer that appeared in *Time Magazine* in 1960.

3. Schaeffer, *Back to Freedom and Dignity*, 1:371.

4. Lewis, *Mere Christianity*, 12.

The thesis of this chapter is that metaphysical realism formed the basis of the evangelistic approach, which they called pre-evangelism, of both Lewis and Schaeffer. Realists affirm the idea that there is an objective reality, or, reality is mind independent. Reality is not something constructed by the mind; rather, reality is comprehended by the mind although not perfectly. This is what makes science possible. Metaphysical reality goes further and affirms reality extends beyond experience into the realm of the transcendent. Universals give meaning to the particulars. Without universals everything becomes mechanistic, including man. In a mechanistic world everything is simply a biological or chemical matter of cause and effect, meaning the particulars are derived solely from their function.

## PRE-EVANGELISM

Although a fuller discussion of the apologetic value of metaphysical realism comes a little later, for now it is sufficient to understand there is a reality in which all live and it is not created in human minds. This means, in general, a belief about the world can be measured for truth value by submitting it to reality itself. The contribution of metaphysical realism is that it provides meaning to particular things existing outside the mind as well as the mind itself. As Paul Tyson noted, "No operational understanding of reality is simply pragmatic; every time we plan or perform any activity in what we take to be a realistic manner, we do so by putting our confidence in a set of deeply held beliefs about the nature of reality itself."[5] Like Tyson, both Lewis and Schaeffer realized that one's vision of reality informed their beliefs, hence the point of beginning with modern man was reality. Working from the position of metaphysical realism, Lewis and Schaeffer first engaged man by asking questions that would reveal his vision of reality to see if it could explain reality in a consistent fashion.

Schaeffer called this "pre-evangelism,"[6] which he said was no soft option. Lewis referred to his approach as *praeparatio evangelica*.[7] Their pre-evangelism opened a fresh and rewarding way to find the "door" in evangelism. Grounded in metaphysical realism, pre-evangelism moved from ontology to epistemology. It was a way to have serious conversation with those whose minds had been closed off to objective truth. Pre-evangelism answered what Jacques Ellul had in mind when he spoke of finding a door to present the gospel. He wrote:

---

5. Tyson, *Returning to Reality*, 1.
6. Schaeffer, "Back to Freedom and Dignity," 1:149.
7. Lewis, *Collected Letters of C. S. Lewis*, 2:484–85.

> The gospel no longer penetrates. We seem to be confronted by a blank wall. Now if we want to go further, either we must find a door, or we must break down the wall. But first we must investigate this wall, in order to find out whether there is a door: thus, we need to explore this world in which we are living. If there is not a door (as seems to me to be the case) then we must find (or create) the instruments we need in order to make a breach in it.[8]

Lewis and Schaeffer found such a door based on their vision of reality—metaphysical realism. There is a unity between man and his world as both have been created by God; therefore, beliefs can be measured against the way the world is. This vision of reality is developed from the doctrine of creation as found in Genesis.

Pre-evangelism did not begin by arguing with the non-Christian about her view of truth. Instead of beginning with her view of truth, the pre-evangelist helped her compare her view of truth against the reality in which she lived to see if her beliefs rang true to what is. This was not just the reality of the physical world, but the moral structure of man's mind. Schaeffer noted, "The truth that we let in first is not a dogmatic statement of the truth of the Scriptures, but the truth of the external world and the truth of what man himself is."[9] The Christian ought then lovingly to push the non-Christian until she could see that her beliefs do not fit with herself or her world. One could begin with reality and move to the truth of Christianity. As Schaeffer pointed out: "The truth of Christianity is that it is true to what is there."[10] Lewis and Schaeffer believed this prior work was often necessary for eventual conversation on the truth of the gospel. This was particularly the case where the notion of God had been eviscerated from society's explanation of the world and man. The precise relationship between metaphysical realism and evangelism, however, will be reserved for discussion later in this chapter.

## THE MINISTRIES OF LEWIS AND SCHAEFFER

Anyone familiar with the names Lewis and Schaeffer is most likely to think of them as apologists. It might be more accurate, however, to think of them as evangelists, since that is how they viewed themselves. What Lewis and Schaeffer did is possible for any believer with a heart for evangelism. They

---

8. Ellul, *Presence of the Kingdom*, 115.
9. Schaeffer, "God Who Is There," 138.
10. Schaeffer, "He Is There," 290.

were not intellectual professionals defending the faith (although they were great intellects); they were committed to people confessing Christ as Savior. Of course, they were apologists in the sense they were strong promoters and defenders of the Christian faith. Evangelism, however, was the passion of their souls, and philosophy was seen as helpful in that task. Yet, it was not philosophy in a formal sense, but in the sense of thinking clearly and logically. Lewis once wrote that "the salvation of a single soul is more important than the production or preservation of all the epics and tragedies in the world."[11] Again he wrote, "And woe to you if you do not evangelise."[12] George Sayer wrote of Lewis: "He devoted himself to developing and strengthening his belief, and, almost from the year of his conversion, he wanted to become an evangelist for the Christian faith."[13] In *Mere Christianity*, Lewis argued, "The church exists for nothing else but to draw men into Christ, to make them little Christs. If they are not doing that, all the cathedrals, clergy, missions, sermons, even the Bible itself, are simply a waste of time. God became Man for no other purpose."[14]

To speak of Lewis as an evangelist, however, does not necessarily mean that he launched every conversation with a nonbeliever with a passionate presentation of the gospel. As Philip Ryken pointed out, Lewis was "not very aggressive at personal evangelism."[15] However, Ryken goes on to say, "C. S. Lewis was a man of firm evangelistic convictions. So strong was his fervor for the Christian Gospel that he became an object of ridicule to colleagues and a source of embarrassment to friends, even among the Inklings."[16]

According to Ryken, the salvation of human souls was for Lewis "the real business of life."[17] Nevertheless, Lewis approached the nonbeliever intellectually or in what might be called the mind-directed approach. By that, it is not to say that he disapproved of the more passionate approach of the preacher, only that was not his gifting. He wrote, "Before closing, I must add that the limitation of my own gifts has compelled me always to use a predominately intellectual approach. But I have also been present when an appeal of a much more emotional and also more 'pneumatic', kind has worked wonders on the modern audience. Where God gives the gift,

---

11. Lewis, "Christianity and Literature," 419.
12. Lewis, "Fern-seed and Elephants," 242.
13. Sayer, *Jack: C. S. Lewis*, 138.
14. Lewis, *Mere Christianity*, 199.
15. Ryken, "Winsome Evangelist," 56.
16. Ryken, "Winsome Evangelist," 57.
17. Ryken, "Winsome Evangelist," 57.

the 'foolishness of preaching' is still mighty."[18] This should clear the air on Lewis's view of how best to do evangelism. It is according to a man's gifting. There is no thought put forth that every evangelist must be a philosopher but, whether a philosopher or not, a proper vision of reality and Scripture should inform everyone's evangelistic approach, and it should exhibit the best of proper thinking. The Christian mind must be ready, with whatever training it has, to point others toward the reality and truth of the Christian vision of the world.

On the matter of philosophy and evangelism, Schaeffer thought the relationship to be one of practical importance, not one of intellectual superiority. He wrote, "In fact, I wonder if apologetics which does not lead people to Christ as Savior, and then on to their living under the Lordship of Christ in the whole of life, really is Christian apologetics."[19] Therefore, it is no surprise that Schaeffer thought of himself as a missionary or evangelist, not as an apologist in the professional sense. Interestingly, throughout a 1960 article in *Time*, Schaeffer was referred to as a missionary.[20] Nevertheless, the article noted that the "European intellectual [was] the single object of the Schaeffers's mission in the mountains."[21] The article correctly points to the fact that intellectuals did listen to Schaeffer, but it would be an error to think that was his only audience. Of course, in those days, college-age adults were asking questions of meaning and that might be thought of as "intellectual" by today's standards.

When Schaeffer, just a few years before he died, edited his books for the five-volume set, he set the record straight in *The God Who Is There*:

> People often say, 'What are you?' and I at times have said, 'Well, basically I am an evangelist.' But sometimes I do not think people have understood that does not mean that I think of an evangelist in contrast to dealing with philosophic, intellectual, or cultural questions with care. I am not a professional, academic philosopher—that is not my calling, and I am glad I have the calling I have, and I am equally glad some other people have the other calling. But when I say I am an evangelist, it is not that I am thinking that my philosophy, etc. is not valid—I think it is. . . . I do not see or feel a dichotomy: this is my philosophy, and this is my evangelism.[22]

18. Lewis, "Modern Man and His Categories," 620.
19. Schaeffer, "God Who Is There," 186.
20. "Mission to Intellectuals," 62.
21. "Mission to Intellectuals," 62.
22. Schaeffer, "God Who Is There," 185–86.

Later on Schaeffer pointed out: "Thus apologetics, as I see it, should not be separated in any way from evangelism."[23] A few paragraphs later, he wrote, "To me there is a unity to all reality, and we can either say that every field of study is part of evangelism (especially useful to certain people in the world); or we can say that there is no true evangelism that does not touch all of reality and all of life."[24] In this sense, Schaeffer saw no tension between philosophy and evangelism. For Schaeffer, the nature of reality shaped his evangelism, which was why he often spoke of Christianity providing a unified field of knowledge. The Christian message was unified because it was grounded in God and corresponded to the world humans inhabit. It was on this vision of reality that both men argued for the truth of Christianity as providing proper understanding of the truth of things. Both men sought to inculcate in others the Christian mind.

## REALISM NOT RATIONALISM

Lewis and Schaeffer understood that each vision of reality, when practiced consistently, determined what one makes of his world and how one thinks about truth. Naturalistic realism (or scientism) admits only empirical evidence approved by science as material for truth. This vision puts the discussion of God and things of the transcendent realm off limits.[25] Thoughts of God are only wishful thinking, a point Lewis made clear in *The Pilgrim's Regress*.[26] In his circle of influence, atheism had found a home in the minds of many in the mid-nineteenth century.

Another vision of reality that had gained currency in the twentieth century was that of anti-realism (philosophically known as Idealism). When speaking to one holding such a view, to begin with a logical argument for truth would be meaningless. In this view, each truth claim enjoys equal status with contrary truth claims. Anti-realists are not bothered by holding contrary beliefs within their system. Richard Weaver noted this when he summarized the loss of rational thought characterizing the twentieth century. He wrote, "Multiplying instances show complacency in the presence of contradiction which denies the heritage of Greece."[27] It was precisely in this intellectual climate that Schaeffer stressed the importance of antithesis showing that relativism failed the test of reality. He wrote, "If we do not

23. Schaeffer, "God Who Is There," 186.
24. Schaeffer, "God Who Is There," 187.
25. The implications of scientism for ethics are discussed in greater detail in chapter 9 of this volume.
26. Lewis, *Pilgrim's Regress*, 52–54.
27. Weaver, *Ideas Have Consequences*, 10.

communicate clearly on the basis of antithesis, many will respond to their own interpretation of the gospel, in their own relativistic thought-forms, including a concept of psychological guilt-feelings rather than of true moral guilt before the holy, living God."[28] Schaeffer noted, "These are the first steps of classical logic. In other words, in antithesis if this is true, then its opposite is not true."[29]

According to Lewis and Schaeffer, Christianity could be presented and defended on rational grounds, but getting to that point involved pre-evangelism. Their commitment to rational presentation did not necessarily mean formal arguments such as theistic arguments for God's existence. What was meant was there "are good and sufficient reasons to know that Christianity is true."[30] Rational discourse meant that the Christian message made sense in the face of what is. This meant it fit with the moral and rational structure of the universe where the canons of logic prevailed. As Schaeffer pointed out: "Rational means that the things which are about us are not contrary to reason; or, to put it another way, man's aspiration of reason is valid. And so the Judeo-Christian position is rational, but it is the very antithesis of rationalism."[31] The world in which man lived as well as man himself was the creative work of a rational being, God. All creation was the outworking of God's mind, materialized by the power of his word (Heb 1:1–4).

Although Lewis and Schaeffer believed in rational discourse, they warned against making the defense of the Christian faith rationalistic. Their point was that Christianity is not irrational and can be defended in reasonable terms, but one must not forget that the Scripture and Holy Spirit are essential parts of the rational discourse. In a letter to Dorothy L. Sayers, Lewis wrote, "My own frequent uneasiness comes from another source—the fact that apologetic work is so dangerous to one's own faith. A doctrine never seems dimmer to me than when I have just successfully defended it."[32] Lewis was concerned that evangelism not become rationalistic. The same concern is expressed in *The Great Divorce*. In the discussion between the Spirit (Christian) and the Ghost (non-Christian), Lewis provided this challenging dialogue:

> "Why, if you are interested in the country only for the sake of painting it, you'll never learn to see the country."
> "But that's just how a real artist is interested in the country."

28. Schaeffer, "God Who Is There," 195–96.
29. Schaeffer, "He Is There," 311.
30. Schaeffer, "God Who Is There," 182.
31. Schaeffer, "God Who Is There," 9.
32. Lewis, *Collected Letters of C. S. Lewis*, 2:730.

> "No, you're forgetting," said the Spirit. "That was not how you began. Light itself was your first love: you loved paint only as a means of telling about light."
>
> "Oh, that was ages ago," said the Ghost. "One grows out of that. Of course, you haven't seen my later works. One becomes more and more interested in paint for its own sake."
>
> "One does, indeed. I also have had to recover from that. It was all a snare. Ink and catgut and paint were necessary down there, but they are also dangerous stimulants. Every poet and musician and artist, but for Grace, is drawn away from love of the thing he tells, to love of the telling till, down in Deep Hell, they cannot be interested in God at all but only in what they say about Him. For it doesn't stop at being interested in paint, you know. They sink lower—become interested in their own personalities and then in nothing but their own reputations."[33]

Alister McGrath noted, "Lewis's analysis of the limits of reason makes it clear that we need more than rational arguments to challenge the 'spirit of the age'. If a myth is 'caught', it begins to work its magic of intellectual and moral transformation." [34]

Schaeffer had similar concerns to Lewis. Although he warned against the retreat of pietism, he also understood the dangers of a purely intellectual approach to the gospel. He warned that it could lead to "the development of an intellectual and cultural snobbishness or elitism. This can easily come about unless we help one another not to fall into it. Such an attitude grieves the Holy Spirit, and destroys rather than builds, and is as offensively ugly as anything we can be."[35] Of course, he balanced the work of the Holy Spirit with the labor involved in giving a reasonable defense of the gospel. He argued that the "Holy Spirit should never be minimized, but nowhere in the Scriptures do we find the work of the Holy Spirit as excuse for laziness and lack of love on the part of those with Christian responsibility."[36] Following the example of Lewis and Schaeffer, all conversations with non-Christians must show compassion when speaking in the interest of truth. The goal of the Christian mind is not to dominate, but to persuade in love.

---

33. Lewis, *Great Divorce*, 84–85.
34. McGrath, *Intellectual World of C. S. Lewis*, 73.
35. Schaeffer, "God Who Is There," 191–92.
36. Schaeffer, "God Who Is There," 191.

## PERSONAL NARRATIVES

Apart from the teaching of Scripture on this matter, it seems both were moved in the direction of compassionate reasoning because of events in their personal lives. Lewis and Schaeffer both struggled at different points with the truthfulness of Christianity. Lewis documented his struggle both in *The Pilgrim's Regress* and *Surprised by Joy*, a struggle that eventually led him to embrace Christianity. In reflection of his own journey he wrote, "On the intellectual side of my own progress had been from 'popular realism' to Philosophical Idealism; from Idealism to Pantheism; from Pantheism to Theism; and from Theism to Christianity. I still think this is a very natural road, but I now know that it is a road very rarely trodden."[37] As Lewis worked through the different views of reality, he followed them to their conclusion to see if in fact they could account for what was known about the world. The importance of this matter fueled this struggle until ending in the truth.

Schaeffer, in his early days of working through the issue of the truth of things, did so beginning with Greek philosophy. According to Colin Duriez, as Schaeffer read the Greek thinkers, "He had a growing sense that he was gaining more questions but no answers." Later Duriez wrote, "Having tasted the thinking of the ancient Greeks, he thought it was only fair to read through the Bible, something he had never done. He ought to give it a last chance. So it was that, night by night, alongside his reading of Ovid he began reading the Bible from the beginning (as a book, he thought this was the way to do it)."[38] Six months later Schaeffer had become a Christian. Later, however, not long after moving to Switzerland, Schaeffer faced a new kind of struggle, which was about the truth of the Christian message. This was brought on by his sense that Christianity had lost some of its reality in his own life as well as what also seemed apparent in other Christians. In his book, *True Spirituality*, Schaeffer speaks of the conclusion of this struggle as the foundation of L'Abri. He wrote, "This was and is a real basis of L'Abri. Teaching the historic Christian answers, and giving honest answers to honest questions are crucial, but it was out of these struggles that the reality came, without which a work like L'Abri would not have been possible."[39] Of this time he wrote,

> We were living in Champery at that time, and I told Edith that for the sake of honesty I had to go all the way back to my agnosticism and think through the whole matter. . . . I walked,

---

37. Lewis, *Pilgrim's Regress*, 207.
38. Duriez, *Francis Schaeffer*, 20–21.
39. Schaeffer, "True Spirituality," 196.

prayed, and thought through what the Scriptures taught, as well as reviewing my own reasons for being a Christian."[40]

Was Christianity true? That is, did its claims square with reality—the truth of things? Interestingly, both men came to similar conclusions in their own personal struggles with truth by holding the truths up to reality.

I think it is not a stretch to say that the personal struggles of both Lewis and Schaeffer helped them in dealing with others who were not yet Christians. There seems to be a strong confidence in the truth of Christianity and its importance, but also a compassion when dealing with the non-Christian who had honest questions. Schaeffer wrote, speaking of pre-evangelism, "As I push the man off his false balance, he must be able to feel that I care for him."[41] Both Lewis and Schaeffer knew the importance and the anguish of struggling with the big questions of life. When dealing with others who were in that state as they themselves had been, they took seriously the weight of the struggle. Consequently, they did not trample on humanity but offered respect and compassion as non-Christians were working through answers to their honest questions. To be authentic, the Christian mind must be convinced and not coerced.

## IMPLICATIONS OF REALISM

To this point, I have only suggested that one's vision of reality shapes his view of truth. Whereas this idea is central to the thesis of this chapter, there must be some justification for the claim. Without giving a lengthy philosophical discussion on the matter, I will simply demonstrate the fact by examples.

Consider the anti-metaphysical realism of naturalism or what has been called scientific naturalism or scientism. This view confesses a reality independent of the mind but denies anything existing above experience. Modernity preferred this view of reality that led to relativism. Weaver wrote in 1948: "The denial of universals carries with it the denial of everything transcending experience. The denial of everything transcending experience means inevitably—though ways are found to hedge on this—the denial of truth. With the denial of objective truth there is no escape from the relativism of 'man the measure of all things.'"[42] It is not difficult to see how a naturalistic vision of reality leads to relativism when it comes to truth claims. It is not that truth is denied, but rather the possibility of absolute universal truth is denied.

40. Schaeffer, "True Spirituality," 195–96.
41. Schaeffer, "God Who Is There," 138
42. Weaver, *Ideas Have Consequences*, 4.

Another example comes from postmodernity, which is committed to anti-realism (Idealism). This vision of reality is anti-realism at every level. It denies any concept of objective reality and hence objective truth. Postmodernist Richard Tarnas says, "The postmodern paradigm is by its nature fundamentally subversive of all paradigms, for at its core is the awareness of reality as being at once multiple, local, and temporal, and without demonstrable foundation."[43] The postmodernist denies objective reality, concluding that reality is plastic and relative to the individual or community, and truth is relative. This is not just the idea that truth cannot be fully known by humans in this life, but that truth itself is variegated in quality over a given population, with each individual possessing his own version of truth. This was very much in step with the existentialism of the 1960s portrayed so well in the film *Dead Poet's Society*.

It is interesting to see the reaction of the scientific community to the anti-realism of postmodernity. Non-theistic biologist Edward O. Wilson argued, "Reality, they [postmodernists] propose, is a state constructed by the mind, not perceived by it. In the most extravagant version of this constructivism, there is no 'real' reality, no objective truths external to mental activity, only rivaling versions disseminated by ruling social groups. Nor can ethics be firmly grounded, given that each society creates its own codes for the benefit of the same oppressive forces."[44] A similar criticism is found in the *Humanist Manifesto 2000* which Wilson signed: "Some forms of postmodernism counsel defeatism; at best, they offer no program for resolving the world's problems; at worst, they deny that solutions are either possible or achievable. The effects of this philosophical-literary movement are counterproductive, even nihilistic."[45] This is not the warning of someone in the Christian community or even sympathetic to the Christian faith. Yet, the point is made regarding the power of one's vision of reality to shape a corollary view of truth.

While Wilson and others demand an alternative vision of reality to the anti-realists, the alternative offered in the *Humanist Manifesto 2000* is a tried and failed alternative—that of modernity which is remembered as anti-metaphysical realism. The signers of that document offer a realist view of reality, but a naturalistic vision of reality. According to the *Humanist Manifesto 2000*, "Scientific naturalism enables human beings to construct a coherent worldview disentangled from metaphysics or theology and based

---

43. Tarnas, *Passion of the Western Mind*, 401.
44. Wilson, "Back to the Enlightenment," 21
45. Kurtz, *Humanist Manifesto 2000*, 22.

on science."[46] That is, truth claims can never rise higher than experience because there is nothing above experience in this vision of reality.

However, one's vision of reality not only shapes how one views truth, it is also how one interprets common words. For example, the statement "Man is unique" could be interpreted functionally or ontologically depending on one's vision of reality. If one has a naturalistic vision of reality, then man's uniqueness is found in what he can do, that is, a functionalist view of man. On the other hand, if one has a metaphysical vision of reality, then uniqueness could mean man is unique because he is created in the image of God. There could be agreement in the words of the statement but clearly not on the interpretative side of things. Without understanding this, miscommunication results, which is problematic for evangelism.

Schaeffer understood the fact that with anti-metaphysical realism there was the loss of antithesis, which meant common words could mean something quite different depending on one's vision of reality. He wrote, "In such a setting the problem of communication is serious; it can only be overcome by negative statements that clearly say what we do *not* mean, so that the twentieth-century man understands the positive statements we *do* mean.... Without this, in an age of relativity, we cannot expect the evangelical, orthodox Church to mean much to the surrounding culture or even to the Church's own children."[47]

One is reminded of the apostle Paul on Mars Hill when he addressed the Stoics and the Epicureans. First, he spoke to the matter of reality; namely, the true nature of reality is that God does not need something from men, but men need something from God. He corrected their false understanding of reality before speaking to them of the resurrection. He could have spoken of immortality for neither group would have challenged that, but Paul confronted them with Christian truth within a metaphysical realism that allows for resurrection. Indeed, resurrection only makes sense within a metaphysical realism.

## REALISM IN APOLOGETICS

Lewis's and Schaeffer's metaphysical realism informed their apologetic approach. In particular, it shaped their practice of pre-evangelism. It seems clear that pre-evangelism works because there is a reality independent of the mind, including the transcendent realm. Reality being independent of the mind allows for a common rubric by which each person's beliefs are

---

46. Kurtz, *Humanist Manifesto 2000*, 24.
47. Schaeffer, "God Who Is There," 196.

judged. Universals provide the moral ordering that judges all alike, king and servant, as well as giving meaning to life itself.

Metaphysical realism, often associated with Plato, was observed to resonate with Christianity early in church history. While Lewis and Schaeffer agreed for the most part with the Platonic vision of reality, they realized that at points Plato was lacking or even in error as he did not have the benefit of special revelation, or so it seems. They were in agreement that metaphysical reality affirmed that reality consisted of necessary and contingent beings (the uncreated and the created). Reality includes universals and particulars where the universals give meaning to the particulars. Particulars, as Schaeffer explained, "are all the individual things—each individual thing is a particular."[48]

Regarding universals, Schaeffer noted, "The Greek philosophers, and especially Plato, were seeking for universals which would make the particulars meaningful."[49] According to Schaeffer, "The Greeks long before understood that there was a dilemma between the particulars and the universals. It was not only Plato who wrestled with this, but he especially understood exactly what Jean-Paul Sartre has said in our generation: a finite point has no meaning unless it has an infinite reference point. He is right. Unless the particulars have a universal over them, the particulars have no meaning."[50] Schaeffer, however, explained that "Plato understood that you have to have absolutes, or nothing has meaning. But the difficulty facing Plato was that his gods were not big enough to meet the need. So although he knew the need, the need fell to the ground because his gods were not big enough to be the point of reference or place of residence for his absolutes, for his ideals."[51]

Likewise, Lewis presented this Platonic understanding of reality in the *Chronicles of Narnia*. In *The Last Battle* Lord Digory explained why the new Narnia looked something like the old Narnia, only brighter, richer, and more wonderous. He exclaimed, "'All the old Narnia that mattered, all the dear creatures, have been drawn into the real Narnia through the Door. And of course, it is different; as a real thing is from a shadow or as waking life is from a dream.'" After "he added under his breath, 'It's all in Plato, all in Plato: bless me, what *do* they teach them at these schools!'"[52]

---

48. Schaeffer, "Escape from Reason," 215.
49. Schaeffer, "He Is There," 306
50. Schaeffer, "Church at the End," 7.
51. Schaeffer, "He Is There," 287.
52. Lewis, *Last Battle*, 195.

In *The Pilgrim's Regress*, Lewis's idea of the "Island" was a metaphor for how things on this earth (the shadow) point to the Real. The "shadow" causes something to arise in the human heart, a desire or longing for the true, the good and the beautiful or what Lewis spoke of as the "Island." Peter Kreeft's essay, "Lewis's Philosophy of Truth, Goodness and Beauty," discussed this matter: "Our second point is the metaphysics of truth, goodness and beauty: that is, their objective reality. Lewis's polemic against deniers of objective truth, goodness and beauty is wonderfully simple and powerful."[53] Lewis spoke of universals when speaking of the "Law of Human Nature which was [as being] on the order of mathematics."[54] On this vision of reality there is a universal concept of morality just as there is a universal concept of mathematics. It was precisely this vision of reality that gave rise to his view of pre-evangelism.

However, in a letter to Dom Bede Griffiths, OSB, Lewis separated from Plato on the view of matter. He wrote, "But I fear Plato thought the concrete flesh and grass bad, and have no doubt he was wrong."[55] In *The Pilgrim's Regress*, Lewis made the point that the material good is good. He did this through a conversation between Vertue and the Guide.[56] Vertue asked, "Is it wholly wrong to be ashamed of being in this body?" The Guide responded, "The Landlord's Son was not. You know the verses—'When thou tookest upon thee to deliver man.'"[57] According to Lewis, Plato had the right idea, but apparently lacked knowledge of the true and living God.

## CHRISTIAN REALISM

As part of their metaphysical vision of reality, both believed in the historic fall as taught in Genesis 3. Christianity presents a vision of reality different than other religions. For Christianity, creation started out as something good, in fact, very good; and then something happened. Of course, that something was the sin of Adam. In *The Pilgrim's Regress* Lewis gave a wonderful picture of this. John (the pilgrim) and his current traveling companion (Vertue) encounter Mother Kirk. The question to Mother Kirk was:

> "Do you not think this Landlord of yours is a very strange one?" he asked.

53. Kreeft, "Lewis's Philosophy of Truth," 27.
54. Lewis, *Mere Christianity*, 12.
55. Lewis, *Collected Letters*, 2:326.
56. For those not familiar with *The Pilgrim's Regress*, the Landlord is God the creator and his Son is Christ.
57. Lewis, *Pilgrim's Regress*, 189.

"How so?" said she.

"Why does he make a road like this running up to the very edge of a Precipice—unless it is to encourage travelers to break their necks in the dark?"

"Oh bless you, he never left it like that," said the old woman. "It was a good road all round the world when it was new, and all of this gorge is far later than the road."

"You mean," said Vertue, "that there has been some sort of catastrophe."[58]

In the next section Lewis tells the story in allegorical form about the fall of man and subsequent consequences for all creation.

Likewise, Schaeffer's vision of reality included a time-space fall of historic Adam. Christian truth could explain the human dilemma of how man could do both good things and great evil. He wrote, "By the action of one man in a historic, space-time situation, sin entered into the world of men. But this is not just a theoretical statement that gives us a reasonable and sufficient answer to man's present dilemma, explaining how the world can be so evil and God still be good. It is that in reality, from this time on, man was and is a sinner."[59] On the other hand, Schaeffer argued that although man was finite and cruel, man was a noble creature. He wrote,

> Perhaps you do not like the word nobility, but whatever word you choose, there is something great about man. I want to add here that evangelicals have often made a serious mistake by equating the fact that man is lost and under God's judgment with the idea that man is nothing—zero. This is not what the Bible says. There is something great about man, and we have lost perhaps our greatest opportunity of evangelism in our generation by not insisting that it is the Bible that explains why man is great.[60]

This view of man made it possible for Schaeffer to talk with the non-Christian meaningfully as he respected the humanness or what he called the *mannishness* of man.

Based upon this view of reality, both spoke of pre-evangelism in view of objective reality, and this reality is fitted to who human beings are, including both their blameworthy and praiseworthy acts. In a letter to Sister Penelope, CSMV, speaking of his radio talks to the RAF, Lewis explains, "Mine are *praeparatio evangelica* rather than *evangelium*, an attempt to convince

---

58. Lewis, *Pilgrim's Regress*, 79–80.
59. Schaeffer, "Genesis in Space and Time," 61.
60. Schaeffer, "He Is There," 278.

people that there is a moral law, that we disobey it, and that the existence of a Lawgiver is at least very probable and also (*unless* you add the Christian doctrine of the Atonement) imparts despair rather than comfort."[61] That is, before presenting the gospel, Lewis thought it necessary to show modern man where he was wrong. In a Christmas sermon (1940s), Lewis explains what he means by the notion of "despair not comfort." Stephanie R. Derrick wrote concerning C. S. Lewis's Christmas sermon:

> Real Pagans differ from post-Christians, Lewis continued, firstly in that they were actually religious: "To [the Pagan] the earth was holy, the woods and waters were alive." Secondly, they "believed in what we now call an 'Objective' Right or Wrong," that is, that "the distinction between pious and impious acts was something which existed independently of human opinions." Finally, Pagans, unlike "post-Christian man," had "deep sadness" because of their knowledge that they did not obey the moral code perfectly. To compensate for this shortcoming, the Pagan developed a wealth of ceremonies to "take away guilt."[62]

Lewis's point was that in a world of anti-metaphysical realism there is no personal sense of offending a higher power because none exists. The post-Christian man must first learn of the bad news, namely that he is a sinner, before hearing the good news. This is a matter of showing modern man that he has an improper vision of reality, and until that is corrected, the gospel message is meaningless to the post-Christian according to Lewis. In this case, when dealing with modern man the diagnosis is part of pre-evangelism and actually comes first. This is what both Lewis and Schaeffer meant by pre-evangelism.

## TESTING CLAIMS OF REALITY

In contrast to the careful, cultivated pre-evangelism necessary to provide an anchor for Christian belief in an epistemologically unmoored age, Lewis highlighted the concept of Bulverism, which is the idea that you "assume that your opponent is wrong and then explain his error, and the world will be at your feet." On the other hand, if you "attempt to prove that he is wrong or (worse still) try to find out whether he is wrong or right, . . . the national dynamism of our age will thrust you to the wall."[63] Lewis explained, "In other words, you must show *that* a man is wrong before you start explaining

61. Lewis, *Collected Letters*, 484–85.
62. Derrick, "Christmas and Cricket," n.p.
63. Lewis, "Bulverism," 589.

*why* he is wrong."[64] This could be done by having the post-Christian see how her beliefs about the world in general and truth in particular do not fit with the way the world is. For Lewis, reality was a great teacher. He wrote:

> What I like about experience is that it is such an honest thing. You may take any number of wrong turnings; but keep your eyes open and you will not be allowed to go very far before the warning signs appear. You may have deceived yourself, but experience is not trying to deceive you. The universe rings true wherever you fairly test it.[65]

One sees this clearly in book four of *The Pilgrim's Regress*.

Likewise, Schaeffer believed that reality is an effective teacher. One must be shown to be wrong before moving on to what makes correction possible. He explained how pre-evangelism works by using the analogy of removing a roof from a structure. He wrote, "It is like the great shelters built upon some mountain passes to protect vehicles from the avalanches of rock and stone which periodically tumble down the mountain." He went on to say, "The Christian, lovingly, must remove the shelter and allow the truth of the external world and of what man is, to beat upon him. When the roof is off, each man must stand naked and wounded before the truth of what is." A little later he explained, "The Scriptures then show him the real nature of his lostness and the answer to it."[66] Schaeffer reminded us, "This means that we do not try first to move a man away from the logical conclusion of his position but towards it. . . . We should try to move him in the natural direction his presuppositions take him."[67] Schaeffer was certain that any non-Christian vision of reality will fail at the end when carried out far enough. Man intuitively will build a shelter, so to speak, to protect himself from the inconsistencies. But the Christian gently removes the shelter, and allows Reality to judge of the truthfulness of one's beliefs as everybody lives in the same reality—an objective reality. This reality, according to Schaeffer, falls into two parts, "the fact that the universe truly exists and it has a form, and then what I would call the 'manishness' of man—which is my own term for meaning that man is unique. People have certain qualities that must be explained."[68] Once done, now the gospel, the good news, comes to offer man a true place of safety.

64. Lewis, "Bulverism," 589.
65. Lewis, *Surprised By Joy*, 218.
66. Schaeffer, "God Who Is There," 140–41.
67. Schaeffer, "God Who Is There," 138.
68. Schaeffer, "God Who Is There," 178.

## ETHICS, REALITY, AND PRE-EVANGELISM

Schaeffer highlighted the importance of pre-evangelism when recounting an incident when he was speaking at Oxford University to some theology students on communicating the gospel. After his lecture a student stood up and said, "'Sir, if we understand you correctly, you are saying that pre-evangelism must come before evangelism. If this is so, then we have been making a mistake at Oxford. The reason we have not been reaching many of these people is because we have not taken enough time with pre-evangelism.' I said that I totally agree."[69]

Both Lewis and Schaeffer believed one place where reality would judge modern man was in the area of morals. Lewis appealed to the universal of the real Right. He wrote,

> The moment you say that one set of moral ideas can be better than another, you are, in fact, measuring them both by a standard, saying that one of them conforms to that standard more nearly than the other. But the standard that measures two things is something different from either. You are, in fact, comparing them both with some Real Morality, admitting that there is such a thing as a real Right, independent of what people think, and that some people's idea gets nearer to the real Right than others.[70]

Schaeffer agreed when he spoke about all men having a sense of "moral motions." He said, "You may ask why I use the term 'moral motions.' I choose the term simply because I am not talking about specific norms. I am talking about the fact that men have always felt that there is a difference between right and wrong. All men have this sense of moral motions."[71]

Even atheist Marc Hauser agreed, writing, "If there are moral universals, then there must be capacities that all normally developing humans share." For Hauser, the best explanation is that "we are born with abstract rules or principles, with nurture entering the picture to set the parameters and guide us toward the acquisition of particular moral systems." Hauser, as a scientist, simply looked at the reality in which we live and concluded that all men have a sense of right and wrong. If this sense of morality is innate, it must be universal and this reasonably calls for a metaphysical realism, although, of course, Hauser would not agree with that explanation. Nonetheless, this highlights the idea of Lewis and Schaeffer using reality

---

69. Schaeffer, "God Who Is There," 155.
70. Lewis, *Mere Christianity*, 13.
71. Schaeffer, "He Is There," 295.

to test one's belief and to do this as part of pre-evangelism. Christianity fits perfectly with Hauser's observations. Schaeffer noted, "It is not surprising that if a reasonable God created the universe and put me in it, he should also correlate the categories of my mind to fit that universe, simply because I have to live in it."[72]

In "He Is There and He Is Not Silent," Schaeffer wrote, "The Christian has a certainty right from the start that there is an external world that is there, created by God as an objective reality. He is not like the man who has nowhere to begin, who is not sure that there is anything there."[73] As Schaeffer pointed out: "The loss of the certainty of objectivity is a serious thing to the scientist, just as it is for the drug addict."[74] This means, generally speaking, the evangelist's first work is to prepare the unbeliever for the gospel by looking at the truth of things to help him see where his beliefs may run contrary to reality. On this view of evangelism, one should carefully listen to honest questions and find honest answers—answers that fit the way the universe and man are. This is precisely how both Lewis and Schaeffer engaged in pre-evangelism based upon their metaphysical realism. Of course, if a person is ready to listen to the gospel carefully, then there would be no need for pre-evangelism.

## CONCLUSION

The Christian mind, according to both Lewis and Schaeffer, is one that sees the order in the universe as the reflection of the order of the Creator. Communicating that vision enabled Lewis and Schaeffer to reach a broad audience, and continues to enable their work to be effective in evangelism and discipleship today. The Christian mind depends on a reality that makes sense, can be understood by the human mind, and which points to the author and perfecter of our faith.

The way Lewis and Schaeffer employed pre-evangelism in their work of evangelism was dependent on their metaphysical vision of reality. The point here is not to demonstrate that all views of pre-evangelism require this vision of reality. It appears, however, from what has been presented here that pre-evangelism would only be an option for those with a metaphysical vision of reality. The argument here does not necessarily require a commitment to natural theology, only that created reality forms a unity of what is intrinsic and extrinsic to man. That is to say, the mind of man has categories

---

72. Schaeffer, "He Is There," 335.
73. Schaeffer, "He Is There," 334–55.
74. Schaeffer, "He Is There," 338.

of thought that correspond to the way the world is and when one's beliefs are contrary to what is, that person must ignore the conflict, pretending it does not exist. I think the value of this form of pre-evangelism is that it allows the debate about beliefs to begin with the post-Christian's beliefs against the truth of things; not the post-Christian's beliefs against the Christian's beliefs.

## BIBLIOGRAPHY

Derrick, Stephanie L. "Christmas and Cricket: Finding Two Lost C. S. Lewis Articles." *Christianity Today*, December 18, 2017. https://www.christianitytoday.com/ct/2017/december-web-only/christmas-cricket-lost-c-s-lewis-articles.html.

Duriez, Colin. *Francis Schaeffer: An Authentic Life*. Wheaton: Crossway, 2008.

Ellul, Jacques. *The Presence of the Kingdom*. 2nd ed. Colorado Springs: Helmers & Howard, 1989.

Kreeft, Peter. "Lewis's Philosophy of Truth, Goodness and Beauty." In *C. S. Lewis as Philosopher: Truth, Goodness and Beauty*, edited by David J. Baggett et al., 22–36. Downers Grove: InterVarsity, 2008.

Kurtz, Paul. *Humanist Manifesto 2000: A Call for a New Planetary Humanism*. Amhurst: Prometheus, 2000.

Lewis, C. S. "Bulverism." In *C. S. Lewis: Essay Collection and Other Short Pieces*, edited by Lesley Walmsley, 587–90. London: HarperCollins, 2000.

———. "Christianity and Literature." In *C. S. Lewis: Essay Collection and Other Short Pieces*, edited by Lesley Walmsley, 411–20. London: HarperCollins, 2000.

———. *The Collected Letters of C. S. Lewis*. Edited by Walter Hooper. 2 vols. New York: HarperCollins, 2004.

———. "Fern-seed and Elephants." In *C. S. Lewis: Essay Collection and Other Short Pieces*, edited by Lesley Walmsley, 242–53. London: HarperCollins, 2000.

———. *The Great Divorce*. New York: Macmillan, 1946.

———. *The Last Battle*. New York: Harper Trophy, 2000.

———. *Mere Christianity*. San Francisco: HarperSanFrancisco, 2001.

———. "Modern Man and His Categories of Thought." In *C. S. Lewis: Essay Collection and Other Short Pieces*, edited by Lesley Walmsley, 616–20. London: HarperCollins, 2000.

———. *The Pilgrim's Regress*. Wade Annotated Edition. Edited and introduced by David C. Downing. Grand Rapids: Eerdmans, 2014.

———. *Surprised By Joy*. New York: HarperOne, 1955.

McGrath, Alister. *The Intellectual World of C. S. Lewis*. Chichester: Wiley-Blackwell, 2014.

Ryken, Philip. "Winsome Evangelist: The Influence of C. S. Lewis." In *Light Bearer in the Shadowlands*, edited by Angus Menuge, 55–78. Wheaton: Crossway, 1997.

Sayer, George. *Jack: C. S. Lewis and His Times*. San Francisco: Harper & Row, 1988.

Schaeffer, Francis A. "Back to Freedom and Dignity." In *The Complete Works of Francis A. Schaeffer*, 1:355–84. Downers Grove: Crossway, 1982.

———. "The Church at the End of the Twentieth Century" In *The Complete Works of Francis A. Schaeffer*, 4:3–114. Downers Grove: Crossway, 1982.

———. "Escape from Reason." In *The Complete Works of Francis A. Schaeffer*, 1:207–74. Downers Grove: Crossway, 1982.

———. "Genesis in Space and Time." In *The Complete Works of Francis A. Schaeffer*, 2:2–118. Downers Grove: Crossway, 1982.

———. "The God Who Is There." In *The Complete Works of Francis A. Schaeffer*, 1:5–206. Downers Grove: Crossway, 1982.

———. "He Is There and He Is Not Silent." In *The Complete Works of Francis A. Schaeffer*, 1:275–354. Downers Grove: Crossway, 1982.

———. "True Spirituality." In *The Complete Works of Francis A. Schaeffer*, 3:195–280. Downers Grove: Crossway, 1982.

Tarnas, Richard. *The Passion of the Western Mind*. New York: Ballantine, 1993.

Tyson, Paul. *Returning to Reality*. Eugene, OR: Cascade, 2014.

Weaver, Richard. *Ideas Have Consequences*. Chicago: The University of Chicago Press, 1948.

Wilson, Edward O. "Back to the Enlightenment." *Free Inquiry* 18.4 (1998) 21–22.

# 8

## Disinterested Love in *The Screwtape Letters* and *The Great Divorce*

### C. Keith Callis

DISINTERESTED LOVE IS AMONG the most significant characteristics of the Christian mind as it is portrayed by C. S. Lewis. It is possibly the most important and most difficult attribute of the Christian mind to understand and embody. Disinterest characterizes the highest form of love, which Lewis calls Charity or Divine Gift-love. It is love not oriented toward selfish gain. As Lewis writes in *The Four Loves*, "Divine Gift-Love—Love Himself working in a man—is wholly disinterested and desires what is simply best for the beloved."[1] This sort of love is both a gift from God and a gift from any lover to his or her beloved. It demands no return. It is directed towards those who without God's intervention will not be able to return it. "Divine Gift-love in the man enables him to love what is not naturally lovable; lepers, criminals, enemies, morons, the sulky, the superior, and the sneering."[2] As Lewis defines it, the primary characteristic of this highest, purest, and most God-like love is its insistence on loving that which cannot provide a return on investment. Supported by the love of God with the mind, such love as this should be the goal of the Christian life.

---

1. Lewis, *Four Loves*, 164.
2. Lewis, *Four Loves*, 164.

As described by Lewis, disinterested love is possible only when God transforms or converts our normal, daily efforts into selfless love. He writes, "All the activities (sins only excepted) of the natural loves can in a favoured hour become works of the glad and shameless and grateful Need-love or the selfless, unofficious Gift-love, which are both Charity."[3] This is the heart of the Christian life on earth. As is typical, what Lewis exposits in his nonfiction work, *The Four Loves*, he illustrates in his fiction, notably in *The Screwtape Letters* and *The Great Divorce*.

When the ghostly narrator of *The Great Divorce* meets the Spirit of George MacDonald, he learns that Spirits like MacDonald's journey always to greater heights of bliss, having nothing to gain from their ministry to Ghosts. Their descent to "The Valley of the Shadow of Life"[4] to teach Ghosts about heaven is an expression of love, specifically a kind of love that Screwtape calls "disinterested"[5] even though he does not know it firsthand nor the behaviors that flow from it. To Spirits like MacDonald's this love is constant joy.[6] The phrase "disinterested love" appears among Screwtape's letters on the "enemy's" tactics, and his explanations of it connect *The Great Divorce* with *The Screwtape Letters*. The novels are mutually enlightening. Loving without needing an exchange in kind, or indeed, without asking anything in return, is a major theme of both novels. Screwtape grasps it "only with the abstract intellect."[7] The Spirits know it "like the taste of honey" and are "embraced by it as by a bridegroom."[8] It animates the love that flows spontaneously from them. It *is* their life as it flows from God. Discussed in the one book, it is dramatized by the other.

Disinterested love appears in its most subtle and penetrating form when Lewis's narrator meets the Spirit of George MacDonald in Chapter Nine of *The Great Divorce*. The novel's most sensitive and perplexing cruxes appear there, at about the middle of the book, but MacDonald's interactions with the narrator in that chapter reveal Lewis's wisdom about the kind of regard for God that is implicit in the gospel. The dialogue between the Ghost and Macdonald enacts "disinterested love." As ministering Spirit, MacDonald extends his eternal, living form from Christ. Arguably, the narrator is not a Christian, and the passages in which MacDonald's Spirit reveals his wise regard for him uncover the narrator's misunderstandings about the

---

3. Lewis, *Four Loves*, 171.
4. Lewis, *Great Divorce*, 68.
5. Lewis, *Screwtape Letters*, 86; 37–38; 50–56; 60, 64–65; 81–86; 100–102.
6. Lewis, *Great Divorce*, 74.
7. Lewis, *Great Divorce*, 40.
8. Lewis, *Great Divorce*, 40.

kind of choice that leads to Christ and complete Joy. That choice requires the destruction by Christ of every transgressive, self-interested impulse. The Ghost wants to know with finality whether there is freedom of choice in the question of eternal destiny, the decision for or against Christ. On MacDonald's reckoning, he seeks forbidden knowledge.[9] Implicitly, as to this question, the narrator *uses* his travels through The Valley of the Shadow of Life as a means to serve an intellectual appetite. The novel ends without his allowing its destruction so that he might enjoy heaven and Christ for themselves, disinterestedly.

Whereas the narrator of *The Great Divorce* seems inches from setting aside his desire and enjoying heaven as his dream ends, Screwtape reports to Wormwood by the second letter that their "patient" has become a Christian. The devils tempt on. They want to make him a creature of hell. They do not realize that, in light of MacDonald's teaching, their demonic work is futile. They understand "disinterested love," but they cannot love wisely, nor peer inside their "patient's" soul to discern it there, nor know that it is permanent. As MacDonald tells the Ghost, once tasted heavenly joy is forever in the soul.[10] The demons think they have a chance, but their patient's life is already part of heaven. While the narrator of *The Great Divorce* exists in the gap separating him from MacDonald's wisdom, the demons' efforts are the butt of a comic—and a cosmic—irony. Taken together, the novels illustrate that against divine Love, hellish influence is ultimately futile.

Lewis's narrator observes encounters between several Ghosts and Spirits, and by Chapter Nine has begun to doubt the sincerity of the Spirits of "The Valley of the Shadow of Life." The Ghost thinks it questionable, naturally, that ghosts have a second chance after death to choose heaven; he presents his doubts to MacDonald. It is a reasonable question, if posed in a setting past the limits of human reason. His naïve curiosity leads to further questions that are more common—about pity for the damned, or the lack of free will in choosing one's destiny, or the difference between eternity and time—and these lead him till he wakes.[11] This questioning, however gently and reasonably it goes on, implies that he keeps his own terms for entering heaven. That is the problem. The conditions of choice are not his, but as MacDonald makes clear, they are Christ's. The Ghost's understanding of the "nature of [his] choice" grows, but not to the point of abandoning a quest for forbidden knowledge.[12] When morning comes—the novel's symbol for

---

9. Lewis, *Great Divorce*, 143–44.
10. Lewis, *Great Divorce*, 69.
11. Lewis, *Great Divorce*, 140–44.
12. Lewis, *Great Divorce*, 144.

the closing of spiritual possibility—he awakens and enters everyday reality in wartime, an explicit choice of Christ not yet made. Neither ironic, nor comic, this evident failure to choose is jolting, and Lewis's readers have been admonished about—and prepared for—the timely need for decision. It is a decision whether or not to pursue a love for God and others that is disinterested.

## DISINTERESTED LOVE IN SCREWTAPE

Screwtape's role in the ministry of hell is to instruct lesser demons in the ways of humans, especially susceptibility to sin. Early in the novel he teaches Wormwood about the comings and goings of their spiritual strength. From the evidence of Wormwood's correspondence, he observes that the patient is experiencing a "trough."[13] The letter, number eight in the "collection," contains the first in Screwtape's series of lessons on Divine Love, a strong motif in *The Screwtape Letters*, if dangerous for a demon. To speak of it is heretical in hell, and gives rise to one of the novel's incidents of high comedy when Wormwood reports the discussion to a demon higher in the underworld ranks. Because humans live in time, the nearest they come to constancy is "undulation."[14] "As long as [the patient] lives on earth periods of emotional and bodily richness will alternate with periods of numbness and poverty."[15] But Screwtape explains with characteristic half-understanding that "in His efforts to get permanent possession of a soul He relies on troughs even more than on peaks."[16] God will not coerce faith, nor permanently offer His presence as a stay against weakness. "To override a human will . . . would be for Him useless."[17] He can only "woo,"[18] not tempt, nor force. His felt presence overwhelms the human will, and that contradicts the nature of Divine Love. While the demons wish to absorb and consume the will, annihilating individuality, in God's plan "the creatures are to be one with Him, but yet themselves":[19]

> One must face the fact that all the talk about His love for men, and His service being perfect freedom, is not . . . mere propaganda, but an appalling truth. He really does want to fill the

---

13. Lewis, *Screwtape Letters*, 36.
14. Lewis, *Screwtape Letters*, 36.
15. Lewis, *Screwtape Letters*, 37.
16. Lewis, *Screwtape Letters*, 37.
17. Lewis, *Screwtape Letters*, 38.
18. Lewis, *Screwtape Letters*, 38.
19. Lewis, *Screwtape Letters*, 38.

universe with a lot of loathsome little replicas of Himself—creatures whose life, on its miniature scale, will be qualitatively like His own, not because He has absorbed them but because their wills conform freely to His.[20]

During troughs, human beings become both more themselves and more the kind "of creature[s] He wants [them] to be."[21]

The setting of *The Screwtape Letters* might well be thin air though demons inhabit various departments in the hierarchy of hell. In Lewis's imaginative world, fallen angels exist, insofar as they have existence, as mere practical intelligence, energy, appetite, and will. They cannot love, but feel instead only the emotions associated with the will to dominate and consume—envy, malice, and pride.[22] Thus, Screwtape comprehends Divine Love intellectually as abstract truth. So his understanding, like that of the narrator in *The Great Divorce*, has clear limits: he cannot grasp *disinterestedness*. Lewis very cleverly creates a character who can speak of divine love and observe its effects but who cannot discern its activity within human beings. He knows it externally as a "ghastly luminosity"[23] that forms the permanent background of everything: his image of the immanence of Christ's love throughout the universe. What he does not know is that God has a "foothold" inside the patient that cannot be removed.

When the patient passes through his first "trough" and comes out the other side of it, he experiences a "second conversion . . . deeper"[24] than the first. (The phrasing is wishful thinking: Screwtape keeps alive a hope that conversions are discreet and separate events as a corollary of his belief that they can be undone by a later conversion in the other direction.) The trough coincides with the patient's attracting new friends, worldly, intelligent materialists whose conversations reveal assumptions in "direct opposition"[25] to the patient's faith. Wormwood teaches him to be vain about his ability to "take a positive pleasure in the perception that the two sides of his life are inconsistent."[26] Distractions from real self-knowledge, vanity, and pride can give this pleasure "for quite long periods."[27] Wormwood's job is to ensure the patient enjoys these new people and is not "distracted" from them by

20. Lewis, *Screwtape Letters*, 38.
21. Lewis, *Screwtape Letters*, 39.
22. Lewis, *Screwtape Letters*, vii–ix.
23. Lewis, *Screwtape Letters*, 21.
24. Lewis, *Screwtape Letters*, 57.
25. Lewis, *Screwtape Letters*, 46.
26. Lewis, *Screwtape Letters*, 47.
27. Lewis, *Screwtape Letters*, 47.

the "Enemy." Thus, while "being permanently treacherous to at least two sets of people he will feel, instead of shame, a continual undercurrent of self-satisfaction."[28] A conversation about laughter in the midst of it foreshadows the deepening of Love in the patient that eventually occurs. As Screwtape describes the effect of mild humor "among friends and lovers on the eve of a holiday,"[29] he observes, "The smallest witticisms produce laughter."[30] They cannot be the real cause of the laughter, Screwtape reasons. They are not funny enough. "What the real cause is we do not know. Something like it is expressed in much of that detestable art which the humans call Music, and something like it occurs in heaven—a meaningless acceleration in the rhythm of celestial experience, quite opaque to us."[31] He is speaking of a cause for joy that exceeds its occasion, the joy that simply is selfless delight in friends. He does not discern the love that intensifies during such reunions. It is an inner state he cannot perceive, and since it is in excess of its evident, external cause, it is very near in kind to grace. With abundant pride, he remarks that love and joy are all a "direct insult to the realism, dignity, and austerity of Hell."[32]

Wormwood's mistake, which leads to the patient's deepening faith, is that he did not "get him away from those"[33] deepest impulses which the patient indulges for no reason other than the simple pleasures they offer. "The deepest likings and impulses of any man are the raw material, the starting point, with which the enemy has furnished him."[34] He delights in them for themselves, not for any ulterior reasons, nor for the hope of advantage of any kind. Wormwood has allowed the patient to read a book he really enjoyed; he allowed him to take a walk to an old mill for tea, and "through country he really likes."[35] These "likings" are among the basic endowments of the patient's individuality. He takes innocent pleasure in them. It is "disinterested" pleasure. The word is a leitmotif, and it is at the heart of the "Enemy's" idea of love in *Screwtape*. When the patient walks back from the Old Mill, he is surrounded by a "cloud" that prevents Wormwood from attacking him. "It is the Enemy's most barbarous weapon," Screwtape says, "and generally appears when He is directly present to the patient under certain modes not yet

28. Lewis, *Screwtape Letters*, 48.
29. Lewis, *Screwtape Letters*, 50.
30. Lewis, *Screwtape Letters*, 50.
31. Lewis, *Screwtape Letters*, 50.
32. Lewis, *Screwtape Letters*, 50.
33. Lewis, *Screwtape Letters*, 59.
34. Lewis, *Screwtape Letters*, 59.
35. Lewis, *Screwtape Letters*, 58.

fully classified."[36] It is no wonder that Lewis would represent the action of "disinterested love" as impenetrable to Screwtape; the demons Lewis creates know only competition, malice, and appetite, and have no categories for classifying a kind of regard that does not seek a self-indulgent return.

If the patient delights in these pleasures for their sake alone, his likings are a mirror image of God's Love for him. God does not wish to consume him, as Screwtape and his comrades do. He wishes the man to be more himself, more richly and fully himself:

> Of course I know that the Enemy also wants to detach men from themselves, but in a different way. . . . He really likes the little vermin, and sets an absurd value on the distinctness of every one of them. When He talks of their losing their selves, He means only abandoning the glamour of self-will; once they have done that, He really gives them back all their personality, and boasts (I am afraid, sincerely) that when they are wholly His they will be more themselves than ever.[37]

Screwtape's explanations are glosses on what he assumes happens in conversion; the patient accepts the gospel comprised of the preaching of Redemption and Resurrection: "The earliest converts were converted by a single historical fact (the Resurrection) and a single theological doctrine (the Redemption) operating on a sense of sin which they already had—and sin, not against some new fancy-dress law produced as a novelty by a great man, but against the . . . universal moral law which they had been taught by their nurses and mothers."[38] This gospel is the stable, unchanging message of "mere Christianity,"[39] not some version of "Christianity and—."[40] It is not to be combined with anything that can allow its use as a means to some end other than Redemption. If Grace is the heart of the Christian gospel, Christianity should be "mere Christianity," not "Christianity and—," thus turning the gospel to some use, treating it as a means to some worldly end, such as self-advancement, or even to a genuine good, such as social justice. Anything that is a good-in-itself is corrupted when its representatives take Christianity—and Christ—as a means to achieve it, thereby using God "as a convenience" or a political expedience, and turning aside from him and his love.[41]

36. Lewis, *Screwtape Letters*, 58.
37. Lewis, *Screwtape Letters*, 59.
38. Lewis, *Screwtape Letters*, 108.
39. Lewis, *Screwtape Letters*, 115.
40. Lewis, *Screwtape Letters*, 115.
41. Lewis, *Screwtape Letters*, 107–8; 115–16.

At its center, the Christian gospel, like saving faith, is disinterested. There is nothing on earth to be advanced by or gained by embracing it. "Not as the world gives do I give to you" (John 14:27).[42] On Screwtape's reading, God gives new selves with the distinct qualities and gifts of personality the believer originally had. But the gift of new life is so expansive, so large, so different in kind from anything else in creation, that no return from a human being could match it: this redeemed self gives glimpses of the kinds of selves that exist in heaven—transposed selves of those whose natural abilities, talents, and distinct characters have been given a higher nature than their own natural one because God lives in them.[43] Lewis makes such knowledge obscure to Screwtape.

Screwtape writes on the topic of disinterested love throughout the letters.[44] It is a leitmotif at the heart of the book. Other words for "disinterested" are "impartial" and "unbiased." But to put it thus negatively, as Screwtape does, may be to miss the meaning in the New Testament, where it is a positive virtue, as in 1 Corinthians 13, or, with a turn to life in communion, as in Philippians 2:3-4: "Do nothing from selfishness or empty conceit, but with humility of mind regard one another as more important than yourselves; do not *merely* look out for your own personal interests, but also for the interests of others."

Near the end of the book, Lewis illustrates how love penetrates the numbing pains of wartime in acts of courage that remain selfless and disinterested. The patient has nothing to lose and nothing to gain in carrying out his duties. He feels no motivation, sees no reward. Even in despair, just before his death, he perseveres in the kind of actions that, according to Screwtape, are of utmost value to God, even while God seems to have abandoned him: "Sooner or later he withdraws, if not in fact, at least from their conscious experience, all . . . supports and incentives. He leaves the creature to stand up on its own legs—to carry out from the will alone duties which have lost all relish."[45] The patient's behavior was "the worst possible" for the demons until the end. Feeling himself a coward, he has lost all pride. All he knew in the moments before death was hellish: "One moment it seemed to be all our world: the scream of bombs, the fall of houses, the stink and taste of high explosive on the lips and in the lungs, the feet burning with

---

42. All Scripture in this essay is from the NASB.
43. Lewis, "Transposition," 267-78.
44. Lewis, *Screwtape Letters*, 37-38; 50-56; 60-65, 81-86; 100-102.
45. Lewis, *Screwtape Letters*, 39.

weariness, the heart cold with horrors, the brain reeling, the legs aching. In the next moment, he was with the eternally living."[46]

Thus, the patient survives all of the demons' efforts to undermine his faith. In the last of Screwtape's letters (thirty-one), the demons know their efforts to trip up and damn their patient fail. From the moment of his conversion, they were destined to disappointment. The clue for Screwtape appears in his own words: he refers to the "gods" who had accompanied the patient throughout his life as the patient's friends. They are in reality eternal Spirits who never left him. Screwtape observes that the patient seems to have been born for heaven, seems also to have known the Spirits who had served him, sees even Wormwood, then the Lord Himself: "When he saw them, he knew that he had always known them and realized what part each of them had played at many an hour in his life, . . . so that now he could say to them, one by one, not 'Who are you?' but 'So it was *you* all the time.'"[47]

One of the marks of the conversion of Christians is the possibility of transformation of earthly loves into disinterested love. As Lewis notes,

> Only those into which Love Himself has entered will ascend to Love Himself. And these can be raised with Him only if they have, in some degree and fashion, shared His death; if the natural element in them has submitted—year after year, or in some sudden agony—to transmutation. . . . Natural loves can hope for eternity only in so far as they have allowed themselves to be taken into the eternity of Charity; have at least allowed the process to begin here on earth, before the night comes when no man can work.[48]

Just as the demons in *The Screwtape Letters* had lost their battle when their patient began to show disinterested love, so the need to enjoy disinterested love is a mark of readiness for heaven in *The Great Divorce*.

## DISINTERESTED LOVE IN *THE GREAT DIVORCE*

In the early chapters of *The Great Divorce*, Lewis's readers find hell a paradoxical place. It is a transparency, almost a nothing, yet infinitely extended by the turbulent imaginations of its inhabitants: "The trouble is that they're all so quarrelsome," the narrator learns from a comrade in hell. "As soon as someone arrives he settles in some street. . . . Before the week is over

---

46. Lewis, *Screwtape Letters*, 140.
47. Lewis, *Screwtape Letters*, 147.
48. Lewis, *Four Loves*, 171.

he's quarreled so badly that he decides to move."[49] The process is endless, leaving expanses of empty streets in an infinite underworld sprawl. As the narrator's companion says, "You've only got to think a house and there it is. That's how the town keeps growing."[50] Likewise, only think them, and there are urban centers, shops, factories, theaters, but all in a Grey Town with an atmosphere like dusk and looming rain. This growth is that only of shadows, not realities, an appropriate symbol of insatiable desire, the opposite of disinterested love. Despite its infinitude, the entirety of hell is no larger than a pinprick. It would slip through a tiny crevice in the surface of heaven.

By contrast, heaven is all substance—more than tangibly real, supernally beautiful, and infinite, but with an infinitude different in kind from that in hell. "Heaven is reality itself. All that is fully real is Heavenly," MacDonald says.[51] In heaven, every earthly good is transposed to its heavenly archetype, and its goodness becomes fully present to the perfected senses. Every delight is pristine, and perfection itself is delight. Yet when Ghosts visit the "Valley of the Shadow of Life," below the foothills of the mountains of "deep heaven,"[52] they are painfully alive to their difference.

To the Ghosts, heaven is the Valley of the Shadow of Life; thus at points beneath its highest bliss, it is more than the perfect consummation of every earthly beauty or good. It is terrifying. They are unfit for it. They are attracted, and they are repulsed. When the narrator steps out of the fantastic bus that transports Ghosts to the Valley, he finds, "The light and coolness that drenched me were like those of summer morning, early morning a minute or two before the sunrise, . . . I had the sense of being in a larger space, perhaps even a larger sort of space, than I had ever known before."[53] It "made the Solar System seem an indoor affair."[54] When he tries to pluck a daisy, he finds that "the little flower was hard, not like wood or even like iron, but like diamond."[55] He is thoroughly unprepared. When he becomes aware of his fragility, he says, "I noticed that I could see the grass not only between my feet but *through* them. I also was a phantom."[56] He feels exhilarating

---

49. Lewis, *Great Divorce*, 10.
50. Lewis, *Great Divorce*, 10.
51. Lewis, *Great Divorce*, 70
52. Lewis, *Great Divorce*, 68.
53. Lewis, *Great Divorce*, 20.
54. Lewis, *Great Divorce*, 20.
55. Lewis, *Great Divorce*, 20.
56. Lewis, *Great Divorce*, 20.

freedom, and he also feels "exposure [to] danger," even "terror," feelings, he says, that "continued to accompany me through all that followed."[57]

As a consequence, the narrator offers a mixed outlook on heaven. What he sees troubles him; *how* he sees should trouble him as well. When he first observes heavenly Spirits, his dream-vision combines memory of mere earthly appearances with sensory knowledge of supernal Spirits:

> Some were naked, some robed. But the naked ones did not seem less adorned, and the robes did not disguise in those who wore them the massive grandeur of muscle and the radiant smoothness of flesh. . . . One gets glimpses, even in our country, of that which is ageless—heavy thought in the face of an infant, and frolic childhood in that of a very old man. Here it was all like that. . . . I did not entirely like it.[58]

The Ghost cannot escape this "double vision,"[59] as he calls it in his encounter with the Spirit of MacDonald. Time-bound, he encounters eternal beings utterly different in kind from himself. He cannot see beyond the limitations his condition as a guest from hell impose upon him. The result is that for him vestiges of earth combine with heaven and hell in his visionary dream. Lewis wrote this narrative to separate heaven and hell, to "divorce" them. As every encounter between Spirits and Ghosts shows, the narrator can enjoy this separation only by abandoning every transgressive impulse and choosing Christ. Once "in Christ" and, as it were, outside himself, he gains the objectivity needed to see that he is trying, as MacDonald puts it, to bring something of hell into heaven. Indeed, his mere presence in The Valley of the Shadow of Life accomplishes that. In the meantime—the length of the entire dream—he is troubled by this limited perspective, which inherently unites heaven and hell and from which come the persistent questions about freedom that delay his choice until it is too late.

It is one of the beauties of this narrative that the dialogue between the Ghosts and Spirits suggests interior depths of love and insights into its nature that far exceed those of the narrator. In chapter 9, when the Ghost meets the Spirit of MacDonald, he finds MacDonald solicitous, and by a deft and subtle dramatic irony, more knowing and insightful than he can comprehend. MacDonald's wisdom becomes evident when the narrator tells MacDonald that he had bought his novel, *Phantastes*, at sixteen. He explains that reading it had been to him like the first sight of Beatrice to

---

57. Lewis, *Great Divorce*, 20.
58. Lewis, *Great Divorce*, 24.
59. Lewis, *Great Divorce*, 65.

Dante, the beginning of the *Vita Nuova*. He seems to think that he is speaking of salvation. MacDonald knows better:

> *Here begins the New Life.* I started to confess how long that life had delayed in the region of imagination merely; how slowly and reluctantly I had come to admit that his Christendom had more than an accidental connexion with it, how hard I had tried not to see that the true name of the quality which first met me in his books is *Holiness*. He laid his hand on mine and stopped me.[60]

He "stopped me." The narrator identifies his spiritual condition well, if unawares. MacDonald gets quickly to it. It is not Dante nor the *Vita Nuova*, nor the narrator's notion of holiness, but the narrator's still-to-be-determined "destiny" that at this moment preoccupies MacDonald: "'Ye had started,' said my Teacher, 'to talk of something more profitable.'"[61]

The surrounding context presents what MacDonald means by this "something more profitable." In the previous chapter, the Ghost sees a female ghost on the verge of choice. This choice is revealed in a conversation between a Spirit and a female ghost painfully self-conscious of her insubstantiality, like a partygoer aware of being underdressed. She has seen the otherworldly splendor of the Spirits. "How can I go out like this among a lot of people with real solid bodies?"[62] "You can step out . . . at any moment . . . into infinite happiness,"[63] her own guiding Spirit tells her with the same wise love that guides MacDonald: "Shame is like that," the Spirit says. "If you will accept it—if you will drink the cup to the bottom—you will find it very nourishing: but try to do anything else with it and it scalds."[64] If she traces the source of her shame to overreaching self-regard, sees it for what it is as the bar to Joy, and then allows Christ to destroy it, she will know the happiness of the Spirits. She says, "You really mean . . .?"[65] She breaks off. Lewis represents the condition of such Ghosts as an insuperable disability. She cannot grasp the heavenly meaning until she chooses it. She almost turns. The narrator, too, comes almost to the end of his doubts: "My suspense was strained up to the height. I felt that my own destiny hung on her reply. I could have fallen at her feet and begged her to yield."[66] Just then,

---

60. Lewis, *Great Divorce*, 67.
61. Lewis, *Great Divorce*, 67.
62. Lewis, *Great Divorce*, 60.
63. Lewis, *Great Divorce*, 61.
64. Lewis, *Great Divorce*, 61.
65. Lewis, *Great Divorce*, 61.
66. Lewis, *Great Divorce*, 61.

as a last resort, the Spirit attempts to shake her free, to "fix" her "mind on something not"[67] herself, by sending in a herd of unicorns to astonish her out of herself. The "interview" ends ambiguously, however, without evidence of her choice. The narrator is left with lingering anxiety about the question of her destiny. He little realizes how much that anxiety matters to MacDonald.

If there is a climax—a moment of decision that clears the narrator's doubts—it must happen in the gap between chapters 8 and 9. Just after that gap, when the narrator meets MacDonald, he explains that a question—he does not say which one—that has recently caused him anxiety has disappeared. "I have no anxiety about the answer now."[68] True to the nature of dreams, this anxiety unaccountably evaporates. The narrator never learns the female Ghost's spiritual decision, and anxiety about *that* should not have resolved since anxiety about her choice had also been, implicitly, anxiety about his own. The narrator felt that his destiny had hung on hers, so like her, he, too, comes vicariously to the brink of change. Perhaps in that gap between episodes, in the no-man's land of conjecture between chapters, the narrator made his decision to stay in heaven. But Lewis chose not to dramatize his choice. There is no narrative episode showing it. And the narrator does remain a ghostly figure in a dream. Vicarious experience *is* imaginative, after all, so MacDonald wisely turns the conversation back to the "choice," the "something more profitable" that he wishes the narrator would consider. To be clear, the choice is between pursuing disinterested love, which is the threshold of salvation, and a continued pursuit of selfish gain.

The "nature of the choice" is that it requires repentance, an act of will allowing Christ to destroy besetting sins. The Ghost who lets him destroy the red lizard of lust riding him illustrates it well. It involves the "heart,"[69] and the "heart" is metonymy for the entire sentient self, all of its natural endowments, all of its depths and shallows. Upon this choice, all of the soul's capacities become illuminated by and lived in by Christ himself, who is much more and far other than a projection of the imagination or abstract idea grasped by the intellect. Once allowed in, the higher Nature of Christ animates everything from within, though he is himself objectively apart from the believer.[70]

---

67. Lewis, *Great Divorce*, 62.
68. Lewis, *Great Divorce*, 67.
69. Lewis, *Great Divorce*, 67.

70. Lewis, "Transposition," 267–78. See esp. 277: "In varying degrees the lower reality can actually be drawn into the higher and become part of it"; but also the humble qualification at 273: "But who dares claim to be a spiritual man? In the full sense, none of us."

MacDonald's *Phantastes* is thoroughly Romantic.[71] If one were to attempt at least a partial profile of the narrator of *The Great Divorce*, the attempt would likely end in the conclusion that he, too, has a Romantic bent. For the most part, Romantic poets like Wordsworth, Coleridge, Keats, Byron, and Shelley omitted reference to a personal God. Christ as mediator was, for most, beside the point. Hence, in *The Pilgrim's Regress*, Lewis represents them mockingly in an allegorical character named "Halfways."[72] Arguably, to Lewis the poetry of the Romantics did not celebrate the disinterested love of God or creation, but instead advanced an ideology: as one critic has put it, Romanticism claims "for the imaginative human spirit the rights and responsibilities traditionally attributed to a transcendent God."[73]

In *The Great Divorce* the narrator mentions Keats in relation to holiness: "'Keats was wrong, then, when he said he was certain of the holiness of the heart's affections.'"[74] It is as if the error has just occurred to him. MacDonald sets Keats aside altogether and affirms "holiness" as exclusive to God and those who turn to him:

> I doubt if he [Keats] knew what he meant. But you and I must be clear. There is but one good; that is God. Everything else is good when it looks to Him and bad when it turns from Him. And the higher and mightier it is in the natural order, the more demoniac it will be if it rebels.[75]

The narrator's feelings towards the beauty of Spirits and the supersensory beauty of the landscapes of The Valley of the Shadow of Life also call Romanticism to mind, particularly the Romantic Sublime. The sublime is a feeling of extreme attraction and repulsion existing in the soul simultaneously—attraction to beautiful and overwhelming landscapes, mountain ranges, for instance, and repulsion from the terror of eternity, the sense of which such overwhelming natural vistas can evoke.[76] A remarkable symbol of it is the waterfall in chapter 6. The narrator's perception reveals tensions associated with the sublime in his response: "An immense yet lovely noise vibrated though the forest.... Here once again I realized that something had happened to my senses so that they were now receiving impressions

---

71. See, for example, Brawley, "Ideal and the Shadow," 91–112.

72. Lewis, *Pilgrim's Regress*, 29, 63.

73. Lundin, "Christ, Culture, and the Romantic Quandary," 233. Cf. Netland, "Modest Apologia for Romanticism," 297–317.

74. Lewis, *Great Divorce*, 106.

75. Lewis, *Great Divorce*, 106.

76. This evocative power of natural vistas is the very subject under consideration in Lewis's first chapter of *The Abolition of Man*.

which would normally exceed their capacity."[77] When he hears a voice also coming from it, he says, "I knew that the waterfall itself was speaking: and I saw now (though it did not cease to look like a waterfall) that it was also a bright angel who stood, like one crucified, against the rocks and poured himself perpetually down towards the forest with loud joy."[78] In addition to his attraction to its loveliness, he feels revulsion: "I could not bear the presence of the Water-Giant,"[79] as he calls it. Like everything else, except the Ghosts, it is both natural and supernatural, itself and more than itself, but, above all, a picture of the immanence of the self-giving love of Christ, which pours out in self-sufficing Joy. The waterfall presents the narrator a perfect opportunity to comprehend and to feel the superabundant joy that Christ disinterestedly gives. The narrator's response is a measure of his distance from it, of his inability to take comfort and joy from it and to love joyously in return.

Some of Lewis's most encouraging theological reflection occurs when the narrator presses MacDonald about the relation between eternity and time. He reconciles temporal experience with eternity perhaps as far as language allows. He tells the Ghost that heaven and hell are absolutely separated by a choice whose full eternal significance is available in the present, in human time, if not fully open to human perception:

> "Son," he said, "ye cannot in your present state understand eternity: when Anodos [the central character of *Phantastes*] looked through the door of the Timeless he brought no message back. But ye can get some likeness of it if ye say that both good and evil, when they are full grown, become retrospective. Not only this valley but all their earthly past will have been Heaven to those who are saved. Not only the twilight in that town, but all their life on earth too, will then be seen by the damned to have been Hell."[80]

MacDonald's words in the remarkable paragraph following this passage embrace a wide range of related Scriptural teaching—from Christian mysticism, in which the lives of believers are "hidden" in God in eternal union (Col 3:3), to the immanence of God in believers by the presence of the Holy Spirit (Rom 5:1–5), to life as a process of continuous grace as believers recognize their sins and repent (1 John 1:9). Unrecognized sin is covered, as well, since it is in his character to know of it and to include it in loving

77. Lewis, *Great Divorce*, 49.
78. Lewis, *Great Divorce*, 49.
79. Lewis, *Great Divorce*, 51.
80. Lewis, *Great Divorce*, 169.

regard for fallible believers (1 John 3:20). In sum, MacDonald explains that alive on earth in time, or in the presence of God's glory in eternity, believers participate in the reality of heaven. They do so in efforts to imitate him, in their failures to do so, and in their endurance of suffering. As MacDonald puts it, "Heaven, once attained, will work backwards and turn even . . . agony into a glory."[81] As an eternal event, the choice of Christ encompasses all of the believer's life in time. On MacDonald's reading—and Lewis's—it is as if the life of a repentant believer, all of it, were at once colored by an eternal dye. All of this is a disinterested gift, lovingly bestowed. Just at this point, the novel makes its most compelling symbolic reach towards lived experience as opposed to the purely imaginary experience of a dream.

In creating this dream, and this narrator, Lewis writes of things beyond language, beyond sight, and conception. In consequence, his narrator faces a doubled boundary: the ontological one that separates time from eternity, and nature from super-nature, but also the internal boundary that separates the narrator from full self-awareness about his need for intellectual humility before the Eternal. "Ye cannot fully understand the relations of choice and Time until you are beyond both," Macdonald urges him.[82] Yet the last question the narrator presses is whether there really is freedom of choice. His persistence keeps the choice of heaven on *his* terms, which require a return on any love given, any curiosity unanswered. This lack of awareness is a restraining influence against joy that he is, as it were, born with; indeed, that everyone is born with. He knows by sensation and later, through MacDonald's reasoning, that he is in the presence of more than natural sights and sounds: He sees everything in this environment by "double vision," as both reminiscent of earth and different in kind from anything he has experienced. Lewis negotiates the ontological boundary with language that suggests what he calls transposition: "In varying degrees the lower reality can actually be drawn into the higher and become part of it."[83] He never negotiates the internal one.

MacDonald tells him, "Ye are here to watch and listen."[84] The implication is that the narrator needs gentle correction to change his will to corrupt heaven. He presents the example of an artist who once enjoyed light as an intrinsic gift, in and for itself. "Light itself was your first love: you loved paint only as a means of telling about light."[85] Because of this love, he "caught

---

81. Lewis, *Great Divorce*, 69.
82. Lewis, *Great Divorce*, 71.
83. Lewis, "Transposition," 277.
84. Lewis, *Great Divorce*, 78.
85. Lewis, *Great Divorce*, 84.

glimpses of heaven in the earthly landscape."[86] But later he turned to his own technical accomplishments as of more interest and lost interest in light itself. His guiding Spirit tells him, "but for Grace," every artist "is drawn away from love of the thing he tells to love of the telling."[87] Eventually, they care only about their personalities, their reputations, and "nothing about God at all but only in what they say about Him."[88] The Ghost has lost the capacity for disinterested love of God and created things, and with others like him, he wishes to enjoy heaven but to use it to satisfy a personal desire to exercise his gifts or pursue self-interest of one kind or another. Such Ghosts care "nothing about joy."[89] They mistake "the means for the end."[90] The narrator responds with the usual ignorance about himself: "How fantastic!" But "with a piercing glance," MacDonald says, "It is nearer to such as you than ye think."[91] MacDonald explains more extreme forms of the use of heaven for ulterior purposes: there were "materialistic Ghosts" who tried to persuade the Spirits that heaven "was a hallucination"[92] and others who "in thin, bat-like voices urged the blessed spirits to shake off their fetters, to escape from their imprisonment in happiness . . . and to seize Heaven for their own."[93] In the attempted coup, they offered the "co-operation" of hell.[94] MacDonald's penetrating ironies are hard to miss. The narrator seems to miss them. He offers no comment. The artist is not yet a "Person" in the heavenly sense, according to his spirit. Implicitly, neither is the narrator.[95]

Perhaps predictably, he presents unawares his own effort to bring hell into heaven. His particular form is a misunderstanding of divine love as including pity for the damned: "I asked why the Solid People, since they were full of love, did not go down into hell to rescue the Ghosts. Why were they content simply to meet them on the plain?"[96] To MacDonald, such misunderstanding must be set aside. So there follows a lecture on pity for the damned. Lewis illustrates it with an encounter between the most beautiful image of transposed love in the novel—that of Sarah Smith of Golders

---

86. Lewis, *Great Divorce*, 83.
87. Lewis, *Great Divorce*, 85.
88. Lewis, *Great Divorce*, 85.
89. Lewis, *Great Divorce*, 73.
90. Lewis, *Great Divorce*, 73.
91. Lewis, *Great Divorce*, 73.
92. Lewis, *Great Divorce*, 81.
93. Lewis, *Great Divorce*, 80.
94. Lewis, *Great Divorce*, 80.
95. Lewis, *Great Divorce*, 84.
96. Lewis, *Great Divorce*, 74.

Green—and the grotesque image of human disfigurement by sin, that of Sarah's husband, Frank, as Tragedian and Dwarf, a metaphor for the double-mindedness of the will to manipulate another person to one's purposes. The episode illustrates "a desire very common among the Ghosts," MacDonald says—"the desire to *extend* Hell, to bring it bodily, if they could, into Heaven."[97]

Sarah is divinely beautiful, a lovely masque-like image, the embodiment of transposed and perfected love—that is, disinterested love, joyous and free, the more comely for being so. "Every beast and bird that came near her had its place in her love. In her they became themselves. And now the abundance of life she has in Christ from the Father flows over in to them."[98] She, too, appears to the narrator as a double image. He cannot tell whether she is naked or clothed, "For clothes in that country are not a disguise: the spiritual body lives along each thread and turns them into living organs. A robe or crown is there as much one of the wearer's features as a lip or eye."[99] The Ghost of her husband, once moved presumably by natural desire and affection, turns to pity as a means to manipulate the Spirit of his wife into needing him. He presses the need to be needed. Not in the least disinterested, this, too, is a form of self-will that encloses and entraps the Ghost in his own "self-made misery," but Sarah is not taken in.[100] The narrator and MacDonald discuss this scene:

> "Is it really tolerable that she should be untouched by his misery," the Ghost asks.
> "Would ye rather he still had the power of tormenting her?"

The narrator says, no, but presses the point to its climax:

> "What some people say on Earth is that the final loss of one soul gives the lie to all the joy of those who are saved."
> "That sounds very merciful," MacDonald says: "but see what lies behind it."
> "What?"
> "The demand of the loveless and the self-imprisoned that they should be allowed to blackmail the universe: that till they consent to be happy (on their own terms) no one else shall taste

---

97. Lewis, *Great Divorce*, 80.
98. Lewis, *Great Divorce*, 120.
99. Lewis, *Great Divorce*, 118.
100. Lewis, *Great Divorce*, 135.

joy: that theirs should be the final power; that Hell should be able to veto Heaven."[101]

The Ghost never raises the question again. His question about the relation between eternity and choice persists, however. It is a choice that depends on a willingness to learn to submit to and embody disinterested love.

## CONCLUSION

Disinterested love is a part of being a new person in Christ. The Christian mind is, not exclusively but inescapably, characterized by disinterested love. The more our love becomes disinterested, the more like Christ we become. As Lewis argues in *Mere Christianity*,

> It is when I turn to Christ, when I give myself up to His Personality, that I first begin to have a real personality of my own. . . . Christ will indeed give you a real personality: but you must not go to him for the sake of that. As long as your own personality is what you are bothering about you are not going to Him at all. The first step is to try to forget about the self altogether.[102]

The Christian mind, as Lewis presented it and, with reasonable consistency, lived it, entails self-denial in pursuit of the ultimate good. As he so beautifully summarizes,

> The principle runs through all life from top to bottom. Give up yourself, and you will find your real self. Lose your life and you will save it. Submit to death, death of your ambitions and favourite wishes every day and death of your whole body in the end: submit with every fibre of your being, and you will find eternal life. Keep back nothing. Nothing you have not given away will be really yours. Nothing in you that has not died will ever be raised from the dead. Look for yourself, and you will find in the long run only hatred, loneliness, despair, rage, ruin, and decay. But look for Christ and you will find Him, and with Him everything else thrown in.[103]

This is the goal toward which the Christian mind is oriented. It is the *summum bonum* of the Christian life. This disinterested love is a marker of conversion and evidence of progressive sanctification.

---

101. Lewis, *Great Divorce*, 135.
102. Lewis, *Mere Christianity*, 225.
103. Lewis, *Mere Christianity*, 226–27.

As James Como argues in his essay in this volume, Lewis is a master builder. He uses fiction to illuminate and explain important topics that are often difficult to comprehend in more prosaic presentations. Lewis's exposition of disinterested love in *The Screwtape Letters* and *The Great Divorce* is another sterling example of his craftmanship.

## BIBLIOGRAPHY

Brawley, Chris. "The Ideal and the Shadow." *North Wind: A Journal of George Macdonald Studies*. 25.7 (2007) 91–112.

Lewis, C. S. *An Experiment in Criticism*. Cambridge: Cambridge University Press, 1961.

———. *The Four Loves*. New York: HarperOne, 1960.

———. *The Great Divorce*. New York: HarperOne, 2001.

———. *The Pilgrim's Regress*. Grand Rapids: Eerdmans, 1992.

———. *The Screwtape Letters*. Rev. ed. New York: MacMillan, 1982.

———. "Transposition." In *C. S. Lewis: Essay Collection and Other Short Pieces*, edited by Lesley Walmsley, 267–278. London: HarperCollins, 2000.

Lundin, Roger. "Christ, Culture, and the Romantic Quandary." In *The Culture of Interpretation: Christian Faith and the Postmodern World*, 212–35. Grand Rapids: Eerdmans, 1993.

MacDonald, George. *Phantastes and Lilith*. Introduction by C. S. Lewis. Grand Rapids: Eerdmans, 1964.

McSwain, Robert, and Michael Ward, eds. *The Cambridge Companion to C. S. Lewis*. Cambridge: Cambridge University Press, 2010.

Netland, John. T. "A Modest Apologia for Romanticism." *Christian Scholars Review* 25.3 (March 1996) 297–317.

# 9

# An "Inner Ring" or an Open Fellowship?

## An Evaluation of the Company of St. Anne's in *That Hideous Strength*

*Lindsey Panxhi*

THROUGHOUT HIS WORKS OF fiction, Lewis includes figures who embody the love of what is good, glorious, and right: figures such as the talking beasts of Narnia, the *hrossa* and *sorns* of Malacandra, the Green Lady of Perelandra, and the immortal "Solid People" who walk the foothills of heaven in *The Great Divorce*. In every case, Lewis masters that supremely difficult task of making the good immanently beautiful and desirable. Most readers would, if given the chance, readily step through the wardrobe, into the spaceship, or onto the bus that would allow them to join the fellowship of any of the aforementioned figures. But perhaps fewer readers would eagerly take the train out to join the company at St. Anne's from *That Hideous Strength*.

Lewis's portrayal of the company that gathers around Elwin Ransom in the village of St. Anne's on the Hill has been alternately praised, attacked, and misunderstood over the years. Proponents of the book see St. Anne's as a model of the Christian intellectual and spiritual life, while others see unorthodox traits in the group. This chapter examines strengths and weaknesses in Lewis's portrayal of the company at St. Anne's by applying principles from one of Lewis's essays, "The Inner Ring."[1] Lewis's novel and essay both provide insights regarding the danger of exclusive social circles, alongside reflections about the nature of genuine friendship. Ultimately, in his depiction of the company at St. Anne's, Lewis crafts an effective portrayal of Christian minds working in concert to oppose the devious minds within the NICE.

## CRITICISMS AND CONCERNS REGARDING THE COMPANY AT ST. ANNE'S

The company at St. Anne's is a foil to the corruption so obvious in the NICE, but the strangeness of that small community often confuses modern sensibilities. To some readers, the arrangement of the characters around Ransom seems more like a cult than an example of a healthy community. Ten individuals comprise their fellowship: Elwin Ransom, now known as Mr. Fisher-King or the Pendragon, the aged Dimbles, the young Dennistons, the psychologist Grace Ironwood, the housemaid Ivy Maggs, and the stubborn skeptic MacPhee. The agnostic seer Jane Studdock and the wizard Merlin eventually become integral members at the manor, as well. When I first read *That Hideous Strength* (hereafter, *THS*) as a teenager, I was entranced by the idea of Merlin reawakening, and chilled by the convincingly nefarious National Institute of Co-ordinated Experiments (the NICE), but I was troubled by the strange and unconventional community at St. Anne's. I was baffled and somewhat repelled by the forbidding Grace Ironwood, feisty MacPhee, and the wounded Fisher-King, though I wanted to be drawn to them as I was to Narnians or Malacandrans.

Discomfort with the company of St. Anne's is a common response.[2] For example, in a review printed shortly after the book's publication, Graham

---

1. *That Hideous Strength* was published in 1945. However, there is evidence from Lewis's correspondence that he had finished writing a draft of *That Hideous Strength* by late 1943 or early 1944. See Glover, *Art of Enchantment*, 105–6. It is likely that Lewis continued to revise the novel in 1944, the same year in which he wrote "The Inner Ring."

2. Lewis himself records vexed feelings regarding his manuscript of *THS*. On April 29, 1943, he wrote to a correspondent, E. R. Eddison, about his work on the third book of the space trilogy: "I have just read through what is already written (about 300 sheets) and come to the uncomfortable conclusion that it is all rubbish. Has this ever happened to you? A nauseous moment—when the thought of trying to mend it, and of abandoning it, seem equally unbearable." Lewis, *Collected Letters*, 2:571. In May 1943, he wrote to Owen Barfield about his work on *THS*, saying that "the novel at present in progress is bosh." Lewis, *Collected Letters*, 2:574. However, through the process of revising he must have become more satisfied with his work, as he wrote to Dorothy L.

Greene wrote, "Mr. Lewis writes admirably and excitingly when he is describing the Institute . . . but I found Professor Ransom and the 'good' characters peculiarly unconvincing. The allegory becomes a little too friendly, like a sermon at a children's service, or perhaps like a whimsical charade organized by a middle-aged bachelor uncle."[3] Another 1945 review stated that Lewis's characters "tend to be caricatures or at best personifications of certain mental or moral attitudes he is concerned to present."[4] Rowan Williams, though generally favorable towards *THS*, comments that key characters at St. Anne's come off unsuccessfully. He finds Ransom "theatrical," Dr. and Mrs. Dimble "dull," the Dennistons to be "cardboard figures," and Grace Ironwood and Mrs. Maggs to be "compounds of clichés. They're lively and cleverly done, but they have no life apart from the plot's requirements."[5] In my early readings of the novel, I also found it hard to feel readerly affection for the company at St. Anne's. Now, as an adult, I see that Lewis, the master builder, uses existing forms, themselves somewhat boring for their familiarity, to present an unimaginable reality to an audience better equipped to revel in the mundane than the sublime.[6] This unexpected technique helps explain the common thread of criticism.

Most critics object to the characterization of individuals in the company. However, the ethos of the entire company also leads to polarized reactions to St. Anne's. At an Inklings conference, I found myself in conversation about St. Anne's with two scholars, one Christian and the other non-Christian. The Christian scholar spoke ardently of his admiration for the company, singing their praises as a brilliant portrayal of a community of Christians, operating in concert and in freedom under the direction of Ransom and the higher powers of Deep Heaven. In contrast, the non-Christian scholar expressed a deep dislike towards the group at St. Anne's, saying

---

Sayers on December 6, 1945, after the book's publication: "Thanks for the kind things you say about *That Hideous Strength*, all the more welcome because it has got a more unanimous chorus of unfavourable reviews than any book I can remember. Apparently reviewers *will not* tolerate a mixture of the realistic and the supernatural. Which is a pity, because (a) It's just the mixture I like, and (b) We have to put up with it in real life. I am so glad that you liked the descent of the gods. Mr. Bultitude is described by Tolkien as a portrait of the author, but I feel that is too high a compliment." Lewis, *Collected Letters*, 2:682.

3. Cited by Hooper, "That Hideous Strength," 239. The review was originally published in the *Evening Standard* on 24 August 1945.

4. Cited by Hooper, "That Hideous Strength," 239. Hooper does not provide the name for this reviewer, but the critique was published in *The Times Literary Supplement* (25 August 1945), 401.

5. Williams, "Reassessment," 96–97.

6. See James Como's essay in chapter 4 of this volume.

the company felt cult-like, with its exalted leader, its secluded and secretive location, and its small number of eccentric members, not to mention its stances on obedience and gender.[7] Both opinions are somewhat natural to the modern mind, in light of our cultural sensibilities. Interpreting the company at St. Anne's is akin to walking a tightrope: it requires careful attention, and one can easily slip into an alarming and uncertain space where confidence in the protagonists wavers. However, when *THS* is read and understood as Lewis likely meant it to be, St. Anne's stands as a genuine depiction of a faithful Christian community. Yet admittedly, there are moments throughout the novel that awaken a sense of wariness and mistrust towards the company. Reading Lewis's related essay, "The Inner Ring," provides an explanation of the conflicting responses that the company provokes.

## ST. ANNE'S AND "THE INNER RING"

In 1944, Lewis gave a talk, titled "The Inner Ring," in which he addresses the human tendency to pursue acceptance in exclusive social groups.[8] Lewis describes the propensity within educational, governmental, and commercial institutions for individuals to form exclusive inner rings of those "in the know," who possess the power, respect, and envy of those outside. He cautions his listeners to avoid being consumed with the desire to gain admission to these Inner Rings, saying the desire can define one's life, and will never satisfy once attained. Many scholars have noted the way Lewis depicts Mark Studdock as a protagonist who exemplifies the attitudes warned against in "The Inner Ring."[9] Mark has spent every period of his life, from infancy to adulthood, relentlessly driven by the desire to be inside whatever clique presents itself. The reader is clearly made to see Mark's aspirations as unpleasant and pathetic at best, and hypocritical and criminal at worst. Lewis was writing and editing *THS* and "The Inner Ring" concurrently, and the links between the two works are clear. Lewis uses the terms "inner ring" and

---

7. A detailed discussion of gender dynamics in *THS* is beyond the scope of this paper. Much has already been written about Lewis's literary depictions of women, and the risk he runs of straying into sexism. To read about charges of sexism in the Space Trilogy, see Downing, *Planets in Peril*, 147–51. Monika Hilders credits Lewis with developing a feminine heroic for his female characters; see Hilders, "Foolish Weakness," 77–90. Another positive and careful analysis of Lewis's writings on gender can be found in Shogren, "Lewisian Genders," 387–412.

8. "'The Inner Ring' was the annual 'Commemoration Oration' given at King's College, University of London, on 14 December 1944." Hooper, "Introduction," 20.

9. Downing, *Planets in Peril*, 93 and 135; Hooper, "Playing by the Rules," 105–26, esp. 111–16; Gibson, *C. S. Lewis, Spinner of Tales*, 70, 82, 86; Meilaender, *Taste for the Other*, 94–100; Purtill, "That Hideous Strength," 92.

"inner circle" explicitly eleven times throughout the book, by my count.[10] Notably, ten out of the eleven uses of these terms appear when the narration is giving voice to Mark's thoughts because of his desire to be included.

Throughout *THS*, Lewis alternates between depicting Mark's experiences and those of Jane; the two groups they join stand in clear opposition to one another. Mark spends most of his time at NICE's headquarters at Belbury, whose etymology suggests it should be viewed as a "fortress of Ba'al."[11] In contrast, Jane finds her way to a very different community, located in the remote village of St. Anne's on the Hill. Again, Lewis's name-choice is significant; for according to some Christian traditions, St. Anne is the mother of Mary, the mother of Christ,[12] and she is the patron saint of motherhood.[13] The suffix "on the Hill" evokes the image of a city on a hill, clearly implying that St. Anne's is a Christian community representing God's kingdom. Rowan Williams expresses concern about the way Lewis depicts the opposing factions of the NICE and St. Anne's, writing, "Lewis runs a very deep risk in setting up two conflicting groups, two conflicting *companies of interest*, Belbury and the NICE and St Anne's-on-the-Hill—because it's very difficult to portray the seductions of the inner ring . . . when goodness is itself represented by *another* kind of inner ring, another kind of closed circle."[14]

There are points in the novel that seem to support Williams's interpretation. For example, Jane's first conversation with a member of the company at St. Anne's does, at times, echo the language Lewis associates with inner rings. Jane, plagued by her fearsome night-visions, gives into the Dimbles's urgings to travel to St. Anne's and confer with Grace Ironwood. Miss Ironwood, a tall, thin woman with large, bony hands and solemn grey eyes, informs Jane that her dreams are true visions, and that Jane's ability

---

10. Lewis, *That Hideous Strength*, 101, 135, 169, 171–72, 185, 223, 246, 255, 259, 360. There are many other references to social cliques and elitist attitudes throughout the novel; Mark thinks of the Progressive Element within Bracton College as "Curry and his gang," for example. Lewis, *That Hideous Strength*, 17. I chose to take note specifically of uses of "inner ring" and "inner circle" because of their similarity to Lewis's terminology in "The Inner Ring."

11. Fairfield, "Fragmentation and Hope," 146.

12. Schwartz, *Final Frontier*, 94.

13. Traxler, "Pendragon, Merlin, and Logos," 197. Schwartz also associates the Fisher King's Manor at St. Anne's with "the feminine, the maternal, the natural fecundity of the earth, and by virtue of its ties to the celestial presence of Venus, with the divine love that is the source of the affections, sympathies, and charities that sustain an organic community." Schwartz, *Final Frontier*, 94–95. These valences of the name can suggest the positive symbolic significance of St. Anne's to the reader from the outset.

14. Williams, "Reassessment," 97.

to see present and future events is an important and desirable attribute.[15] When Jane says that she only wants help in stopping the dreams, Ironwood states sternly, "The things which you have seen concern something compared with which the happiness or even the life, of you and me, *is* of no importance . . . You cannot get rid of your gift. You can try to suppress it, but you will fail, and you will be very badly frightened. On the other hand, you can put it at our disposal . . . I would advise you, even for your own sake, to join our side."[16] In the context of Lewis's novel, Ironwood's words, though harsh and direct, are true, and thus represent a stark grace of sorts. However, were I in Jane's position, meeting a stern and forbidding stranger, I would be somewhat alarmed by the urging to "join our side." It sounds somewhat cult-like, or, at the very least, rather militant.

Jane responds to Ironwood's exhortation by saying, "'You keep on talking of *We* and *Us*. Are you some kind of company?' 'Yes. You may call it a company.'"[17] While "company" sounds more congenial than "inner ring," the same use of an exclusive "we" appears, which Lewis marks as a signifier of inner rings in his essay.[18] Lewis writes that when an inner ring "is very secure and comparatively stable in membership, it calls itself 'we.'"[19] Lewis also describes a sense of shared, hidden knowledge among those who belong, the sense that "we four or five all huddled beside this stove—are the people who *know*."[20] Ironwood's response suggests that those at St. Anne's are privy to world-changing secretive information, and that unless Jane joins their "side" she cannot be guaranteed protection or be helped by the insights their company possesses.

Jane is put on edge by Grace Ironwood's words, and returns home for a time, but meets with two more of the group from St. Anne's: Camilla and Arthur Denniston. They invite her to join them on a drive so they can talk together, saying, "'We want to be private.' The 'we' obviously meant 'we three' and established at once a pleasant, business-like unity between them."[21] Jane's pleasure at the Dennistons's use of "we" is perhaps meant to show the positive inclusion of Christian fellowship, but it also sounds much like the

---

15. Lewis, *That Hideous Strength*, 64–66.
16. Lewis, *That Hideous Strength*, 67. Emphasis original.
17. Lewis, *That Hideous Strength*, 68.
18. David Downing notes that "company" is "a term for mystical community that Lewis borrowed from Williams's Arthurian books." Downing, *Planets in Peril*, 136. The influence of Charles Williams's writings on *THS* has long been noted. For more on this topic, see Dickieson, "Mixed Metaphors," 81–114, esp. 100–106.
19. Lewis, "Inner Ring," 145.
20. Lewis, "Inner Ring," 147.
21. Lewis, *That Hideous Strength*, 113.

way Mark is thrilled by being part of the "we" of the Progressive Element at Bracton College, and then within the NICE.[22] And as Camilla urges Jane to dedicate her prophetic abilities to the company at St. Anne's, she says, "Oh, Mrs. Studdock, you *must* come in. You must, you must . . . Don't spoil everything. Do join us."[23] The repeated use of the imperative *must*, and the phrasing 'come in' makes Jane feel distinct unease, as it does Williams, who comments, "Now 'you must come in' is dangerously like the sort of thing that the other side is also saying to Mark, and I'm not sure how well Lewis handles this."[24] One of the ways Lewis handles this is by including Arthur's cautions as a balancing voice.

Arthur interrupts Camilla's insistent urgings, emphasizing the importance of free will: "The Pendragon—the Head, I mean, wouldn't like us to do that. Mrs. Studdock must come in freely."[25] Arthur's emphasis on Jane's freedom of choice allays some of the danger of these representatives of St. Anne's coming across as members of a closed, controlling inner ring. But immediately following Arthur's words, Camilla presses on, telling Jane, "But don't you see . . . that you can't be neutral? If you don't give yourself to us, the enemy will use you."[26] Camilla is expressing a larger truth: the inescapable reality of goodness and evil, and the truth that Jane must choose a side with either St. Anne's or Belbury. Williams objects to Lewis's division of the protagonists and antagonists into two "conflicting companies of interest."[27] However, Lewis is portraying a climactic struggle between the forces of darkness and light on Thulcandra (Earth), and as battle lines are drawn, it is inevitable, and necessary, that the two sides stand in opposition to one another. Ultimately, every individual, including Jane and Mark, must choose whether they will give their lives to the service of God or the devil. The novel effectively conveys the dire import of the two protagonists' daily choices regarding whom they will trust, spend time with, and serve. Had Lewis simply avoided some of the more controlling language such as "must come in" and "give yourself to us" on the part of the characters at St. Anne's, he could have avoided echoes of a controlling inner ring, while still emphasizing the importance of Jane's choices.

22. Lewis, *That Hideous Strength*, 17, 128.
23. Lewis, *That Hideous Strength*, 115.
24. Williams, "Reassessment," 98.
25. Lewis, *That Hideous Strength*, 115.
26. Lewis, *That Hideous Strength*, 115.

27. Williams, "Reassessment," 97. See also Bullard, "Narrative Dualism," 11–24, for a discussion of Lewis's deliberate creation of opposing but parallel experiences for Jane and Mark Studdock, and also St. Anne's and Belbury, in *THS*.

Three other key aspects of Lewis's essay on "The Inner Ring" also diminish the strength of Williams's criticism. First, Lewis makes an interesting distinction, stating, "I am not going to say that the existence of Inner Rings is an evil. It is certainly unavoidable. There must be confidential discussions, and it is not only not a bad thing, it is (in itself) a good thing that personal friendship should grow up between those who work together."[28] So to Williams's accusation that St. Anne's seems like an inner ring, Lewis might willingly acknowledge that it is indeed something of the sort, but he might also argue it is not an inner ring characterized by evil intent, as is the circle within the NICE. In "The Inner Ring," Lewis also comments, "In any wholesome group of people which holds together for a good purpose, the exclusions are in a sense accidental."[29] The more the reader comes to know the company at St. Anne's, the more clear it becomes that they are certainly a wholesome group, held together for a good purpose. Their exclusions are not malicious or elitist, but simply motivated by goals of safety and protection against the insidious schemes of the NICE.

Second, it seems that it is often the clarity of the *telos* that holds a community together that reveals its relative goodness. As Alan Jacobs notes, "The draw of the Inner Ring has such profound corrupting power because it never announces itself as evil—indeed, it never announces itself at all."[30] At Belbury, Mark has difficulty determining the purpose of the NICE even after he has been somewhat officially admitted. In contrast, at St. Anne's Jane is brought into the confidence of the company as soon as she commits herself to join, after her torture by Fairy Hardcastle. The lack of clarity of purpose of an Inner Ring necessitates muddled thinking, lest the members recognize the evil they are perpetrating and seek to escape. As Jacobs argues, "There *are* healthier kinds of group affiliation, and one of the primary ways we can tell the difference between an unhealthy Inner Ring and a healthy community is by their attitudes toward *thinking*."[31] Clarity and thought are two things that the NICE is careful to avoid even with its own members, while St. Anne's encourages critical thought, as in the acceptance of MacPhee the skeptic, and is united around a purpose that is communicated clearly to those within the group.

Third, St. Anne's is not presented as a temptation to Jane in the way the NICE is to Mark. The greatest danger Lewis sees in regards to inner rings is the insatiable desire to be accepted, or, as he calls it, "the lust for the esoteric,

---

28. Lewis, "Inner Ring," 148.
29. Lewis, "Inner Ring," 156.
30. Jacobs, *How To Think*, 56.
31. Jacobs, *How to Think*, 59.

the longing to be inside."³² As Lewis explains, "A thing may be morally neutral and yet the desire for that thing may be dangerous."³³ Such is the case with inner rings. Mark Studdock is consumed by the dangerous desire to be accepted as an insider, and he eventually takes part in criminal activities in order to gain acceptance at the NICE.³⁴ He fabricates propaganda to print on their behalf, perfectly illustrating Lewis's observation, "Of all passions the passion for the Inner Ring is most skillful in making a man who is not yet a very bad man do very bad things."³⁵ The lies Mark writes lead to riots and destruction, and advance the power of the NICE across England.³⁶ He commits evil acts not because of an exceptionally bad character, but because of his distorting desire to truly belong.

In contrast to her husband, Jane highly values her independence. As the company at St. Anne's reaches out to her, Jane resolves that she will "not be drawn in. One had to live one's own life. To avoid entanglements and interferences had long been one of her first principles."³⁷ Jane is not at risk of succumbing to "the longing to be inside" which Lewis defines as the chief danger of inner rings; instead, she is at risk because she resists the aid and insight that St. Anne's can offer.³⁸ After Jane's conversations with Ironwood and the Dennistons, her disturbing dreams continue, and she avoids returning to the one place that can offer real help and solace. "She wanted comfort but she wanted it, if possible, without going out to St. Anne's, without meeting this Fisher-King man and getting drawn into his orbit."³⁹ Jane thinks of the influence of the Fisher-King in terms of a force that could pull her into an "orbit," an image reminiscent of a controlling inner ring. Lewis is not unaware of the compelling aura of St. Anne's; instead, he effectively conveys the thoughts and emotions a non-Christian may feel when encountering a circle of committed Christians. There is an undeniable foreignness in Christian belief and behavior when viewed from an agnostic standpoint, and Lewis effectively allows the reader to feel some of Jane's caution as she, looking on from without, wonders if she is facing an inescapable inner ring.

---

32. Lewis, "Inner Ring," 151.

33. Lewis, "Inner Ring," 149.

34. Lewis, *That Hideous Strength*, 130.

35. Lewis, "Inner Ring," 154.

36. Lewis, *That Hideous Strength*, 131–35; Teresa Hooper also analyzes this scene in which Mark knowingly agrees to take part in criminal activities out of the desire to be accepted in the NICE's inner ring. See Hooper, "Great Dance," 114.

37. Lewis, *That Hideous Strength*, 72.

38. Lewis, "Inner Ring," 151.

39. Lewis, *That Hideous Strength*, 124.

Unlike the NICE, which is an inner ring willfully assembled for its own ends by those on the inside, Ransom makes it clear to the community at St. Anne's that he has no power to choose members or expel them. At a point of decision Ransom tells his friends, "You and I have not started or devised this: it has descended on us—sucked us into itself, if you like. It is, no doubt, an organisation: but we are not the organisers. And that is why I have no authority to give any one of you permission to leave my household."[40] Membership and purpose in St. Anne's are defined by their focus outside the group's existence on their mutual commitment to serving the aims of Maleldil (God). St. Anne's is not a true Inner Ring because membership is not the main attraction for its members; those who become part of the company do so because of the purpose for which the company exists.

## ST. ANNE'S AND FRIENDSHIP

Jane, unlike her husband Mark, is free from the relentless drive to gain acceptance in social circles, but that leaves her with a different dilemma. Jane often feels lonely and vulnerable; her independence has an isolating effect. She is in need of a circle of friends. At the end of "The Inner Ring," Lewis describes genuine friendship as the antithesis of toxic and elitist inner rings. He describes how the pursuit of excellence within a profession can lead to a real bond of friendship:

> And if in your spare time you consort simply with the people you like, you will again find that you have come unawares to a real inside: that you are indeed snug and safe at the centre of something which, seen from without, would look exactly like an Inner Ring. But the difference is that the secrecy is accidental, and its exclusiveness a by-product . . . for it is only four or five people who like one another meeting to do things that they like. This is friendship. Aristotle placed it among the virtues. It causes perhaps half of all the happiness in the world, and no Inner Ring can ever have it.[41]

Before Jane chooses to join the company at St. Anne's, she looks on as an outsider, and, just as Lewis states above, the group does seem exclusive and secretive, like an inner ring. Therefore, the initial wariness that she, and perhaps the reader, feels, can be seen as a deliberate narrative technique on Lewis's part. As the story progresses, it is logical that an antidote to the concern over the nature of St. Anne's would be the portrayal of genuine

---

40. Lewis, *That Hideous Strength*, 198.
41. Lewis, "Inner Ring," 157.

friendship between Jane and the members of the company. However, one weakness of the novel is that the narrative advances rapidly, and thus the opportunity for a gradual unfolding of genuine, caring friendship between Jane and the members of St. Anne's is sidelined.

By highlighting the urgency of the larger battle against the NICE, Lewis does not allow much time for Jane to cultivate deep-seated trust and free fellowship with those at St. Anne's. The Dimbles do show care for Jane when she is disturbed by her dreams, but their main response is to recommend that she visit Grace Ironwood. Miss Ironwood tells Jane that Dr. Dimble's primary reason for sending her to St. Anne's was because of the importance of her visions. This bothers Jane, who asks, "Do you mean he sent me here not to be cured but to give information?"[42] Their conversation carries on as Miss Ironwood replies, "'Exactly.' 'I wish I had known that a little earlier,' said Jane coldly, and now definitely getting up to go. 'I'm afraid it has been a misunderstanding. I had imagined Dr. Dimble was trying to help me.' 'He was. But he was also trying to do something more important at the same time.'"[43] In the conversation that follows, Miss Ironwood urges Jane to "join our side."[44] Jane leaves, feeling, justifiably, somewhat used and manipulated. A similar effect results from her encounter with the Dennistons. Arthur and Camilla invite her to join them on a car ride through the misty countryside; this offer of friendship warms Jane, but their conversation centers around the urgency of Jane joining St. Anne's.[45] Jane feels alternately cautious, compelled, and attracted to the company through what the Dennistons share, but the mounting pressure of her foreboding dreams and the company's need to use those dreams to fight the NICE causes any opportunity for a natural friendship to be set to the side.

Jane's confidence in St. Anne's and her dislike for the NICE advance in large strides through two significant encounters: the first with the Head, Ransom, now the golden-haired and ageless Pendragon, and the second with Fairy Hardcastle. These two meetings propel her to fully join the company at St. Anne's. When Jane meets the Pendragon himself, the course of her life alters: "Jane looked; and instantly her world was unmade."[46] Jane's response to Ransom is one of mingled astonishment, adoration, and attraction. But her encounter with Ransom is not the beginning of a close friendship; he is too far above her in experience, wisdom, and intimacy with the powers of

---

42. Lewis, *That Hideous Strength*, 67.
43. Lewis, *That Hideous Strength*, 67.
44. Lewis, *That Hideous Strength*, 67.
45. Lewis, *That Hideous Strength*, 112–18.
46. Lewis, *That Hideous Strength*, 142.

Deep Heaven.[47] Jane learns from him, admires him, and accepts his guidance, but theirs is not a friendship of equals. Jane's subsequent capture and torture at the hands of Fairy Hardcastle serves to confirm her abhorrence of the NICE and her desire to join the group at St. Anne's, both for protection and for consolation.[48] Jane's two encounters are dramatic, but do not provide her with the experience of friendship that can be such a valuable counterbalance to isolation or controlling inner rings.

Once she settles in at St. Anne's, Jane finally begins to share in genuine friendships. One of the foundations of friendship is trust, and the company displays their confidence in Jane by telling her of all their aims. At the Pendragon's request, MacPhee gives Jane a factual description of Ransom's past experiences and of the supernatural struggle in which the company at St. Anne's is currently caught up.[49] Camilla joins Jane after MacPhee finishes his account, and Camilla asks, "'He's been telling you?'. . . Moved by a kind of impulse which was rare to her experience, Jane seized her friend's hand as she answered, 'Yes!' Both were filled with some passion, but what passion they did not know."[50] They then go on a walk in the garden, side by side. This is one of the first times Lewis has mentioned Jane thinking of Camilla as a friend, and reaching out for physical contact. The nameless passion they feel seems to be linked to the Pendragon and all he represents, for as they walk, they discuss Perelandra, Paradise, and Ransom's eventual return to the planet he loves best. Significantly, when Camilla asks Jane if she believed the facts MacPhee related, Jane replies, "Of course."[51] Jane, softened by friendship and by honesty, has shifted from being an agnostic to willingly accepting the supernatural aspects of St. Anne's as part of the fabric of reality. While Lewis's comments on the subject of friendship at the end of "The Inner Ring" are fairly brief, fifteen years later he returns to the topic in *The Four Loves*, writing, "Lovers are normally face to face, absorbed in each other; friends, side by side, absorbed in some common interest."[52] This scene in *THS* showcases Camilla and Jane, literally walking side by side through the manor garden, and drawn close together due to their shared interest in the realities beyond the bounds of their own planet.

The more time Jane spends with her new friends at St. Anne's, the more Lewis's interest in the Christian mind becomes evident. At least seven

---

47. Lewis, *That Hideous Strength*, 142–50.
48. Lewis, *That Hideous Strength*, 153–59.
49. Lewis, *That Hideous Strength*, 189–94.
50. Lewis, *That Hideous Strength*, 194.
51. Lewis, *That Hideous Strength*, 194.
52. Lewis, *The Four Loves*, 61.

of the ten members of the company have academic backgrounds of some sort, and their training is often integral to their usefulness in serving the purposes of Maleldil. Ransom is a philologist by training, and author of a respected book on the subject.[53] His linguistic knowledge has been invaluable in enabling him to speak with the inhabitants of other planets and with the eldila, the angelic beings who serve Maleldil. Cecil Dimble is a fellow of Northumberland, Jane's former tutor, and a scholar of Arthurian legend.[54] Arthur Denniston is also a respected intellectual; Mark Studdock learns that Arthur had been his chief rival for his fellowship, and that many considered Arthur's papers to be better than Mark's.[55] Camilla also seems to be a scholar of some sort, as she is deeply versed in Arthurian legend.[56] These scholarly pursuits could, to most in the modern world, seem irrelevant and useless, but in Lewis's novel, the excellence in their fields of the scholars of St. Anne's enables them to serve God's will and block the NICE in essential ways. Ransom is able to determine that the body of Merlin lies beneath Bragdon Wood, thanks to the shared scholarship of his group: "Dimble and he and the Dennistons shared between them a knowledge of Arthurian Britain which orthodox scholarship will probably not reach for some centuries."[57] (Notably, Ransom describes both of the Dennistons, not just Arthur, as possessors of deep knowledge of Arthuriana.) Other learned members of the company include Merlin, mage of Arthur's court; Grace Ironwood, who introduces herself as a doctor; and Jane, who is in the midst of working on her doctoral thesis on Donne.[58] MacPhee may also be counted as a learned member of the group. His own background and training is never quite specified, but he has a sharp, scientific, and skeptical mind, and plays the role of evaluating and questioning each piece of information St. Anne's acquires.[59] The life of the mind is central to the majority of the members of St. Anne's, and their intellects intersect with their faith and with the actions that they take throughout the entire novel.

53. Lewis, *That Hideous Strength*, 189.
54. Lewis, *That Hideous Strength*, 29, 31–33.
55. Lewis, *That Hideous Strength*, 18–19.
56. See, for example, Lewis, *That Hideous Strength*, 195. Shogren notes that Camilla, "in her familiarity with the difficult Arthuriana of Charles Williams and her overall interest in the Arthuriad—shows that she has some kind of significant involvement with literature." Shogren, "Lewisian Genders," 399.
57. Lewis, *That Hideous Strength*, 200.
58. Lewis, *That Hideous Strength*, 14.
59. It has often been observed that MacPhee is reminiscent of Lewis's old tutor, Kirkpatrick. Downing, *Planets in Peril*, 136.

Lewis does not suggest that scholarly endeavor is the sole qualification for service to God, however. Another unique element that Lewis weaves into the backstories of virtually every member of the company at St. Anne's is their experience of profound trials and sorrows. They are not a band of academics isolated in an ivory tower. They gather at the manor, not to be sequestered from the world's suffering, but in large part because of what they have suffered. For example, the Dimbles must stand by as the NICE tears down their flourishing garden and unjustly drives them from their home.[60] Also, the Dimbles have never been able to have children, which is an enduring grief all its own.[61] Ivy Maggs has likewise been evicted by the NICE, and has a husband who has been imprisoned for theft, whose release she loyally awaits.[62] Grace Ironwood has some painful secret in her past, as evidenced by the moment she pales at the thought of revealing how she came to be a part of St. Anne's, and Ransom assures her that her story does not need to be told.[63] Ransom himself has experienced anguish throughout his interplanetary excursions, as readers of the previous two books of the trilogy know well, and he bears a perpetual wound on his heel, a source of excruciating pain throughout *THS*.[64] Jane is deeply unhappy in her marriage to Mark, and is plagued by the horrific dreams that are in fact visions of real events.[65] The backstories of the last few members of the company—MacPhee, Merlin, and the Dennistons—are more obscure, but regardless of their pasts, they are caught up in the tumultuous and costly struggle against the NICE through the action of the novel. Those who live at St. Anne's have experienced trials, sorrows, and struggles, and yet they persevere in Christian devotion.

By all they have learned, and in all they have suffered, the company at St. Anne's is drawn together in deep and abiding friendship. The novel's most powerful display of the friendship shared among the members at St. Anne's takes place in the unforgettable chapter, "The Descent of the Gods." The majority of the company is gathered in the kitchen in St. Anne's, "drawn a little closer than usual about the fire and with the shutters closed."[66] Upstairs in the Blue Room, Merlin and Ransom await the coming of the five Oyéresu, the angelic spirits of Mercury, Venus, Mars, Saturn, and Jupiter.

60. Lewis, *That Hideous Strength*, 29, 74–75.
61. Lewis, *That Hideous Strength*, 29.
62. Lewis, *That Hideous Strength*, 75, 82, 302.
63. Lewis, *That Hideous Strength*, 198.
64. Lewis, *That Hideous Strength*, 114, 141.
65. Lewis, *That Hideous Strength*, 14–16, for just one example.
66. Lewis, *That Hideous Strength*, 320.

The five powers descend through Deep Heaven into Thulcandra, a heavenly invasion force coming to convey their powers to Merlin, who will then dismantle the forces of the NICE. David Downing succinctly describes the effect the Oyéresu have on the eight individuals gathered in the homely kitchen: "[A]ll of the planetary intelligences meet with Ransom and Merlin, their very proximity making the rest of the company at St. Anne's successively mercurial, amorous, martial, saturnine, and jovial."[67] As the spirit of each angelic being rests upon St. Anne's on the Hill, the company is united in speech, serenity, charity, courage, solemnity, joy, laughter, and merrymaking, successively.

In this wondrous chapter, the company at St. Anne's experiences more genuine fellowship in one night than many friends might in a lifetime. For example, as the spirit of Mars, or Malacandra, descends, "Their love for one another became intense. Each, looking on all the rest, thought, 'I'm lucky to be here. I could die with these.'"[68] As the greatest spirit, Jupiter, Glund-Oyarsa, descends, "In the kitchen his coming was felt . . . the kettle was put on, the hot toddy was brewed. Arthur—the only musician among them—was bidden to get out his fiddle. The chairs were pushed back, the floor cleared. They danced . . . And no one while it lasted thought himself or his fellows ridiculous. It seemed to each that the room was filled with kings and queens."[69] Here in the presence of the spirits of Deep Heaven, Charity reigns, and the group is united without hint of jealousy, insecurity, pride, or envy. Here no inner ring ethos could abide. In this chapter, Lewis successfully depicts the company as a circle of friends I suspect virtually every reader would readily join. Moreover, the unhindered joy and friendship depicted serve as a small foretaste of the eternal fellowship of all the saints in God's kingdom.

Significantly, Lewis does not describe any specific ending to the scene when the company is gathered in the kitchen. There is no cessation of the dancing, no awkward return of self-consciousness, no fading of the joy brought by the spirits who serve Maleldil. Instead, the narrative shifts from the dancing company in the kitchen to the Pendragon and Merlin upstairs, and states that the power of these five planetary spirits enters into Merlin, so that he is ready the next day to invade Belbury and bring down all of the NICE's machinations upon their own heads. By leaving off the narration while the company is still joyfully dancing in the kitchen, Lewis implies that the unity of the friendships at St. Anne's carries on unceasingly while

---

67. Downing, *Planets in Peril*, 78.
68. Lewis, *That Hideous Strength*, 324.
69. Lewis, *That Hideous Strength*, 326.

the fragmented and backstabbing members of the NICE slide into savagery and murder. For the next eleven scenes, all of the action focuses upon Mark as he resists the NICE's efforts to entrap him in their devilish inner rings.[70] Finally, the NICE collapses in sensational fashion, and Mark escapes, joining Jane at St. Anne's.[71]

## CONCLUSION

By analyzing *THS* in light of "The Inner Ring," it becomes clear that the NICE is an adept fictional portrayal of the negative power of inner rings, while St. Anne's provides a positive opposing model of faithful Christian fellowship. Admittedly, there are moments when members of the company at St. Anne's use language that sounds overly exclusive, or when genuine friendships are not solidly established due to concerns over time pressure caused by the growing power of the NICE. Yet, once Jane enters into the company at St. Anne's, she comes to know the open fellowship of a group equipped to serve Maleldil both through their intellectual pursuits and through the things they have suffered. In other words, it is the embodiment of the Christian mind that unites the diverse individuals in the company at St. Anne's. This humble, disparate band of scholars, gardeners, and housewives becomes, in the presence of heavenly powers, a host of "kings and queens."[72]

## BIBLIOGRAPHY

Bullard, Sadie H. "Narrative Dualism in C. S. Lewis's *That Hideous Strength*." *Mythlore* 29.3 (2011) 11–24.

Dickieson, Brenton D. G. "Mixed Metaphors and Hyperlinked Worlds: A Study of Intertextuality in C. S. Lewis's Ransom Cycle." In *The Inklings and King Arthur: J. R. R. Tolkien, Charles Williams, C. S. Lewis, and Owen Barfield on the Matter of Britain*, edited by Sorina Higgins, 81–114. Berkeley: Apocryphile, 2017.

Downing, David C. *Planets in Peril: A Critical Study of C. S. Lewis's Ransom Trilogy*. Amherst: University of Massachusetts Press, 1992.

Fairfield, Leslie P. "Fragmentation and Hope: The Healing of the Modern Schisms in *That Hideous Strength*." In *The Pilgrim's Guide: C. S. Lewis and the Art of Witness*, edited by David Mills, 145–60. Grand Rapids: Eerdmans, 1998.

Gibson, Evan K. *C. S. Lewis, Spinner of Tales: A Guide to His Fiction*. Grand Rapids: Eerdmans, 1980.

Glover, Donald E. *C. S. Lewis: The Art of Enchantment*. Athens: Ohio University Press, 1981.

---

70. Lewis, *That Hideous Strength*, 327–60.
71. Lewis, *That Hideous Strength*, 380–82.
72. Lewis, *That Hideous Strength*, 326.

Hilders, Monika. "The Foolish Weakness in C. S. Lewis's Cosmic Trilogy: A Feminine Heroic." *SEVEN: An Anglo-American Literary Review* 19 (2002) 77–90.

Hooper, Teresa. "Playing by the Rules: Kipling's 'Great Game' vs. 'The Great Dance' in C. S. Lewis's Space Trilogy." *Mythlore* 25.1 (2006) 105–26.

Hooper, Walter. "Introduction." In *The Weight of Glory and Other Addresses*, 1–21. New York: HarperCollins, 1949.

———. "That Hideous Strength: A Modern Fairy-Tale for Grown-Ups (1945)." In *C. S. Lewis: A Companion & Guide*, 231–42. San Francisco: HarperCollins, 1996.

Howard, Thomas. *C. S. Lewis, Man of Letters: A Reading of His Fiction*. San Francisco: Ignatius, 1987.

Jacobs, Alan. *How to Think: A Survival Guide for a World at Odds*. New York: Currency, 2017.

Lewis, C. S. *The Collected Letters of C. S. Lewis*. Edited by Walter Hooper. 2 vols. New York: HarperCollins, 2004.

———. *The Four Loves*. New York: Harcourt Brace, 1960.

———. "The Inner Ring." In *The Weight of Glory and Other Addresses*, 141–57. New York: HarperCollins, 1949.

———. *That Hideous Strength*. New York: Scribner, 1996.

Meilaender, Gilbert. *The Taste for the Other: The Social and Ethical Thought of C. S. Lewis*. 2nd ed. Grand Rapids: Eerdmans, 1998.

Newman, Barbara. "Charles Williams and the Companions of the Co-inherence." *Spiritus: A Journal of Christian Spirituality* 9.1 (2009) 1–26.

Purtill, Richard L. "*That Hideous Strength*: A Double Story." In *The Longing for a Form: Essays on the Fiction of C. S. Lewis*, edited by Peter J. Schakel, 91–102. Kent: Kent State University Press, 1977.

Schwartz, Sanford. *C. S. Lewis on the Final Frontier: Science and the Supernatural in the Space Trilogy*. New York: Oxford University Press, 2009.

Shippey, T. A. "The Ransom Trilogy." In *The Cambridge Companion to C. S. Lewis*, edited by Robert MacSwain and Michael Ward, 237–50. Cambridge: Cambridge University Press, 2010.

Shogren, Benjamin. "Those Kings of Lewis's Logres: Arthurian Figures as Lewisian Genders in *That Hideous Strength*." In *The Inklings and King Arthur: J. R. R. Tolkien, Charles Williams, C. S. Lewis, and Owen Barfield on the Matter of Britain*, edited by Sorina Higgins, 387–412. Berkeley: Apocryphile, 2017.

Traxler, Janina P. "Pendragon, Merlin, and Logos: The Undoing of Babel in *That Hideous Strength*." *Arthurian Literature* 20 (2003) 191–206.

Van Leeuwen, Mary Stewart. *A Sword between the Sexes? C. S. Lewis and the Gender Debates*. Grand Rapids: Brazos, 2010.

Williams, Rowan. "That Hideous Strength: A Reassessment." In *C. S. Lewis and His Circle: Essays and Memoirs from the Oxford C. S. Lewis Society*, edited by Roger White et al., 91–109. Oxford: Oxford University Press, 2015.

# 10

## Ethics among Men without Chests

*Andrew J. Spencer*

LEWIS IS KNOWN FOR his writing in several different genres. He is a poet, writer of science fiction, reteller of Greek myth, children's author, apologist, literary critic, and polemicist. Many of these facets of Lewis's work are highlighted in the essays of this volume. One aspect of his work that is less often considered is his ethics, which are woven throughout his work in all genres. A major theme in much of what Lewis wrote was the depiction of the Christian mind and a presentation of how it would look to apply the Christian mind to life in the modern world. This application is the heart of Christian ethics.

Lewis used stories to illustrate and demonstrate the ideas he outlined more explicitly in his essays. In fact, none of Lewis's works of fiction were written merely to entertain; each one carries the message of Christianity within it. Sometimes that message leans more toward apologetics, as with *The Lion, the Witch and the Wardrobe*. At other times the main message behind Lewis's fiction is ethical, as in *That Hideous Strength*. Frequently, in our own lives and in the work of Lewis, there is little difference between convincing people of the truthfulness of Christian ethics and convincing them of the reality of the Christian God. Very often, as one reads Lewis's fiction, the connections between his essays and nonfiction books seem to leap off the page. He imaginatively portrayed the arguments from his essays in his stories, which makes them all the more powerful.

This chapter explores Lewis's ideas about ethics in a world of men without chests. It is clear that Lewis had a vision of where the world was headed, particularly with respect to the prevalence of scientism in the ethics of the modern world. Lewis moves beyond mere cultural criticism, however, when he shows part of the reason society has moved to accept scientism—as in *The Abolition of Man*—as well as how it will impact the human world and how it can be effectively resisted—as in *That Hideous Strength*. In those two works particularly, Lewis contrasts the ethics of the Christian mind with ethics shaped by a misplaced faith in the ability of science to show how one should live in this world.

## SCIENTISM

A common myth, which Lewis dealt with and which continues today, is that science and Christianity are fundamentally at odds. Sometimes skirmishes are waged under these banners on the front of the interpretation of particular passages, such as the age of earth and the possibility of special creation. However, increasingly often, there is conflict in the field of ethics between Christianity and particular interpretations of scientific data. The nature of the apparent battle between religion and science has not changed significantly since Lewis's day, though the topics of division are different. The conflict, however, is not actually between science and Christianity, but between scientism and Christianity.

According to philosopher J. P. Moreland, scientism is "the view that the hard sciences provide the only or at least a vastly superior knowledge of reality compared to other disciplines."[1] This is not a scientific claim, but a philosophical claim that empirical study is the ultimate arbiter of truth. In reality, one can be both a Christian and an ardent supporter of legitimate scientific endeavors; indeed, Christians *should* be vocal advocates for scientific truth. Conflict arises when people attempt to reduce the proper field of human knowledge to those things that can be empirically verified. This reduction leads to a shift in ethics "from positive *duty and virtue* to do-no-harm *minimalism*."[2] The nature of scientism is to demand the primacy and authority over all areas of life, which leads to inevitable conflict with competing systems like Christianity.

Lewis recognized the ethical reductionism of scientism and rejected its totalitarian tendencies by advocating for the Christian mind. He affirmed the good of science while resisting the claims of scientism. He notes,

---

1. Moreland, *Scientism and Secularism*, 205.
2. Moreland, *Scientism and Secularism*, 35. Emphasis original.

> When I accept [Christian] Theology I may find difficulties, at this point or that in harmonizing it with some particular truths which are imbedded in the mythical cosmology derived from science. But I can get in, or allow for, science as a whole.... If, on the other hand, I swallow the scientific cosmology as a whole, then not only can I not fit in Christianity, but I cannot even fit in science.[3]

The "scientific cosmology" Lewis calls out is a form of scientism.

Popularizers of scientism are often bold in their proposals for a world dependent solely on science for truth, seeming not to recognize their categorical errors. For example, astrophysicist Neil DeGrasse Tyson has proposed a country called Rationalia where all decisions are made based on evidence. In his admittedly whimsical land, he fails to acknowledge the inability of empirical evidence to indicate what goals the nation should have.[4] Recently deceased scientific popularizer Stephen Hawking affirmed his belief that everything can be explained by metrics in an interview with Ira Flatow on the popular radio show, *Science Friday*:

> I believe there are no questions that science can't answer about the physical universe. Although we don't yet have a full understanding of the laws of nature, I think we will eventually find a complete unified theory. Some people would claim that things like love, joy, and beauty belong to a different category from science and can't be described in scientific terms. But I think they can all be explained by the theory of evolution.[5]

For Tyson and Hawking, the truth of the whole can be discovered by dissecting reality until each constituent part is understood in the minutest detail.

Both Tyson and Hawking portray their vision of an empiricist world as perfectly democratic. However, both fail to recognize that such an approach concentrates power among the few whose experiments get funded and whose research papers are approved as interesting and suitable by those already in power. Scientism functions as a religion—one without a grounding objective morality—that uses the laboratory as the temple and the latest peer-reviewed journal as the holy writ. As Michael Aeschilman observes, "It is this religion and this historical concentration of amoral knowledge and power of the few over the many and over nature itself that Lewis called 'that hideous strength.'"[6]

3. Lewis, "Is Theology Poetry?," 20–21.
4. Tyson, "Reflections on Rationalia."
5. Flatow, "Stephen Hawking Looks Back," 0:40–1:13.
6. Aeschliman, *Restitution of Man*, 27.

Proponents of scientism seem unaware of the limitations of their own epistemology, which frees them to criticize religious adherents without understanding them first. For example, philosopher and critic of religion Stephen Asma feels secure in arguing, "The fideism or faithism tradition, from Kierkegaard to C. S. Lewis, has defended religion on the grounds that its truths are above and beyond the regular faculties of knowledge."[7] This confident assertion comes in the context of a volume whose thesis is to ostensibly defend religion for its empirically verifiable benefits for society. For Asma, who was previously a militant critic of all religion, it is now permissible for people to have some religious beliefs, since studies have shown that faith can be useful to curb some antisocial behaviors, to comfort those in sorrow, and to give hope in an otherwise hopeless world.

Asma's argument depends on the assumption that the epistemology of contemporary scientism is the essence of rationality, with all belief in non-material ideas functioning as an irrational addition to true knowledge. In presenting his understanding of the irrationality of religious belief, Asma gives the perspective of the "more extreme atheist": "Beliefs, we are told, must align themselves to evidence and not to mere yearning. Without rational standards, like those entrenched in science, we will all slouch toward chaos and end up in pre-Enlightenment darkness."[8] Asma indicates his general agreement with these sentiments, but supports the continuance of irrational belief among the unenlightened devotees of religion because it seems to have an analgesic function, providing meaning for those who cannot get it in the supposedly pure rationalism of scientism.

The argument in *Why We Need Religion* reflects a shift in tone from the militant scientism of Neil Degrasse Tyson, Richard Dawkins, and other popular proponents of scientism, but it is the same perspective, nonetheless. The continued existence of such confident but unfounded assumptions is what helps keep C. S. Lewis relevant for contemporary ethics and apologetics. Within the brief quotations already provided, we can detect signs of the fallacy of chronological snobbery and the self-referentially incoherent view that a dependence on empirical evidence can, apart from non-material ideals, support an ultimately rational perspective.

While historical realities, like the religious tones of the Crusades, are often seen as defeaters of religious belief, the negative effects of scientism are generally given a pass by evangelists for agnosticism. Eugenics, the Holocaust, and the Soviet Gulag system are a few testaments to extreme abuses of scientism, but they are rarely considered by those anxious to avoid religious

---

7. Asma, *Why We Need Religion*, 3.
8. Asma, *Why We Need Religion*, 3.

belief. Those horrific events in human history were possible because they were rationally justified on the scientific grounds that blacks, Jews, homosexuals, or other selected outgroups were scientifically unfit to reproduce or even, in the most extreme cases, to live. The German program was enabled by the conflation of scientific theory with divine revelation.[9] The Gulags were founded on the militantly rational belief that national progress depends on absolute support for the endeavors of the Soviet program.[10] There is a significant difference between the role of Christianity in the Crusades and the role of scientism in various historical horrors: When Christianity is used to abuse, it is implemented contrary to its internally normative structure; when scientism is used for abuse, it is a result of the system, which demands empirically determined theories be used normatively instead of descriptively.

## LEWIS *CONTRA* SCIENTISM

Subverting scientism in its various forms was a major emphasis in all of Lewis's writing. He made his arguments against radical empiricism in rational terms through multiple essays and especially through his short volume *The Abolition of Man*. Arguably the most powerful attack Lewis levied against scientism, however, is in his imaginative work, particularly in *That Hideous Strength*. In both these works Lewis shows the capability and probable trajectory of scientism. Notably, these imaginative works precede the awareness of the horrors of the Nazi extermination camp and Soviet Gulags. They remain the more powerful argument because the materialist proponent of scientism can always retreat to the complexity of social influences as confusing the *real* cause of such horror. Readers of *That Hideous Strength*, however, cannot escape the imaginative power of the novel for which the prose of *The Abolition of Man* provides complementary commentary.

In the face of religious diversity, scientism falls back on its universal accessibility to all humans. Though the Buddhist and Christian disagree about fundamentals of theology, all people have the innate ability to access empirically validated knowledge. Or, at least, that is how the case is often presented.

---

9. It is impossible to understand the political and religious realities in Germany during the Nazi reign without seeing the power of scientism to justify inflicting harm on select populations. The German Christian support of the supposed scientific basis for the ghettoization of the Jews, and their later extermination, is a principal basis for Karl Barth's rejection of natural revelation as authoritative for ethics. See, Barth, "No!," 65–128.

10. Solzhenitsyn, *Gulag Archipelago, 1918–1956*, 142–49.

The genius of Lewis, and the Christian mind that he promotes, is recognizing that while scientism claims to reside in a common sense of reality, it depends almost wholly for its power on the rejection of the common sense.[11] Though scientism claims to democratize ethics by putting normative claims into universally accessible terms, it effectively concentrates power into the hands of those who control the laboratories, the journals, and, perhaps, even the news.

In a Chestertonian reversal, *That Hideous Strength* demonstrates that the supposed liberation of the common man through the efforts of the NICE leads to tyranny. This is seen most clearly when Mark and Cosser go to the picturesque village of Cure Hardy to find the "facts" they will present to support the destruction of the village and its replacement with a model one. Cosser insists on Mark writing the report on Cure Hardy in advance of the visit, beginning with the assumption of the nature of the hamlet:

> "I think you'll find it consists almost entirely of the two most undesirable elements—small *rentiers* and agricultural labourers."
>
> "The small *rentier* is a bad element, I agree," said Mark. "I suppose the agricultural labourer is more controversial."
>
> "The Institute doesn't approve of him. He's a very recalcitrant element in a planned community, and he's always backward. We're not going in for English agriculture. So you see, all we have to do is verify a few facts. Otherwise the report writes itself."[12]

When they actually make the journey, the description of the visit indicates the logical conclusion of the worldview of scientism and Mark's status as partially, but not fully converted:

> They walked about that village for two hours and saw with their own eyes all the abuses and anachronisms they came to destroy. They saw the recalcitrant and backward labourer and heard his views on the weather. They met the wastefully supported pauper in the person of an old man shuffling across the courtyard of the almshouse to fill a kettle, and the elderly *rentier* (to make matters worse, she had a fat old dog with her) in earnest conversation with the postman. It made Mark feel as he were on a holiday, for it was only holidays that he had ever wandered about an English village. For that reason he felt pleasure in it. It did not quite escape him that the face of the backward labourer was rather more interesting than Cosser's and his voice a great

11. Aeshliman, *Restitution of Man*, 2–15.
12. Lewis, *That Hideous Strength*, 85.

deal more pleasing to the ear. The resemblance between the elderly *rentier* and Aunt Gilly (When had he last thought of *her*? Good Lord, that took one back.) did make him understand how it was possible to like that kind of person. All this did not in the least influence his sociological convictions. Even if he had been free from Belbury and wholly unambitious, it could not have done so, for his education had had the curious effect of making things that he read and wrote more real to him than things he saw. Statistics about agricultural labourers were the substance; any real ditcher, ploughman, or farmer's boy, was the shadow.[13]

The NICE was intent on putting "science" to work for the benefit of humanity, but not for the sake of humans. In fact, as the narrator informs us, Mark's education had the effect of pushing him away from seeing the good in humans for the sake of a universalized, faceless, collective idea.

One of the most powerful means of indoctrinating a population is through education. Lewis makes this evident through his description of Mark Studdock,[14] but he states it clearly in the first chapter of *The Abolition of Man*. Of a younger Mark it might be said that he is "a boy who thinks he is 'doing' his 'English prep' and has no notion that ethics, theology, and politics are all at stake. It is not a theory they put into his mind, but an assumption, which ten years hence, its origin forgotten and its presence unconscious, will condition him to take one side in a controversy which he has never recognized as a controversy at all."[15] In this instance, the Cure Hardy controversy was whether the village could be more usefully arranged. At a more basic level, however, the controversy was over the worthiness of the common people in that village.

Scientism is compelling to its advocates because it is supposed to free humans from the constraints of nature. Lewis undermines this theory, noting, "what we call Man's power over Nature turns out to be a power exercised by some men over other men with Nature as its instrument."[16] This is later narrowed down to a more precise picture of the reality of most great progressive programs: "Man's conquest of Nature, if the dreams of some scientific planners are realized, means the rule of a few hundreds of men over billions upon billions of men."[17] This was the reality of Nazism and Communism, as history now reveals. To a certain degree, it is the reality of

---

13. Lewis, *That Hideous Strength*, 87.
14. Lewis, *That Hideous Strength*, 185.
15. Lewis, *Abolition of Man*, 5.
16. Lewis, *Abolition of Man*, 55.
17. Lewis, *Abolition of Man*, 58. Cf. Lewis, *That Hideous Strength*, 177–78.

the Silicon Valley idea of society. It is also, to a great degree, the heart of the so-called democratic socialism that is growing in popularity in the United States. "Progress" often entails handing control of a larger portion of life to experts and technocrats who are supposed to have the skill to run our lives better. Often, stated goals are humane—feeding the hungry, educating more children, etc.—but the preference for which goals are most important is often assumed rather than discussed, which leads to disagreement.

As Lewis argues, "Progress means movement in a desired direction, and we do not all desire the same things for our species."[18] It is exactly this disagreement that the NICE must root out. The quickest way to do that is through the power of the state by ensuring the right sorts of people are placed into power. This oligarchy, Lewis argues, "must more and more base its claim to plan us on its claim to knowledge. If we are to be mothered, mother must know best. This means they must increasingly rely on the advice of scientists, till in the end the politicians proper become merely the scientists' puppets."[19] He goes on, "I dread government in the name of science. That is how tyrannies come in. In every age the men who want us under their thumb, if they have any sense, will put forward the particular pretension which the hopes and fears of that age render most potent."[20] These pretensions can be sown, watered, and fertilized through the crafting of elementary school curricula for the next generation and propaganda for the present generation.

## THE POWER OF PROPAGANDA

Mark Studdock served as the engine for the NICE in inventing propaganda (along with Fairy Hardcastle, the chief of police), to shape public opinion for the centralization of control. To gain support for an independent police force, the NICE coordinated riots and then invented the news that would tell the stories of the riots. Mark, because he was desperately seeking to maintain his place in the Inner Ring, [21] knowingly violated his conscience to fabricate the news in advance of the events.[22] When he fled into the teeth of the riots, Mark saw the fruit of his labor when the conversation in the pub indicates a general trust in the contents of the newspaper rather than the testimonies of the continuous stream of refugees from the city. "Fragments

---

18. Lewis, "Is Progress Possible?," 346.
19. Lewis, "Is Progress Possible?," 350.
20. Lewis, "Is Progress Possible?," 351.
21. See Lindsey Panxhi's essay on this topic in chapter 9 of this volume.
22. Lewis, *That Hideous Strength*, 130–35.

of articles which Mark himself had written drifted to and fro. Apparently he and his kind had done their work well; Miss Hardcastle had rated too high the resistance of the working classes to propaganda."[23] The populace was not equipped to resist carefully crafted propaganda.

Resisting in the face of overwhelming propaganda takes obstinate belief, a critical mind, and, very often, a great deal of personal pain. It is often the person least impacted by modernistic educations—and thus the most reliant on common sense—who is best at sniffing out foolishness. In *The Silver Chair*, Puddleglum reveals the sort of sacrifice necessary to overcome the mental control of the ruling class when he stomps on the Queen of the Underland's enchanted fire. The smell of burnt Marsh-wiggle cleared the air for the whole party, and "the pain itself made Puddleglum's head for a moment perfectly clear and he knew exactly what he really thought."[24] This clarity of thought enables him to declare that the half-forgotten reality the Queen debunked was, to him, a great deal better and wiser than the muted presentation of reality she offered. He declares,

> Suppose this black pit of a kingdom of yours *is* the only world. Well, it strikes me as a pretty poor one. And that's a funny thing, when you come to think of it. We're just babies making up a game, if you're right. But four babies playing a game can make a play-world which licks your real world hollow. That's why I'm going to stand by the play-world. I'm on Aslan's side even if there isn't any Aslan to lead it. I'm going to live as like a Narnian as I can even if there isn't any Narnia.[25]

Puddleglum is capable of pulling himself back from the brink of enchantment with the Queen's progressive vision, in part, because he was the least modern of the characters in the room at the time. It may be better to be uneducated than half-educated by modern standards. Thankfully, through his painful sacrifice, he draws the others back with him.

To commit the heroic acts of a Puddleglum, one must value heroic things. It is just this sort of virtue that living in a modern, scientifically dominated world demands. However, such virtue is rooted out by our culture. Neil Postman's classic, *Amusing Ourselves to Death*, shows how one ideology replaces another in the modern mind.[26] Perpetual entertainment has tilled the ground of minds for the seeds of scientism and helped push out more classical forms of thought. The mechanism may have been different in

23. Lewis, *That Hideous Strength*, 215.
24. Lewis, *Silver Chair*, 181.
25. Lewis, *Silver Chair*, 182.
26. Postman, *Amusing Ourselves to Death*.

Lewis's day, when newspaper articles were the means of formation instead of conspiracy theory websites, Russian-funded Twitter bots, and an ideologically stilted media industry. However, the result is the same: the creation of "men without chests"—men who do not value virtue and are thus without moral character.

Unlike many other dystopian novels, there is hope within Lewis's *That Hideous Strength*. Both Huxley and Orwell provide a warning, but little chance of a solution. In Narnia, Edmund is redeemed[27] and Eustace is un-dragoned.[28] Readers watch Jill transform in a less dramatic fashion.[29] None had an immediate and permanent cure, but the influence of Narnian air and exposure to a cause outside themselves, as well as contact with Aslan, help undo some of the damage wrought by the modern educational system. In *That Hideous Strength*, both Jane and Mark Studdock are converted from their modernity because of their severe trials.[30] Most clearly in the cases of the Studdocks and Eustace, the key step was to leave the supposed objectivity of Modernity, and therefore scientism, behind.

## OBJECTIVITY AND SCIENTISM

The pursuit of objectivity is central to becoming a full-fledged member of the NICE. Objectivity, on the most basic level, means emotional detachment from observation of the world. Thus, the scientist observes the phenomena before her, reporting the killing of a giraffe by a pride of lions according to its actual course of events rather than as a struggle between good and evil. Or, the journalist reports on a bill under consideration by the legislature without intentionally inserting his own desires into the article reporting on the nature of the legislation. This is the sort of objectivity Bill "the Blizzard" Hingest pursued, and which results in his murder by the NICE police force.[31] It might be more helpful to describe this sort of objectivity as fairmindedness or intellectual honesty. Hingest's interest is in science, properly understood, but what is being served at Belbury is scientism, which purports to obliterate value structures, but places naturalism as the ultimate value.

Scientism pretends to offer objectivity by classifying values as emotions.[32] Mark Studdock recognizes that rejecting values external to science

27. Lewis, *Lion, the Witch and the Wardrobe*, 138–39.
28. Lewis, *Voyage of the Dawn Treader*, 105–11.
29. Lewis, *Silver Chair*.
30. Lewis, *That Hideous Strength*, 380–82.
31. Lewis, *That Hideous Strength*, 70–72.
32. Lewis, *That Hideous Strength*, 295.

prevents making judgments of quality about the work at Belbury. As Lewis represents it, however, the objectivity of science for the NICE is simply the acceptance and application of the naturalistic fallacy. Professor Frost articulates this view:

> Existence is its own justification. The tendency to developmental change which we call Evolution is justified by the fact that it is a general characteristic of biological entities. The present establishment of contact between the highest biological entities and the Macrobes [i.e., supernatural beings] is justified by the fact that it is occurring, and it ought to be increased because an increase is taking place.[33]

No clearer representation of the naturalistic fallacy can be made. This occurs in contemporary discourse often. Studies show that an increasing number of couples cohabitate prior to marriage, which is used to argue that society should approve of couples sleeping together outside of marriage. The system itself supplies its values because what is is what ought to be.

The process to arrive at this version of objectivity is to dehumanize. Frost took Mark into an empty room, which was aesthetically disconcerting. The narrator noted, "A man of trained sensibilities would have seen at once that the room was ill-proportioned, not grotesquely so, but sufficiently to produce dislike."[34] Everything was off-balance, in a way intended to disorient the room's occupants. There were spots on the ceiling at disconcertingly irregular intervals. After some time in this ugly, disorienting room, Mark recognized that was the point of it:

> To sit in the room was the first step toward what Frost called objectivity—the process whereby all specifically human reactions were killed in a man so that he might become fit for the fastidious society of the Macrobes. Higher degrees in the asceticism of anti-Nature would doubtless follow: the eating of abominable food, the dabbling in dirt and blood, the ritual performances of calculated obscenities.[35]

The goal of the training in objectivity was to drive the idea of "normal" or "natural" from the mind of the subject, replacing it with an acceptance of whatever exists.

Though the intentions of the authors of the volume that Lewis critiques in *The Abolition of Man* are not so sinister as the NICE, their methods are

33. Lewis, *That Hideous Strength*, 295.
34. Lewis, *That Hideous Strength*, 297.
35. Lewis, *That Hideous Strength*, 299.

little different. As Lewis observes, "The schoolboy who reads this passage in *The Green Book* will believe two propositions: firstly that all sentences containing a predicate of value are statements about the emotional state of the speaker, and secondly, that all such statements are unimportant."[36] The only significance left to an object under observation can be cataloged in its measurable qualities.

Such an approach to reality, however, ignores its own dependence upon an external value structure. Even Frost in his assertion that "existence is its own justification" was making a value judgment, because it is not self-evident that existence should be preferable to nonexistence without appeal to something outside the system. Borrowing value from a metaphysical source is inescapable. As Lewis argues,

> Natural Law or Traditional Morality or the First Principles of Practical Reason or the First Platitudes, is not one among a series of possible systems of value. It is the sole source of all value judgements. If it is rejected, all value is rejected. If any value is retained, it is retained. The effort to refute it and raise a new system of value in its place is self-contradictory. There has never been, and never will be, a radically new judgement of value in the history of the world.[37]

Objectivity in the context of modernity, especially as it is represented in the fairy tale world of *That Hideous Strength*, is itself an unrealizable myth that, having abandoned the foundation upon which later discoveries were built, has devolved to something quite insidious in pursuit of progress.

## SCIENTISM AND PROGRESS

The myth of progress is at the heart of this pursuit of so-called objectivity. Lewis held a dim view of this myth, noting that much of the supposed progress was really simply an advance of technocracy and greater government in the name of science.[38] Progressive movements, even those more beneficent than the NICE, tend to fail because they forget qualities that led to the possibility of their existence. Often such progressive movements are not advancement in any real sense, but simply change. In relation to Christian doctrine Lewis argues,

---

36. Lewis, *Abolition of Man*, 4.
37. Lewis, *Abolition of Man*, 43
38. Lewis, "Is Progress Possible?," 346–53.

> For change is not progress unless the core remains unchanged.... In other words, wherever there is real progress in knowledge, there is some knowledge that is not superseded. Indeed, the very possibility of progress demands that there should be an unchanging element. New bottles for new wine, by all means: but not new palates, throats and stomachs, or it would not be, for us, "wine" at all.[39]

Objectivity, as represented in *That Hideous Strength* and *The Abolition of Man*, emphasizes changing the palate rather than changing the substance offered for consumption.

Lewis shows in another essay that the supposed objectivity of scientism is really a form of subjectivity. He writes,

> If "good" and "better" are terms deriving their sole meaning from the ideology of each people, then of course ideologies themselves cannot be better or worse than one another. Unless the measuring rod is independent of the things measured, we can do no measuring. For the same reason it is useless to compare the moral ideas of one age with those of another: progress and decadence are alike meaningless words.[40]

In other words, objectivity, as endorsed by scientism, is functionally equivalent to arguing that humanity is the measure of all things. Such arguments are, therefore, incompatible with the goal of the Christian mind, which is to bring itself into conformity with the God-saturated reality that surrounds it.

Thus, the conquest of nature is really the conquest of humans, because the supposed defeat of nature denies its real attributes. Technological advancement, including increasing material wealth, reduction in disease, and many of the fruits of science, is seen as justification for the demise of the pursuit of the divine mind. This fundamentally changes humanity's relationship with the created order. As Lewis observes, "For the wise men of old the cardinal problem had been how to conform the soul to reality, and the solution had been knowledge, self-discipline, and virtue. For magic and applied science alike the problem is how to subdue reality to the wishes of men: the solution is a technique."[41] At some point, however, having unmoored the purpose of humanity from any fixed reality, the logical outcome of this technique is self-destruction.

---

39. Lewis, "Dogma and the Universe," 32.
40. Lewis, "Poison of Subjectivism," 91.
41. Lewis, *Abolition of Man*, 77.

## Spencer—Ethics among Men without Chests

The scientists of Belbury admitted to their goal to eliminate humanity. It begins with Filostrato's suggestion that real trees be replaced with aluminium ones. Such a tree would be "so natural, it would even deceive."[42] No inconvenience of dropped leaves and the convenience of being able to move the tree when it suited a homeowner's purpose. This, however, would be but a preview to the end goal of abolishing organic life. At this point, *That Hideous Strength* becomes its most satirical, as Filostrato discussed the sort of progress that would fulfill the vision of the NICE:

> In us organic life has produced Mind. It has done its work. After that we want no more of it. We do not want the world any longer furred over with organic life, like what you call the blue mould—all sprouting and budding and breeding and decaying. We must get rid of it. By little and little, of course. Slowly we learn how. Learn how to make our brains live with less and less body: learn to build our bodies directly with chemicals, no longer have to stuff them full of dead brutes and weeds. Learn how to reproduce ourselves without copulation.[43]

After his dinner companion's assertion that this does not sound very enjoyable, Filostrato explained that the process has already begun and must, therefore, be allowed to continue, as if guided by an external force:

> Nature herself begins to throw away the anachronism. When she has thrown it away, then real civilization becomes possible. You would understand if you were peasants. Who would try to work with stallions and bulls? No, no; we want geldings and oxen. There will never be peace and order and discipline so long as there is sex. When man has thrown it away, then he will become finally governable.[44]

This is, ultimately, the abolition of man.

## HUMANITY'S NEED FOR PURPOSE

In Lewis's discussion of ethics in *Mere Christianity* he highlights three basic aspects of Christian ethics: (1) human social relationships; (2) internal peace; and (3) the purpose of humanity.[45] The second and third pieces are notably absent from the moral calculus, such as it is, of the NICE. Most

---

42. Lewis, *That Hideous Strength*, 172.
43. Lewis, *That Hideous Strength*, 173.
44. Lewis, *That Hideous Strength*, 173.
45. Lewis, *Mere Christianity*, 72.

significantly, it is the telos or purpose that has, figuratively, gelded the men of Belbury. As Frost asserted, "Existence is its own justification."[46] There is no purpose except to be. However, humans as individuals and humanity as a whole cannot exist for long without a purpose.

Victor Frankl's book *Man's Search for Meaning* highlights the tragic inability of humans to survive in desperate situations apart from meaning. Conversely, Frankl also reveals that purpose has the ability to sustain existence even in the face of unthinkable evil.[47] Such individually and socially sustaining meaning is exactly the part of humanity that is most quickly eradicated by the so-called objectivity of scientism. The virtue to apprehend meaning is destroyed by scientism, so that any progress made by scientism is likely to be toward the wrong goal.

The irony of the myth of progress, which is perpetuated by scientism, is that what has been abandoned for the sake of advancement is often what is most longed for. That is, the process of advancing undermines the ability to enjoy the advancement. As Lewis famously concluded in *The Abolition of Man*, "In a sort of ghastly simplicity we remove the organ and demand the function. We make men without chests and expect of them virtue and enterprise. We laugh at honour and are shocked to find traitors in our midst. We castrate and bid the geldings be fruitful."[48]

Even during Lewis's lifetime, his readers assured him that the satirical vision of the decadence of modernity was much closer to reality than he recognized.[49] Both *That Hideous Strength* and *The Abolition of Man* were being secretly realized even as Lewis wrote them, as the Allied soldiers would bring to light once they uncovered the horrors of the Nazi concentration camps.[50] Modernity has only continued to dull the perceptions of humanity as euphemistic language disguises the horrors of infanticide and elimination of the sick and old for mere convenience. Instead of discussing the processes head-on, we hear of "abortion care" and "euthanasia" or "death with dignity."

The best response to escape the horrors of modernity is to turn from the myth of progress toward the truth that was understood in the past. For Lewis, on a social level, this entails a greater focus on personal relationships, especially through feasting and drinking together for the sheer enjoyment of it. Thus, when the White Witch's regime is lifting, the Narnians are

---

46. Lewis, *That Hideous Strength*, 295.

47. See especially Frankl, *Man's Search for Meaning*, 78–87.

48. Lewis, *The Abolition of Man*, 46.

49. Brown, *The Lion in the Waste Land*, 250–251

50. Lewis recognizes the connection between scientism and the Nazi death camps in his essay "Is Progress Possible?," 348–49.

discovered sharing a meal together, listening to the sound of water melting.[51] The vision of progress at Belbury is one of sanitization of the loose ends created by biology—an elimination of the common, coarse, and seemingly unrefined. The happiness of the individual should be secondary to the goods of the collective. In contrast, Lewis argues, "Progress, for me, means increasing goodness and happiness of individual lives."[52]

Lewis's political philosophy has many similarities with that of John Locke.[53] In his essay, "Membership," Lewis teases out the competing demands of collectivism and individualism. He writes:

> The secular community, since it exists for our natural good and not for our supernatural, has no higher end than to facilitate and safeguard the family, and friendship, and solitude. To be happy at home, said Johnson, is the end of all human endeavor. As long as we are thinking only of natural values we must say that the sun looks down on nothing half so good as a household laughing together over a meal, or two friends talking over a pint of beer, or a man alone reading a book that interests him; and that all economics, politics, laws, armies, and institutions, save insofar as they prolong and multiply such scenes, are mere ploughing the sand and sowing the ocean, a meaningless vanity and vexation of spirit. Collective activities are, of course, necessary, but this is the end to which they are necessary.[54]

According to Lewis, progress should be focused on real discernible goods for individuals rather than a dehumanized vision of the common good. This vision is neither of Randian individualism nor of socialistic collectivism, but something between those poles. The Christian mind recognizes both the integrity of the individual and the necessity of collective cooperation.[55]

In *That Hideous Strength* the tragedy of progress is that its proponents have forgotten the purpose of its advance. As Lewis notes, "There is, in fact, a fatal tendency in all human activities for the means to encroach upon the very ends which they were intended to serve."[56] Thus, the authors of *The*

---

51. Lewis, *Lion, the Witch and the Wardrobe*, 114–17.
52. Lewis, "Is Progress Possible?," 347.
53. Dyer and Watson, *Lewis on Politics*, 83–103.
54. Lewis, "Membership," 161–62.
55. The roots of healthy individualism can be seen in the Old Testament as a significant advance over other ancient Near Eastern religions. Unterman, *Justice for All*, 18–19.
56. Lewis, "Membership," 162.

*Green Book* attempt to enable their students to resist propaganda by removing the means to recognize it. The progress of modernity has lost its purpose. Or, returning to Lewis's metaphor for ethics from *Mere Christianity*, the performance of modern progress is failing because it has been engaged to provide dance music and actually is playing nothing but funeral dirges. The fleet was commissioned to sail to New York and has actually arrived at Calcutta.[57]

## CONCLUSION

For Lewis, the solution is to determine what the *telos* of human life should be. The purpose, which is stated clearly in *The Abolition of Man*, is for humans to conform themselves to nature rather than trying to conquer it.[58] As he illustrates through the visitation of Venus at St. Anne's and particularly the relationship of Mark and Jane Studdock in *That Hideous Strength*, real freedom comes by yielding control to the designer and submitting to the order of the universe.[59] At a basic level, this entails deference to Natural Law, or the *Tao*, as Lewis calls it in *The Abolition of Man*, but it also requires submission to Christ. Discovering and obeying the truth rather than seeking to overcome nature becomes the aim of the Christian mind and, indeed, of all ethics.

Although technology has provided the means to conquer nature, rejection of technology is not Lewis's proposed response. Instead he encourages study of those who better understood life's purpose, particularly through the study of what might now be called Great Books or Classical Studies. Lewis argues, "To study the past does indeed liberate us from the present, from the idols of our own market-place. But I think it liberates us from the past too." In contrast, "The unhistorical are usually, without knowing it, enslaved to a fairly recent past."[60] Freedom is found not in the pursuit of the novel, but in the exploration of the permanent. The selection of Old Western culture is Lewis's field of choice because there is evidence of the pursuit of the permanent and because that material is both relatively accessible and widely available.

As Lewis explains in his introductory essay to Athanasius's *On the Incarnation*, new books are suspect because they are on trial. In contrast, old books have been curated, with the better material being maintained. Old

---

57. Lewis, *Mere Christianity*, 72.
58. Lewis, *Abolition of Man*, 77.
59. Lewis, *That Hideous Strength*, 374–82.
60. Lewis, "De Descriptione Temporum," 12.

books also help correct the blindness caused by our temporal limitations. Lewis writes,

> None of us can fully escape this blindness, but we shall certainly increase it, and weaken our guard against it, if we read only modern books. Where they are true they will give us truths which we half knew already. Where they are false they will aggravate the error with which we are already dangerously ill. The only palliative is to keep the clean sea breeze of the centuries blowing through our minds, and this can be done only by reading old books. Not, of course, that there is any magic about the past. People were no cleverer then than they are now; they made as many mistakes as we. But not the *same* mistakes.[61]

The point of study, then, is not merely to gain knowledge, but wisdom. More specifically, the Christian mind should be formed for the pursuit of truth by the pursuit of truth through intellectual "conversation" with those who have pursued truth throughout history. Seeking truth along with authentic Christian faith is the most helpful, but even reading those who were attempting to find truth rather than manufacture it will prove to be a formative experience.

Though Lewis compares minds improperly formed by modernity to geldings, that metaphor fails when discussing the solution. A gelding cannot be made fertile again, but the human mind can be better formed by seeking to conform itself to reality. Mark was drawn into the belly of despair in hopes of joining the Inner Ring of the NICE, yet there was a way out by yielding to the *Tao* and submitting to his role as husband.

To live ethically in a world—to be a human with a chest—is to recognize the integrity of the created order. As Lewis concludes in his essay, "The regenerate science which I have in mind would not do even to minerals and vegetables what modern science threatens to do to man himself. When it explained it would not explain away. When it spoke of the parts it would remember the whole."[62] The Christian mind will teach humans to see without seeing through and to experience reality as it is; that is, to see the sublimity of the waterfall beyond our own emotions.

## BIBLIOGRAPHY

Aeschliman, Michael D. *The Restitution of Man: C. S. Lewis and the Case Against Scientism*. Grand Rapids: Eerdmans, 1998.

---

61. Lewis, "On the Reading of Old Books," 440.
62. Lewis, *Abolition of Man*, 79.

Asma, Stephen T. *Why We Need Religion*. New York: Oxford University Press, 2018.

Barth, Karl. "No!" In *Natural Theology*, by Emil Brunner and Karl Barth, 65–128. Eugene, OR: Wipf & Stock, 2002.

Brown, Janice. *The Lion in the Waste Land*. Kent, OH: Kent State University Press, 2018.

Dyer, Justin Buckley, and Micah Watson. *C. S. Lewis on Politics and the Natural Law*. New York: Cambridge University Press, 2016.

Flatow, Ira. "Stephen Hawking Looks Back." https://www.sciencefriday.com/segments/stephen-hawking-looks-back/.

Frankl, Victor. *Man's Search for Meaning*. Boston: Beacon, 1992.

Lewis, C. S. *The Abolition of Man*. New York: HarperCollins, 2001.

———. "De Descriptione Temporum" In *Selected Literary Essays*, 1–14. Cambridge: Cambridge University Press, 1969.

———. "Dogma and the Universe." In *God in the Dock*, 24–35. Grand Rapids: Eerdmans, 1970.

———. "Is Progress Possible?" In *God in the Dock*, 346–53. Grand Rapids: Eerdmans, 1970.

———. "Is Theology Poetry?" In *C. S. Lewis: Essay Collection and Other Short Pieces*, edited by Lesley Walmsley, 10–22. London: HarperCollins, 2000.

———. *The Lion, the Witch and the Wardrobe*. New York: Harper Trophy, 1994.

———. "Membership." In *The Weight of Glory*, 158–76. New York: HarperCollins, 2001.

———. *Mere Christianity*. New York: HarperCollins, 2001.

———. "On the Reading of Old Books," In *C. S. Lewis: Essay Collection and Other Short Pieces*, edited by Lesley Walmsley, 438–43. London: HarperCollins, 2000.

———. "The Poison of Subjectivism." In *Christian Reflections*, 89–102. Grand Rapids: Eerdmans, 1967.

———. *The Silver Chair*. New York: Harper Trophy, 1994.

———. *That Hideous Strength*. New York: Scribner, 1996.

———. *The Voyage of the Dawn Treader*. New York: Harper Trophy, 1994.

Moreland, J. P. *Scientism and Secularism: Learning to Respond to a Dangerous Ideology*. Wheaton: Crossway, 2018.

Postman, Neil. *Amusing Ourselves to Death*. New York: Penguin, 1985.

Solzhenitsyn, Aleksandr. *The Gulag Archipelago, 1918–1956: An Experiment in Literary Investigation III–IV*. New York: Harper & Row, 1975.

Tyson, Neil Degrasse. "Reflections on Rationalia." https://www.facebook.com/notes/neil-degrasse-tyson/reflections-on-rationalia/10154399608556613.

Unterman, Jeremiah. *Justice for All: How the Jewish Bible Revolutionized Ethics*. Philadelphia: Jewish Publication Society, 2017.

# 11

## Lewis on Lament

### Heath A. Thomas

"A MAN IS BORN for trouble as the sparks fly upward" (Job 5:7).[1] Eliphaz aims his comments at Job to help the great sufferer understand his situation. Eliphaz argues humanity is born into distress and suffering, and, as Job is a human being, he too will experience suffering. In the book of Job, Eliphaz sits within his rights to note that human beings are born to trouble but Job, too, is within his rights to note that Eliphaz's description of his specific situation is, in fact, wrong. And further, Job correctly notes Eliphaz (and his friends Zophar and Bildad) wrong Job by misreading his plight. They accuse him of misdeeds when he is innocent of their charges. Job's exclamation captures his sense of being wronged by his friends: "Miserable comforters are you all!" (Job 16:2). But Job is not alone in recognizing the experience of being wronged by another.

C. S. Lewis argues that the innate sense of being wronged, and the ability to reflect upon that terrible experience, enables one to realize that some standard for right and wrong exists. After all, how would one be able to sense wrong, or reflect upon the experience, unless some general standard by which to measure justice or injustice exists? This is because, as C. S. Lewis says, human beings are "haunted" by the idea of the kind of behavior that we

---

1. All Scripture quotations derive from the author's translation, unless otherwise noted.

ought to practice, and thereby ought not to practice. We long for "fair play, or decency, or morality, or the Law of Nature."[2] When it is not enforced and we are wronged by another, we tend to cry foul.

But why do human beings long for fair play? Why do we cry foul when we are wronged? Lewis leads his readers to reason that the standard for "fair play," for right and wrong, stands external to ourselves—it is objective. Further, because we sense an objective standard for right and wrong (even if we grope towards it rather than grasping it wholly) human beings query from whence comes this moral standard. Lewis responds that standard does not come from the material world; it derives from God, who is just and moral.

Lewis's reasoning on the desire for "fair play" informs his configuration of justice in his later work on the Psalms. His work *Reflections on the Psalms* (1958) stands out in Lewis's written corpus: "C. S. Lewis, the great twentieth-century creator of Narnia, English professor at Oxford and Cambridge, and apologist for the Christian faith, wrote only one book on a portion of Scripture—the Psalms."[3] No doubt because of its richness of vision and poetic expression, Lewis engages this book. But there is something beyond the poetic that Lewis tackles in *Reflections on the Psalms*. This work touches upon the theme of justice, right and wrong, and fair play that one finds throughout Lewis's corpus.

An analysis of Lewis's engagement with the elements of lament in *Reflections on the Psalms* shows a place where Lewis allowed his own preferences to overwhelm a fuller apprehension of the Christian mind. Specifically, by rejecting as wicked or embodying self-righteousness psalms that call for judgment on evildoers, Lewis misses the significance of certain psalms of lament for life in a world broken by sin. And yet, despite his criticism of those psalms, there is within Lewis's broader work (especially his later work) material that helps the reader to understand the value of those psalms of lament for the Christian life.

This essay explores Lewis's conception of justice in *Reflections on the Psalms* through his engagement with the idea of "lament" in the Psalms. I argue that Lewis under-reads the value of lament for the Christian life in *Reflections on the Psalms*; his viewpoint may be augmented by (a) recent research on lament and by (b) Lewis's own perspective on petitionary prayer in *Letters to Malcolm*. From this engagement, a deeper understanding on Lewis, lament, and the Christian mind will be offered.[4]

2. Lewis, *Mere Christianity*, 16.

3. Travers, *Encountering God in the Psalms*, 12.

4. It is with great respect and love that I offer this essay in honor of my colleague and friend, Michael Travers. Michael loved C. S. Lewis and the poetry of the book of Psalms. His research in both will be reflected throughout this essay. May his memory

## REFLECTIONS ON THE PSALMS

*Reflections on the Psalms* is one of Lewis's more mature pieces of spiritual contemplation in his corpus. This is because his *Reflections on the Psalms* ruminates upon the ways the Psalter negotiates the pain and joys of living before God in and through poetry. Lewis does not write as an expert on the Psalms but rather as a practitioner; he is one who worships using the book of Psalms rather than one who dissects them academically. He writes this work from the perspective of a devout Christian interested in the ways that the book of Psalms informs the life of faith.

From his perspective of a practitioner rather than an academic, Lewis deals with several topics throughout the book of Psalms which he finds interesting or stimulating for the Christian life. He investigates:

- the concept of "judgment" in the Psalms,
- the imprecatory psalms that curse the enemy,
- the concept of death in the Psalms,
- what it means to delight in the Lord,
- reflection on the law of the Lord,
- the feeling of moral superiority and self-righteousness that he believes emerges in the Psalms,
- the preponderance of the Psalms to describe the natural world,
- praising God in the Psalms,
- Christological interpretation and "second meanings" of biblical texts, and
- the conception of the Psalms as the word of God that reveals Jesus Christ.

In this rather random assemblage of topics, one finds an unsystematic presentation of Lewis's thoughts and reflections, even provocations, from the Psalms. He attempts not to summarize the Psalms, as one would do in an introduction to the corpus, but to respond to them and reflect upon how these texts generate and elicit Christian spirituality, an essential attribute of the Christian mind. His engagements are many and varied. As one might expect, some of his reflections rise to the level of towering insight, while others fail to reach those lofty heights. Judgment/justice remains a key theme he introduces in the opening chapter and one to which he returns in the closing chapter.

---

be forever blessed.

Judgment/justice as a theme emerges from his discussion on lament. I define lament as follows: *lament is a kind of prayer that voices a complaint to God about distress, and it is uttered to persuade God to act on the sufferer's behalf.*[5] Lewis devotes a good deal of time talking about texts like these in the Psalms: Pss 6, 7, 10–13, 16–17, 22–23, 26–28, 31, 35–36, 39–43, 52, 54–55, 57, 58, 63, 69, 86, 88, 102, 109.[6] Although Lewis never identifies these explicitly as lament psalms, one notes that scholars flag each of these psalms formally as laments, as Claus Westermann's classic work on the Psalms exemplifies.[7]

It is in place to note that Lewis never employs the technical language of "lament" as defined here. In fact, Lewis neglects to mention the term "lament" at all in his *Reflections*, on this author's count. How is it possible, then, to link Lewis and lament in this essay? Lewis likely fails to make the generic identification because formal categorization of these psalms as generically as "laments" was not yet in vogue. Such generic categorization began with Hermann Gunkel in Germany during the 1930s (through Joachim Begrich's collation and editing of Gunkel's seminal research on the Psalms in 1933) and continued for the next thirty years in German biblical scholarship.[8] Only later did the insights of German biblical scholarship trickle into the English-speaking world. And these insights did not receive the interpretative weight one might think if the reader or interpreter of the Psalms was not a biblical scholar. As a result, one should not expect the generic insights of Gunkel, Begrich, Westermann, and others to play a significant role, if any, in Lewis's *Reflections on the Psalms*. Still, in this work he clearly engages the psalms scholars identify as laments, and he rightly recognizes concepts in these psalms scholars associate with laments. Therefore, it is appropriate to link Lewis and lament in this essay and assess his understanding of the idea.

As the definition above implies, a lament is a kind of speech whose primary import is to plead to God for help.[9] In this way, it is a form of petitionary prayer that, as shall be explored below, concerns itself with questions of justice in our shared human experience.

---

5. Thomas, *Habakkuk*, 67.

6. For full listing of psalms mentioned or discussed, see "Appendix II" in Lewis, *Reflections on the Psalms*, 175–78.

7. Westermann, *Der Psalter*, 29, 47.

8. Gunkel and Begrich, *Einleitung in die Psalmen*.

9. Specifically, Job 6:22–30; 7:11–21; 13:20–14:22; Habakkuk 1–2; and Jeremiah's 'confessions' (Jer 11:18—12:6; 15:10–21; 17:14–18; 18:18–23; 20:7–18). For discussion and other complaints in prose texts in the Pentateuch and Prophets, see Balentine, *Prayer in the Hebrew Bible*, 89–139, 146–98. For fuller discussion, see Miller, *They Cried to the Lord*, 55–134; Greenberg, *Biblical Prose Prayer*.

In his opening chapter, "'Judgement' in the Psalms," Lewis rightly argues that some psalms that cry out to God for help are juridical in tone because they appeal for God to right the wrongs of the afflicted.[10] These psalms call God to be the judge of their appeal for help (their complaint). As a just judge, God will hear and give a moral verdict. Lewis states,

> The ancient Jews, like ourselves, think of God's judgement in terms of an earthly court of justice. The difference is that the Christian pictures the case to be tried as a criminal case with himself in the dock; the Jew pictures it as a civil case with himself as the plaintiff. The one hopes for acquittal, or rather for pardon; the other hopes for a resounding triumph with heavy damages.[11]

Lewis proceeds to describe the way these psalms cry out for justice, alerting the reader to the juridical language of these psalms. On the one hand, Lewis confirms the appropriateness of the cries of the one who complains to God: often the one uttering these cries lies in the dust; the lamenter is so oppressed and disadvantaged that all the speaker wants is for God to hear the case. Lewis's insight here stands as fundamentally appropriate. To bolster his point, Lewis draws into his discussion the parable of the persistent widow from Luke 18, whose cry for justice surely is admirable and justified, not least because Jesus taught it. But more to the point, the kinds of prayers one finds in the psalms that cry for justice resonate with the widow's appeal. Crying to God for justice remains understandable and justifiable in the life of faith. As it was with the widow in Jesus's parable, so it is with Christians in the life of faith.

Nonetheless, lament psalms remain dangerous. Why so? Because they teeter upon the precipice of self-righteousness, Lewis argues. Laments in the Psalms are juridical, Lewis argues, and they rise from the voice of one positioned as a plaintiff in a courtroom scene. The plaintiff in these Psalms, Lewis charges, is one who is "quite sure, apparently, that his own hands are clean" even as he raises a charge to God the judge against a wicked oppressor.[12] On this, Lewis rightly recognizes one of the key elements one finds in scholarship on the laments: these psalms gain their force from their juridical structure. God is the judge, the plaintiff is the afflicted who testifies about an experience of wrong that needs to be set right.[13] But Lewis takes this further as he identifies the lamenters in these psalms as being righteous

10. Lewis, *Reflections on the Psalms*, 12.
11. Lewis, *Reflections on the Psalms*, 12.
12. Lewis, *Reflections on the Psalms*, 19–20.
13. Mandolfo, *God in the Dock*, 30–42, 135.

in their appeal. But in this construction, Lewis fingers a problem. Lewis reasons that there is no sense in which those who know and love God can ever view themselves as righteous before God, the judge. Far from it! But he argues that no human stands as righteous before God, the righteous judge. At this point, Lewis's theological convictions emerge in his reading of the Psalms. Because humanity stands condemned before a holy God, any shadow of self-righteousness in prayer misfires from the outset. Instead, what is needed in prayer is penitence rather than complaint. The only appropriate prayer for humanity in this case is a cry for mercy rather than justice.

Because of the shadow of self-righteousness Lewis identifies in lament prayer, he distinguishes between two realities of such prayer in the psalms: being right in a specific case, and being "righteous" in the sense of being a good person. One can be right about being wronged in a specific case, but one cannot be right about having no wrong or being "righteous." He says,

> I think it is important to make a distinction: between the conviction that one is in the right and the conviction that one is "righteous" is a good man. Since none of us is righteous, the second conviction is always a delusion. But any of us may be, probably all of us at one time or another are, in the right about some particular issue.[14]

He thinks that the laments are on stable ground when they pray about particular issues of injustice. After all, they are right to identify wrong. His point on the imprecatory psalms (the psalms that pray for vengeance) holds for laments as well:

> If the Jews cursed more bitterly than the Pagans this was, I think, at least in part because they took right and wrong more seriously. For if we look at their railings we find they are usually angry not simply because these things have been done to them but because these things are manifestly wrong, are hateful to God as well as to the victim. The thought of the "righteous Lord"—who surely must hate such doings as much as they do, who surely therefore must (but how terribly He delays!) "judge" or avenge, is always there, if only in the background.[15]

To apply this sentiment to his view of laments: if laments utter complaint righteously to God, the judge, about experiences of wrong, then they do this in part because they take right and wrong more seriously than perhaps we do in our modern world. The innate sense of being wronged has value

---

14. Lewis, *Reflections on the Psalms*, 20.
15. Lewis, *Reflections on the Psalms*, 35.

in that it leads us to the natural law and God's standard of fairness. It also points to the belief that the divine judge is not impartial to the instances of injustice. The cries of lament draw God to move to act concerning the specific situations of injustice identified by the lamenter. So, Lewis argues, the laments rightly present instances of injustice.

But laments remain misdirected when they position the lamenter as being just or righteous in terms of one's legal status before God, the judge. No human, Lewis reckons, is without sin before God. Because of this fact, it is impossible to interrogate the righteousness of another or to accuse another of moral injustice before God when the accuser is as unrighteous as the accused. God judges both. So why would the psalms veer towards this misdirected path?

Lewis sees the problem of self-righteousness lurking in the laments as evidence of the "Jewishness" of these psalms. "All this [accusation and complaint in the psalms] of course has its spiritual danger. It leads into that typically Jewish prison of self-righteousness which Our Lord so often terribly rebuked."[16] (As Philip and Carol Zaleski note, "One winces at the adverb."[17]) In this understanding, lament psalms teeter on the edge of impiety or the prison of self-righteousness, which is a particularly Jewish problem. Impiety emerges in the laments because they promote a perspective of the plaintiff as better than the defendant when in fact *all are sinners before God*. Self-righteousness emerges in laments when the plaintiff believes that she is right and the defendant plainly wrong. Self-righteousness and impiety in the laments lead to what Lewis will later call "Pharisaism" in the psalms.[18]

It is worth pausing to note anti-Semitic leanings in Lewis's characterization.[19] One of the most stinging reviews of Lewis's *Reflections on the Psalms* comes from Stanley Rosenbaum, who offers Lewis's presentation of Judaism as overwhelmingly negative and thoroughly uninformed. Lewis misunderstands basic concepts of the Hebrew Bible, including law, sacrifice, and Hebrew poetry. As a result, he gravely misrepresents Judaism and the Jewish people throughout his *Reflections on the Psalms*, and Lewis's presentation of self-righteousness in the laments would give substance to his critique.[20] The depth of his portrayal of the Jewish religion was a consis-

16. Lewis, *Reflections on the Psalms*, 20.
17. Zaleski and Zaleski, *Fellowship*, 458.
18. Lewis, *Reflections on the Psalms*, 77.

19. It is also notable that in the two-part essay on the Psalms, which likely was an earlier draft of chapters 2 and 3 of *Reflections*, Lewis's criticism of Judaism is much more muted and fair. Lewis, "Psalms," 218–31.

20. Rosenbaum, "Our Own Silly Faces," 486–89.

tent weakness in Lewis.[21] According to the Zaleskis, "Lewis's impression of Judaism rested largely on his reading of the Old Testament, viewed largely through the lens of philosophical monotheism."[22]

Rosenbaum's reading of Lewis alerts us to the dangers of an anti-Semitic reading of the Hebrew Scriptures. To be fair, Lewis clearly admires the Jewish people and Judaism in general in other works, especially emerging in correspondence.[23] Still, admiration expressed in other works does not diminish the damaging characterization (or mischaracterization) in *Reflections on the Psalms*. His reading of Judaism and the Jewish people there is flat and angular. Scholarship has gone a long way to reconnect Jesus and Judaism and to highlight the various Judaisms present in Jesus's day.[24] Because of this, it is worth noting that Jesus's characterization of the faithful life before God was a specific thread in Judaism amongst others before the parting of the ways between Judaism and Christianity, some many decades after Jesus's life. So, it will not do to characterize the Psalms as somehow "Jewish" in a kind of theological slur.

Moreover, his reading of the Psalms as tending towards "self-righteousness" is, I believe, profoundly misguided, as shall be demonstrated below. I do not see the problem of self-righteousness as a particularly "Jewish" problem as much as it is a human problem. For Lewis's critique of "self-righteousness" in the psalms to hold, then, this problem must be identified as distinctively Jewish only to be critiqued in the New Testament. But one finds that the Old Testament clearly decries self-righteous positioning in each of its three sections (Law: Deut 9:4; Prophets: Isa 64:6; Jer 2:34–5; Ezek 28:2; Hos 12:8; Writings: Prov 16:2; 18:12; 20:9; 21:4; 30:12), just as one finds in Jesus's teaching in the New Testament. So, something different must be afoot in the Psalms than what Lewis sees.

Lewis's way out of the particularly "Jewish" problem of self-righteousness in lament comes in what he identifies as a Christian reading of these psalms. In his final chapter in the book ("Second Meaning in the Psalms"), Lewis returns to this theme of judgment in the psalms which he began in the first chapter. He argues that self-righteous tendencies in the psalms (like those he discusses in the first chapter) find their answer in the righteousness

---

21. For example, his thin discussion of Judaism as a religion with little concept of an afterlife in Lewis, "Religion Without Dogma?," 163–64.

22. Zaleski and Zaleski, *Fellowship*, 306.

23. One might also note that he married Joy, herself a Jewish convert to Christianity. Lewis also notably helped pay for the rabbinical studies of his stepson, David Gresham. Hooper, *Companion and Guide*, 110–12.

24. See, for instance, the now-classic works: Wright, *Jesus and the Victory of God*, and Wright, *New Testament and the People of God*.

of Christ, when Jesus is read as the speaker of these psalms. Reading the psalms as a Christian means that they are read with Jesus as the central speaker of the laments. In this interpretation, Jesus gives voice to the laments and utters the cries of complaint:

> Our Lord therefore becomes the speaker in these passages when a Christian reads them; by right—it would be an obscuring of the real issue if He did not. For He denied all sin of Himself.[25]

In this way, the self-righteousness of the speaker in the lament psalms is justified: Christ was perfectly righteous before God, and thereby his accusation against others before God is right. Humans may not be able to utter laments of the psalms without teetering on the edge of impiety and self-righteousness. But Jesus, as the perfect human, can utter laments and embody a righteous disposition precisely because Jesus is holy, just, and righteous before God.

A practical effect of Lewis's characterization of lament in *Reflections on the Psalms* is to undercut the validity of lament prayer in the life of faith—only to reinforce its validity as lament reveals Jesus. In the next section of this essay, I would like to rehabilitate the validity of lament in the Christian life by reconsidering lament in the light of recent research.

## RESEARCH ON LAMENT AND THEOLOGICAL CONSIDERATIONS

Lewis's understanding of lament would be helped in light of studies on lament in the latter half of the twentieth century. In fact, research on lament has blossomed since Lewis's *Reflections on the Psalms* in 1958. This research shows that lament may be subcategorized into different kinds of lament.[26] It can be marked by several formal elements that do not necessarily occur in a fixed sequence,[27] but true to *all* lament stands a general appeal to God about

---

25. Lewis, *Reflections on the Psalms*, 158–59.

26. E.g., individual complaints to God about being falsely accused (Pss 7, 26, 27), general individual pleas to God about distress (Pss 17, 22, 57, 59, 61), individual pleas to God about illness (Pss 38, 88), individual complaints against God's own activity (Pss 6, 35, 39), and community complaints to God (Pss 44, 74, 79, 80; Lam 5). For discussion, with bibliography, see Day, *Psalms*, 19–38.

27. Invocation to the Lord, plea for help, descriptions of distress with complaint (concerning God's activity or inactivity, the activity of enemies, negative experiences of the individual like sickness or sin, for example), reasons why God should respond (though not always), statements of trust in God (though not always), praise to God (though not always). See the helpful discussion of Gillingham, *Poems and Psalms*, 214–15.

distress. Often individual laments like Psalm 22 begin with a cry out to God about a distress and then move to praise to God about his salvific action; still, not all laments follow this turn from lament to praise.[28] Whether laments turn to praise or not, foundational to all these psalms is the direction of their focus.

Laments stand out as such because they are directed *to God*. Lament is often distinguished from praise speech, as evidenced in the Hallelujah psalms (Pss 146–50), where the focus lay upon declarative tribute to God's goodness and character. Both praise and lament, however, are habits in the life of faith that are expressed before God. These habits of praise and lament are earthy and contextual: they praise God about specific situations and experiences, as do laments. Claus Westermann unfortunately bifurcates praise and lament as "polar opposites," but his understanding surely is exaggerated. Broyles shows that lament *presupposes* the Lord's goodness and justice; lament depends upon divine fidelity and justice to ground its prayer.[29] The primary difference between these forms of speech lay in their temporality: lament *anticipates* God's goodness/justice to extol him, whilst praise *participates* in God's goodness/justice and rejoices in him. Both expressions before God must be allowed to work together instead of contesting one another.

In terms of function, lament suffers from some misconceptions, and we have seen one already in Lewis's presentation of lament: an expression of self-righteousness in a "Jewish" mode. Lewis's characterization aside, in the popular imagination some may understand lament to be merely an expression of grief, something people do when they are sad, or depressed, or upset. Because of this, lament can be misunderstood as unhinged emotionalism or as speech that strikes out against God without taking a sober look at one's situation.[30] This view may arise out of uncritical reflection on what is going on in the biblical material or simple terminological confusion (confusing biblical lament with grief), but nonetheless, this perspective does not hold true to biblical lament prayer. Lament is a sober and emotion-filled expression to God about a real wrong experienced or perceived; lament looks to the good and just God to set things right.

---

28. Community complaint prayers do not return to praise as a (general) rule (Pss 44, 74, 79; Lam 5). Note that some individual laments depict only petition (Pss 25, 77, 88, 141, 143), and some laments move from lament to praise then back to lament (Ps 86; Lam 3). For discussion, see Villenueva, *Uncertainty of Hearing*.

29. Westermann, *Praise and Lament in the Psalms*, 11; Broyles, *Conflict of Faith and Experience*, 36–37.

30. We see this in Lewis's critique of his own grief and, likely, prayers of lament in Lewis, *Grief Observed*, 34–35.

Another misconception comes through psychological readings of lament, where scholars and/or ministers advocate lament as cathartic and healing speech that ameliorates grief and suffering through its very vocalization.[31] In this view, lament may be seen as something that needs to be "released" in order to move to reorientation in one's own personal or spiritual life.[32] Lament speech is, no doubt, an impetus to healing when faced with trauma. Therefore, it remains illegitimate to diminish either lament's palliative capacity or its cathartic potentiality. However, palliative care and/or self-actualization does not comprise lament's primary function.[33] Lament is a form of prayer which expects something from its addressee, namely, divine response. Psychological readings tend to reduce lament's emphasis upon divine response in favor of an inward affect. Lament certainly generates catharsis, but always in relation to the Other who listens and responds to prayers.

Finally, lament may be mischaracterized as irritating complaint or rebellious protest and turning away from the Lord. Imagine an angry person striking out at, and turning away from, God, protesting the Lord's failures and calling him into account for his inability to meet the individual's needs. In this latter position, lament may be thought to deny one's relationship with God, or to denigrate theodicy.[34] But such a perspective treats lament as the kind of speech that is unbecoming of God's people. Especially so when laments carry with them imprecations against enemies.

But lament is not God-denying speech, as the logic of its direction (to God) presupposes radical faith in the deity. Lament is a spiritual habit that depends upon the Lord to respond when called upon out of his goodness and justice. Lament properly functions as prayer that anticipates divine response.[35] Lament presents petitions (often centering upon the question of justice, as Lewis rightly understands) before the throne of God:

> My God! My God! Why have you forsaken me? (Ps 22:1; Matt 27:46; Mark 15:34)

> Awake, O Lord! Why do you sleep? Rouse yourself!
> Do not reject us forever! (Ps 44:23)

> Hear, O Lord, my righteous plea; listen to my cry.

---

31. Though without determining lament as a form of cathartic speech, Patricia Huff Byrne does move in this direction: Byrne, "Give Sorrow Words," 255–64.
32. Brueggemann, *Psalms and the Life of Faith*.
33. Note the nuanced discussion of Swenson, *Living Through Pain*, esp. 221–56.
34. See the discussion of Holzem, "'Kriminalisierung' der Klage?," 153–81.
35. Miller, *They Cried to the Lord*, 55–134, esp. 57, 126.

Give ear to my prayer—it does not rise from deceitful lips. (Ps 17:1)

The issue of justice and rightness that was *formerly* known or experienced in the world—but is not so now—is set firmly in God's view *presently*. The tacit assumption of all lament prayer is that God, in his goodness and tacit "rightness," will hear the prayer and respond: "May my vindication come from you; may your eyes see what is right" (Ps 17:2).

Lament's language leans upon a theological bulwark of God's goodness, justice, and power primarily in two ways: God as just and orderly Creator of the world and God as the covenant partner of Israel.[36] Israel can expect God to respond to her pleas on the basis that he is the just convener of the covenant and the just ruler of creation. As Walter Brueggemann rightly argues, the tacit belief in the justice of the Lord as the judge of the earth enables his covenant people to challenge him on areas they perceive to be fundamentally unjust in life, as Psalm 17:2 implies.[37] Thus, there is *expectation* and *hope* built into lament that is not necessarily present in mere expressions of grief, catharsis, protest, or doubt. Miller beautifully summarizes the essence of biblical prayer that coheres with lament: "There is, therefore, in the character of Scriptural prayer a powerful suggestion that the one who prays can truly engage the deity, can urge reasons upon God for acting in behalf of the one in need, just as God in giving the law urges reasons upon the people for responding and obeying."[38]

The issue of hope, too, flags the reality that lament prayer is not *objective* but *subjective* speech in need of divine response, whatever it may be. There is a hope that, despite the lamenter's position, God will respond. Differentiation between these perspectives is crucial. If lament is indeed *objective* speech, then it functions as an indictment against God from the perspective of one who sees his or her situation objectively; this stance then provides the foundation that warrants protest against the Lord and his action or inaction that is somehow unjust.

Lament simply does not embody this perspective. It functions as subjective speech—grounded in a tacit belief in divine goodness, justice, and power—represented internally from the perspective of the sufferer. One may note that interrogatives appear frequently in the lament form, as Psalm

---

36. Psalm 19 correlates covenant and creation in this manner. It looks back to the lament of Psalm 17 and anticipates the lament of Psalm 22, responding to them by affirming an implicit order and just structure to both the created order and covenantal relationship between God and Israel.

37. Brueggemann, *Theology of the Old Testament*, 235–36.

38. Miller, "Prayer as Persuasion," 361.

22:1 indicates: "Why?"[39] Raising a question is not the same linguistically as declaring something spoken with full knowledge or authority about a situation. Lament raises questions, admitting the limited knowledge and perspective of the lamenter. But even if the lament form uses indicative statements or imperatives to demand things of God, it still does so with the expectation of divine response.[40] Rhetorically, then, when it does offer statements or demands, lament still depends upon a logic of divine response. Lament's hope for divine encounter—*the* objective response—depends upon God rather than stands over and against him.[41] To the best of human understanding, the lamenter presents a situation of distress to God in hopes that he will change it. And from the lamenter's perspective, the world *is* out of joint, but it is up to God to respond: to correct any error of the petition, to change the lamenter's perspective, to deliver one from distress, but ultimately to enact justice in the situation of distress. Divine justice and order in both creation and the covenant comprise the substance of the faith and hope of lament.

Lament, then, is petitionary prayer through and through. Therefore, when they appeal to God for justice (which they do), the psalms of lament look to God to be the one who sets the world to rights. Lament remains fundamentally *prayer*.

And because of their focus on prayer to God, psalms of lament provide the vocabulary and grammar to the people of God to utter their requests, hopes, and fears to him in the life of faith. Michael Travers beautifully sets this point on display: "Prayers in the Psalms originate from our human needs and express our dependence on God for all of life. Paradoxically, prayer also gives testimony to our faith in God."[42] Travers precisely puts his finger on the issue of faith in lament. The paradox within lament lay in the fact that this form of speech raises questions to God (which may be misunderstood as an absence of faith or a sense of self-righteousness), but because those very questions are offered to *God*, the lamenter humbles herself before the one who is powerful, just, and good to set things right.

---

39. Generally, interrogatives in the complaint against God remain prevalent within community laments, but also appear in individual laments (e.g., Ps 22:1; Hab 1:2, 13; Gen 25:22; Job 13:24)

40. "Beside these accusatory questions are complaints in the form of statements. They appear frequently in the [individual lament] and often with startling bitterness. They tread that thin line between reproach and judgment. But never do they condemn God, for the utterances are never objective statements. They always remain personal address." Westermann, *Praise and Lament*, 177; see also 181–88.

41. For a somewhat different view see Brueggemann, *Psalms*, 51–122.

42. Travers, *Encountering God in the Psalms*, 14.

Lament is speech that embodies the Christian mind in the face of injustice; it is fundamentally humble and faith-filled speech by the faithful offered in humility to a gracious God.

Therefore, it is unlikely that lament positions itself as self-righteous. Its mode of being, as speech offered to God, originates from the humility of a creature who, in desperate need for God's help and vindication, calls to the Creator to provide justice as only God can see fit. Lament does not demand as if the petitioner can leverage God's response: God is no automaton. Lament, rather, pleads with God to see whether he will respond and, if so, how. The stance of lament is humble and dependent rather than self-righteous. Because of this fact, the force of Lewis's critique on the lament psalms as "self-righteous" misfires.

## LEWIS ON LAMENT RECONSIDERED

I have identified limitations to Lewis's perspective on lament in *Reflections on the Psalms*. Because he characterizes lament prayer as tending towards self-righteousness, Lewis does not rightly represent the paradoxical faith on display in it. Lament is valid, even necessary, in the life of faith. Prayers, like those offered in lament, "express our dependence on God for all of life."[43] In this last section of the essay, I offer a reading of Lewis on lament by exploring his affirmation of the validity of petitionary prayer, especially in his posthumous *Letters to Malcom: Chiefly on Prayer*.

Lewis dealt with prayer occasionally in his earlier nonfiction works,[44] but his most thorough treatment on the topic was his *Letters to Malcolm*. This latter work comprises a series of letters written by Lewis to a fictional friend called "Malcolm." In them, Lewis explores the conditions, spirit, and efficacy of prayer, and he considers why it remains vital in the Christian life.

For our purposes, this essay focuses upon the tenth letter. In it, Lewis discusses the necessity of petitionary prayer in the life of faith. He says, without flinching, that petitionary prayer offers human needs to God so that the Lord might change the situation of the one uttering the prayer. The petitioner utters cries for help because he or she believes that God is good and will give good, just response to the one praying. As one sees, this belief is drawn from an understanding of the goodness and justice of God. Lewis says of petitionary prayer:

> We can bear to be refused but not to be ignored. In other words, our faith can survive many refusals if they really are refusals and

---

43. Travers, *Encountering God in the Psalms*, 14.
44. For example, Lewis, "Petitionary Prayer," 197–205.

not mere disregards. The apparent stone will be bread to us if we believe that a Father's hand put it into ours, in mercy or in justice or even rebuke.[45]

The radical faith offered in petitionary prayer is that the "Father" will respond in some way rather than disregarding the petitioner. What the petitioner cannot abide is the assumption that God simply disregards or ignores the prayers. Real faith, Lewis contends, is one which presses into the Father through prayer and understands that whatever response God gives is "bread" rather than an "apparent stone."

I argue that the stance of petitionary prayer Lewis depicts here resonates with the view of lament offered above. Lament, as argued above, is petitionary prayer that looks to God to answer the appeal of the distressed. As creatures, human beings cry out to God about a sense of wrong and they look to him to make it right as the divine judge. God's response to the appeal remains his own, but the stance of the petitioner is one of utter dependence and trust in the justice of a good and holy God. Lament, as argued above, and petitionary prayer, as Lewis contends in *Letters to Malcolm*, are analogous. Both anticipate God's good response, but the prayers never demand a certain response: lament—as a subset of petitionary prayer—looks to God to give his response, whatever that may be. In both petitionary prayer and lament, God is understood as the one who offers "mercy" or "justice" or "rebuke." The point is that both lament and petitionary prayer look to God to make things right and lean upon God to give whatever response he sees fit.

In this way, I offer that Lewis's perspective on petitionary prayer in the tenth letter in *Letters to Malcolm* provides a different valence on Lewis's conception of justice and lament in *Reflections on the Psalms*. If the two are set in dialogue, one notes the deficiencies of his view of lament in *Reflections on the Psalms*, the resonance of Lewis's perspective on petitionary prayer in *Letters to Malcolm* with recent scholarship on lament, and a renewed vitality for lament for the Christian mind as a form of petitionary prayer.

## BIBLIOGRAPHY

Balentine, Samuel E. *Prayer in the Hebrew Bible*. Minneapolis: Fortress, 1993.
Broyles, Craig C. *The Conflict of Faith and Experience in the Psalms: A Form-Critical and Theological Study*. Sheffield: Journal for the Study of the Old Testament, 1989.
Brueggemann, Walter. *Psalms and the Life of Faith*. Minneapolis: Fortress, 1995.
———. *The Psalms*. Cambridge: Cambridge University Press, 2014.
———. *Theology of the Old Testament: Testimony, Dispute, Advocacy*. Minneapolis: Fortress, 1997.

45. Lewis, *Letters to Malcolm*, 75.

Byrne, Patricia Huff. "'Give Sorrow Words': Lament—Contemporary Need for Job's Old Time Religion." *Journal for Pastoral Care & Counseling* 56.3 (2002) 255–64.

Day, John. *Psalms*. New York: Continuum, 2003.

Gillingham, S. E. *The Poems and Psalms of the Hebrew Bible*. Oxford: Oxford University Press, 1994.

Greenberg, Moshe. *Biblical Prose Prayer as a Window to the Popular Religion of Ancient Israel*. Berkeley: University of California Press, 1983.

Gunkel, Hermann, and Joachim Begrich. *Einleitung in die Psalmen: die Gattungen der religiösen Lyrik Israels*. Göttingen: Vandenhoeck & Ruprecht, 1933.

Holzem, Andreas. "'Kriminalisierung' der Klage? Bittgebet und Klageverweigerung in der Frommigkeitsliteratur des 19. Jahrhunderts," In *Klage*, edited by M. Ebner et. al, 153–81. Neukirchen-Vluyn: Neukirchener, 2001.

Hooper, Walter. *C. S. Lewis: A Companion and Guide*. New York: HarperCollins, 2001.

Lewis, C. S. *A Grief Observed*. New York: Bantam, 1976.

———. *Letters to Malcolm: Chiefly on Prayer*. San Francisco: HarperOne, 2017.

———. *Mere Christianity*. New York: HarperCollins, 2001.

———. "Petitionary Prayer." In *C. S. Lewis: Essays and Other Short Pieces*, edited by Lesley Walmsley, 197–205. London: HarperCollins, 2000.

———. "The Psalms." In *C. S. Lewis: Essays and Other Short Pieces*, edited by Lesley Walmsley, 218–30. London: HarperCollins, 2000.

———. *Reflections on the Psalms*. New York: HarperOne, 2017.

———. "Religion Without Dogma?" In *C. S. Lewis: Essays and Other Short Pieces*, edited by Lesley Walmsley, 163–78. London: HarperCollins, 2000.

Mandolfo, Carleen. *God in the Dock: Dialogic Tension in the Psalms of Lament*. Sheffield: Sheffield Academic Press, 2002.

Miller, Patrick D. "Prayer as Persuasion: The Rhetoric and Intention of Prayer." In *Word and World* 13.4 (1993) 356–62.

———. *They Cried to the Lord: The Form and Theology of Biblical Prayer*. Minneapolis: Fortress, 1994.

Rosenbaum, Stanley N. "Our Own Silly Faces: C. S. Lewis on the Psalms." In *Christian Century*, May 18, 1983.

Swenson, Kristin M. *Living Through Pain: Psalms and the Search for Wholeness*. Waco: Baylor University Press, 2005.

Thomas, Heath A. *Habakkuk*. Grand Rapids: Eerdmans, 2018.

Travers, Michael E. *Encountering God in the Psalms*. Grand Rapids: Kregel, 2003.

Villenueva, Federico. *The "Uncertainty of Hearing": A Study of the Sudden Change of Mood in the Psalms of Lament*. Leiden: Brill, 2008.

Westermann, Claus. *Der Psalter*. Stuttgart: Calwer, 1967.

———. *Praise and Lament in the Psalms*. Louisville: Westminster John Knox, 1987.

Wright, N. T. *Jesus and the Victory of God*. London: SPCK, 1996.

———. *The New Testament and the People of God*. Minneapolis: Fortress, 1992.

Zaleski, Philip, and Carol Zaleski. *The Fellowship: The Literary Lives of the Inklings*. New York: Farrar, Straus & Giroux, 2015.

# 12

## "As Ever in My Great Task-Master's Eye"
Milton's Sonnet 7 and Productivity in the Christian Mind

### Leland Ryken

READING LEWIS'S *A PREFACE to Paradise Lost* first awakened in me a desire to specialize in Milton.[1] For the past three decades, my primary scholarly project has been to place selected Miltonic sonnets in a Puritan context, and my explication of Sonnet 7 in this essay is part of that effort. My enterprise exhibits several key elements of C. S. Lewis's theory and practice as a literary critic, including an insistence that a poem is a work of verbal artistry before it is a philosophic statement, that literature needs to be placed

---

1. This essay represents a convergence of important aspects of my scholarly life, including Milton, the Puritans, the literary theory of C. S. Lewis, and my personal and professional friendship with Michael Travers. Before Michael became known for his expertise in the Bible as literature and C. S. Lewis, he was a specialist in the poetry of John Milton, and I first knew Michael as a fellow Miltonist. Michael's dissertation and first book were on the devotional mode in the poetry of John Milton and were something that any evangelical scholar would aspire to write—rooted in the Christian faith, meeting all the requirements of scholarship in the secular academy: uncluttered, unpretentious, and solid. My dissertation and first book were also on the poetry of Milton, and in many of my scholarly interests I have felt myself to be a kindred spirit to Michael Travers. One way in which this is evident is that over the course of half a century of teaching Milton's poetry I have told my students that virtually all of Milton's poetry can be read devotionally, a claim that approximates Michael's thesis in his dissertation.

into the milieu of its origin before we can understand its nuances, and that "Milton's thought, purged of its theology, does not exist."[2]

At the level of content, Milton's Sonnet 7 ("How Soon Hath Time") touches upon issues that were important in Michael Travers's life and dear to his heart. The poem is a college poem, written as Milton was finishing his college education at Cambridge University. It is a defense of the scholarly and intellectual life. The framework into which Milton casts this defense is a quest to find vindication when the quick passing of time leaves a person in the position of having achieved less than hoped. As always, Milton takes the experiences and issues of real life and transmutes them into a work of high art.

Milton's Sonnet 7 illustrates an aspect of the Christian mind that well characterizes the Puritans. It also characterizes, to some extent, the lives of C. S. Lewis and Michael Travers. Though we marvel at the productivity of Lewis, he lived with a sense of desire to do more for the glory of God. For example, in a letter to Don Giovanni Calabria, dated 10 September 1949, Lewis apologizes profusely for a belated response to a letter: "For nothing else was responsible for it except my perpetual labour of writing and (lest I should seem to exonerate myself too much) a certain Accidia, an evil disease and, I believe, of the Seven Deadly Sins that one which in me is the strongest—though few believe this of me."[3] Michael, too, often apologized for inconsequential delays in his work and correspondence, even in the midst of his cancer treatments. These men shared the sentiment with Milton's Sonnet 7—a common one for Christians conscious that their days on earth are numbered by God—that at the end, their effort and the heart behind it would be judged; therefore, there was no time to waste.

My procedure in this essay will be first to demonstrate some of the elements of Lewis's literary theory are being applied in this analysis of Milton's sonnet. Then I will explicate Milton's poem on its own terms as a poem, and explore how certain key features of Milton's Puritan milieu can further illuminate the poem. I will assume but not seek to prove the conclusion of theologian Augustus Strong that Milton was "a Puritan of the Puritans."[4]

## LEWIS ON LITERARY CRITICISM

Consideration of Lewis's literary criticism must begin by noting that Christian literary scholars in Britain, operating without the impetus of a network

---

2. Lewis, *Preface to Paradise Lost*, 65.
3. Lewis, *Collected Letters*, 2:979.
4. Strong, *Great Poets and Their Theology*, 231.

of Christian colleges with their philosophy of the integration of faith and learning, have generally avoided drawing explicit connections between their faith and their literary theory. This means that we need to *infer* what the links are. Applied to Lewis, we can begin with the premise that when he plies his trade as a literary critic we are, indeed, observing his Christian mind at work because we know that Lewis was a Christian thinker.

We should also note that Lewis wrote only one work of literary theory: *An Experiment in Criticism*. But this turns out to be misleading because one of the strengths of Lewis's literary criticism is that he continuously tucks in bits of literary theory from which we can piece together a coherent theory about what literature is and does. These passages often occur in unexpected places, so that (for example) one of his best statements of literary theory comes in an essay entitled "The Language of Religion"[5] instead of an essay entitled "Christianity and Literature"[6] in the same anthology of essays.

The fact that Lewis did not explicitly formulate a Christian poetic or overtly integrate his literary analysis with his Christian faith does not mean that he regarded literary criticism as unrelated to his Christian faith and mind. In the same passage in which Lewis asserts that "Milton's thought, when purged of its theology, does not exist," he also claims regarding his personal faith that "for the student of Milton my Christianity is an advantage," just as it would be an advantage "to have a real, live Epicurean at your elbow while reading Lucretius."[7] While Lewis does not explicitly tie his literary scholarship to his Christian faith, we can nonetheless operate on the premise that whatever Lewis says about literature represents the theory and practice of his Christian mind.

The starting point for Lewis is that literary works have integrity in themselves as the expression of an author. Lewis has tremendous respect for literary works and a corresponding humility to receive what they have to offer. He writes, "The first demand any work of any art makes upon us is surrender. Look. Listen. Receive. Get yourself out of the way."[8] When we come to read a novel or poem, therefore, "Attention to the very objects they are is our first step."[9]

If we ask what Christian doctrine underlies this respect for works of literature as created objects, the answer is the doctrine of God's creation of the universe. We catch a glimpse of this in a passage where Lewis theorizes

---

5. Lewis, "Language of Religion," 255–66.
6. Lewis, "Christ and Literature," 411–20.
7. Lewis, *Preface to Paradise Lost*, 65.
8. Lewis, *Experiment in Criticism*, 19.
9. Lewis, *Experiment in Criticism*, 82.

that it "is appropriate, almost inevitable, that when that great Imagination which in the beginning . . . had invented and formed the whole world of Nature" came to express itself in the words of the Bible, "that speech should sometimes be poetry"—that is, a work of art.[10] Literature is worthy of honor because the creativity that produced it is akin to divine creativity.

Lewis's theory of reading begins with the text itself, but the overwhelming quantity of Lewis's published literary scholarship is devoted to the context rather than the text of literary works. He does not assert this as part of his literary theory, so we need to infer it from his published work. The chief example is *English Literature in the Sixteenth Century: Excluding Drama*, a seven-hundred-page book that contains only intermittent explications of texts.

The third pillar of Lewis's approach to literature is again one that we need to infer, and we can do so by combining the first two points I have established. For Lewis, the right approach to literary analysis is to operate on the premise that while a reader's primary goal is to receive "the thing the poet has made for us,"[11] we cannot do that fully without placing a work into its historical and biographical context. The text does not exist as data for establishing a context, but the reverse: we recover the context in order to illuminate the text. This is what I propose to do with Milton's sonnet on the subject of the swift passing of time.

## "RECEIVING" MILTON'S POEM

Although my primary purpose in this essay is to relate the content of Milton's sonnet to Puritan ideas and experience, I want to begin with the poem itself. C. S. Lewis performed a great service to his discipline by advocating that when we assimilate a work of art we need to receive it first of all. Further, Lewis famously said that a poem "is not merely *logos* (something said) but *poiema* (something made). . . . Attention to the very [poem] is our first step."[12] I accordingly propose to look at Milton's Sonnet 7 as Lewis prescribed—by "entering fully into the opinions, . . . attitudes, feelings and total experience" of the poet.[13] The text of Milton's poem is as follows:

> How soon hath Time, the subtle thief of youth,
>
> Stolen on his wing my three and twentieth year!
>
> My hasting days fly on with full career,

10. Lewis, *Reflections on the Psalms*, 5.
11. Lewis, *Experiment in Criticism*, 82.
12. Lewis, *Experiment in Criticism*, 19, 82.
13. Lewis, *Experiment in Criticism*, 85.

> But my late spring no bud or blossom showeth.
> Perhaps my semblance might deceive the truth
> That I to manhood am arrived so near,
> And inward ripeness doth much less appear,
> That some more timely-happy spirits endueth.
> Yet be it less or more, or soon or slow,
> It shall be still in strictest measure even
> To that same lot, however mean or high,
> Toward which Time leads me, and the will of Heaven.
> All is, if I have grace to use it so,
> As ever in my great Task-Master's eye.

I will begin my scrutiny of the poem where C. S. Lewis believed analysis of any poem should begin—by identifying the genres to which the poem belongs and exploring how these explain the text. Lewis's oft-quoted insistence on this principle comes in the very first sentence of *A Preface to Paradise Lost*, where he writes, "The first qualification for judging any piece of workmanship . . . is to know *what* it is," by which Lewis meant the genre of a work.[14]

The first genre to which Sonnet 7 belongs is known as the occasional poem—a poem arising from a specific event in the life of the poet or the social life of the time. Sonnet 7 is a birthday poem, in at least a general sense. Early editors affixed the title "On His Having Arrived at the Age of Twenty-Three" to the poem, a title still in circulation. This title identifies Milton's twenty-third birthday (or the time close to it) as the occasion of the poem. The current scholarly consensus argues that Milton's twenty-fourth birthday is the occasion around which Milton composed the poem. I favor the traditional view that the birthday in view is Milton's twenty-third. According to line 2 of the poem, Milton's twenty-third year has already been taken from him. As we ordinarily calculate the matter, an infant on a first birthday (for example) has already completed one year of life, so it would have been on Milton's twenty-third birthday that he could say that twenty-three years had been taken from him.

An important component in the commentary surrounding this poem is the fact that in the Cambridge Manuscript of Milton's poems, the sonnet is inserted into a letter to a friend. The letter refers to a conversation of the previous day in which the friend had accused Milton of "too much love of Learning" and of dreaming away his "Yeares in the armes of a studious

---

14. Lewis, *Preface to Paradise Lost*, 1.

retirement."[15] But Milton did not *compose* the sonnet on the occasion of the conversation. He plainly states that the enclosed sonnet was the product of "some of my nightward thoughts some while since."[16] "Some while since" is the equivalent of "quite a long time ago," or "so long ago that I do not remember the exact date," not "yesterday" or "a few days ago."

In much recent criticism of the poem, the discussion imperceptibly and perhaps unconsciously slides into treating the poem as though *written* in refutation of the friend. In fact, however, the letter belongs to the afterlife of the poem, not its composition. Milton did, indeed, think that the sonnet refuted the friend's criticism, but he did not *compose* it as a rebuttal. In the letter, Milton states that he included it with the letter because it "[came] in not altogether unfitly," adding that "by this I believe you may well repent of having made mention at all of this matter."[17] In much recent commentary on this poem, especially among critics who argue that the sonnet was written around the time of Milton's twenty-fourth birthday and after his graduation from college, the letter to the friend has become the proverbial tail that wags the dog.

Placing the poem into a Puritan context is completely unaffected by the dating of the poem. If we simply follow the contour of the poem itself, putting the letter out of our mind as contributing to the composition of the poem, we will possess the poem that Milton wrote. The later dating of the poem, combined with a misuse of the letter to the friend, has been a gigantic red herring in the interpretation of Sonnet 7.

In my reading of the poem, then, we have a second occasion for the poem, namely, the last months of Milton's time at college. The poem itself tells us how Milton felt as he took stock of his development and future plans during his final days on campus. One commentator pictures the poem as being written "some eight months before [Milton] was to round off his education at Cambridge, and so bring to a conclusion the first stage of his life, that of youth and preparation, with the necessity of beginning a second, that of young manhood."[18] I am fond of two interpretations pinned on the poem by my students. One of them called Sonnet 7 "Milton's graduation poem." Another correctly claimed that the octave of the poem is a Miltonic version of "senior panic." The octave of the poem expresses feelings that are universal among students as they face graduation from college. Milton's silencing

---

15. Milton, *Complete Prose Works of John Milton*, 1:319. Hereafter abbreviated *CPW*.

16. Milton, *CPW*, 1:320.

17. Milton, *CPW*, 1:320.

18. Cheek, "Of Two Sonnets by Milton," 127.

of his opening self-distrust is, among other things, a defense of the stage of preparation for life that college represents.

In addition to being an occasional poem, Sonnet 7 is an Italian sonnet, a genre to which it adheres with complete faithfulness. In conventional manner, the octave, rhyming *abba abba*, poses a problem that requires a solution. The problem is twofold: the swift passing of time, and the speaker's immaturity and underachievement. The universal human experience expressed in the octave is a young person's confronting a personal feeling of under-accomplishment, accompanied by an awareness that time is marching on. The reversal or *volta* in an Italian sonnet comes at the beginning of the ninth line and is here signaled by Milton's word *yet*. The sestet (final six lines) then finds a solution to the problem that has been posed (a solution that I will explore in the second half of this essay). The rhyme scheme of the sestet of an Italian sonnet is variable rather than fixed, and Milton's chosen rhyme scheme is *cde dce*. A conventional Italian sonnet does not end in a rhyming couplet as the English or Shakespearean sonnet form does. However, even though Milton's sonnet does not end with a rhyming couplet, Milton adds an original touch by conflating the two sonnet forms available to him: his last two lines are a self-contained epigrammatic climax to the poem, just as Shakespeare's concluding couplets are.

I do not have space to conduct a detailed explication of the poem, so I will be content with the following brief "program notes." The sequence of thoughts is this: three lines establish the occasion of time's swift passing; then five lines detail the poet's lack of maturity (both internally and physically), as contrasted to his peers; the next four lines assert confidence in God's providential direction of the speaker's future life; and a concluding two-line epigram expresses the poet's resolve to persist on his chosen path, having attained a satisfactory solution to his opening anxiety attack. This line of thought is embodied in a rich poetic texture, consisting of such techniques as the personification of time, metaphors of plants and their growth or lack of it, and evocative allusions to God as guide and taskmaster.

What I have briefly unfolded are the poem's intrinsic poetic qualities, such as any classroom teacher of the poem would explicate. My further enterprise is to see what nuances emerge that would otherwise be hidden when we place the poem into a Puritan context.

## THE PURITAN GENRE OF INTROSPECTIVE MEDITATION

I have already placed the poem into the literary families of the occasional poem and the sonnet, but an additional genre exists as well. Sonnet 7 is a meditative poem, but of a specific type, namely, introspective self-examination. Such self-examination was a regular and even daily practice for the serious Puritan. Its goal was self-knowledge and holy reformation of one's life, and I will note in passing that Stanley Fish's highly influential book on *Paradise Lost* made the bold claim that Milton's intention in his grand epic, despite its high art, "differ[s] little from . . . many devotional writers [by endeavoring] 'to . . . show how a man may come to a holy reformation.'"[19]

The Puritan preoccupation with self-examination was rooted in the Reformation itself. John Calvin famously begins his *Institutes of the Christian Religion* with the statement, "Nearly all the wisdom we possess . . . consists almost of two parts: the knowledge of God and of ourselves."[20] Loosely speaking, the octave of Milton's sonnet focuses on knowledge of self and the sestet on knowledge of God.

The Puritans embraced Calvin's ideal of self-knowledge. William Perkins claimed that "every man hath a calling to search into himself."[21] "Consider the profitableness of a serious faithful examination of thy [spiritual] estate," wrote George Swinnock.[22] William Hook admonished, "Omit not a day without reviewing your actions and repentings."[23] William Burkitt, writing specifically to students, encouraged "Serious Self-examination, by which we make a daily enquiry into the State of our Souls."[24] And Richard Rogers noted in his diary written during his years at Cambridge University that he desired "to know mine own heart better, where I know that much is to be gotten in understanding of it, and to be acquainted with the diverse corners of it and what sin I am most in danger of."[25] Half a century ago Macon Cheek helpfully labeled Sonnet 7 "a brief essay in critical self-examination, both retrospective and prospective."[26] In being such, the poem is a vintage Puritan document.

One more thing to note about the genre of introspective meditation is that the Puritan practice of engaging in spiritual self-assessment was sometimes occasioned by an external event. Guides to meditation, for example, variously encouraged self-examination in times of spiritual crisis, at the end of the calendar year, and in February or March (as being a time when death

19. Fish, *Surprised by Sin*, ix.
20. Calvin, *Institutes*, 1:35.
21. Perkins, *Workes*, 1:73.
22. Swinnock, *Works*, 3:292.
23. Hook, *What Gifts of Grace*, 2:688.
24. Burkitt, *Poor Man's Help*, 40.
25. From Richard Rogers's diary in *Two Elizabethan Puritan Diaries*, 62.
26. Cheek, "Of Two Sonnets by Milton," 129.

seemed especially near and/or a season emblematic of human sinfulness).[27] One of the occasions that the guides mention is one's birthday, and Milton's poem fits the pattern. Additionally, the sonnet was written at a crucial transition point of Milton's life (a crisis of sorts), and inasmuch as Milton's birthday was December 9, the composition occurred around the annual change of calendar.

Recent criticism on this poem overstates the importance of the conversation with the friend to whom Milton sent a letter with Sonnet 7 enclosed, so I need to say again that Milton composed his poem on the occasion of his birthday, well before (probably more than a year before) the conversation with the friend. Sonnet 7 is not about the friend's criticism of Milton; it is a poem of self-assessment and (in the octave) self-criticism, in standard Puritan fashion.

## PURITAN VIEWS OF TIME

The first three lines of Milton's poem state the crisis that the speaker confronts on the occasion of his birthday, namely, the swift passing of time. This had been a common poetic subject for classical and Renaissance poets, but for poets in these humanistic traditions the passing of time did not produce a personal crisis. To understand why it did so for Milton, I propose that we inquire into a well-thought-out set of ideas that the Puritans generated on the subject of time. I note in passing that Richard Baxter said in the conclusion of a treatise on redeeming the time that he had written at such length on this subject "because it is of unspeakable importance."[28] Milton sometimes incorporates the stock vocabulary of Puritan writing and sermons into his sonnets, which becomes evident when Milton's words are placed in proximity to similar comments from Puritan authors.

To begin, the Puritans simply placed an extremely high value on time. For John Howe, time is "a precious thing that . . . is to be redeemed,"[29] while John Downame called time "the most precious treasure."[30] Willam Whately regarded time as "a thing most precious,"[31] and Robert Bolton declared similarly that "time is precious."[32]

---

27. Hambrick-Stowe, *Practice of Piety*, 169–74.
28. Baxter, *Practical Works of Richard Baxter*, 1:246.
29. Howe, *Works of John Howe*, 3:33.
30. Downame, *Guide to Godlinesse*, 270.
31. Whately, *Prototypes*, 235.
32. Bolton, *General Directions*, 183.

Secondly, the Puritans viewed time as fleeting and brief. In his sonnet, Milton speaks of time as "hastening," and so does Richard Baxter: "Remember the swift and constant motion of your neglected time. What haste it makes! ... It hasteth as fast while you play, as while you work."[33] For John Flavel, too, "the precious inch of time" that comprises a human life is "in hasty motion."[34] "Man's time is short in this world," Richard Eaton declared in a funeral sermon.[35]

Another strand in Puritan thinking about time is the conviction that God calls all creatures to account for their use or misuse of time. Richard Sibbes asserted that "we shall give an account to God how we have spent our time. ... It will be a fearful account when we have spent our time idly."[36] "God will call you to account," wrote Richard Baxter, "for every hour of your misspent time."[37] Robert Bolton spoke in similar terms: "We must be accountable for time. At the dreadful bar of that last tribunal, ... we must ... give up a strict account for the expense of every moment of time."[38]

All of these ideas about time fed into the most important one, namely, the Puritan phobia about misspent time. "Abhor all pastimes and triflings that would rob you of your time," wrote Baxter.[39] The person who pursues his or her calling as God intended "cannot endure to spend any idle time," wrote John Cotton.[40] For John Downame, misspent time "exceedeth all other losses, and ... the wasting of it is the greatest unthriftiness."[41] Downame also bequeathed what we can use as a summary formula on this point when he wrote of "the prodigal misspending of ... time."[42]

The broader context here is the Puritan work ethic, which produced a climate in which work was highly and often obsessively valued. The opposites of diligence are sloth and idleness, which unleashed unending scorn and denunciation from the Puritans. The accompanying assumption was that those who worked diligently (the omnipresent virtue extolled by the Puritans in regard to work) would have something to show for their

---

33. Baxter, *Practical Works*, 1:235.
34. Flavel, *Works of John Flavel*, 3:231.
35. Eaton, *Sermon Preached at the Funeralls*, 10.
36. Sibbes, *Complete Works*, 6:498.
37. Baxter, *Practical Works*, 1:234.
38. Bolton, *General Directions*, 190.
39. Baxter, *Practical Works*, 4:977.
40. Cotton, *Christ the Fountain of Life*, 119.
41. Downame, *Christian Warfare*, 270.
42. Downame, *Christian Warfare*, 271.

diligence. Puritan Thomas Watson said aphoristically that "God will reward our diligence, not our laziness."[43]

The plain inference of statements by Puritan preachers and writers is that if people do not produce effects from their labors, they have been lacking in diligence and the wise use of their time. Richard Baxter titled a treatise on time "Directions for Redeeming or Well Improving Time."[44] "To redeem time," writes Baxter, "is to see that we cast none of it away in vain," that is, without producing something. To "improve" time likewise implies that something discernible has been gained during a given segment of time. This is the issue at stake in Sonnet 7. Milton does not chastise himself for not having chosen or entered a profession (a currently popular interpretation of the poem) but rather for having accomplished less than he feels would have been a reasonable expectation after twenty-three years of life.

For many years I was resistant to an interpretation that claimed that "behind the sonnet lies the age-old topic of 'time neglected.'"[45] After all, Milton was a dynamo of academic diligence and industry, rarely leaving his studies before midnight. But the plain drift of the octave of the poem is that Milton's time has slipped away from him so imperceptibly (the meaning of the adjective *subtle*) that he finds himself without the maturity and productivity that should have occurred by now. A late spring season that produces no bud or blossom and a person who lacks inward ripeness commensurate with his age are a spectacle of time not functioning as it should. The octave is partly a lament about things not under Milton's control (such as his immature external appearance) and partly self-criticism about not having progressed as he should have.

To sum up, to view time as fleeting and as a thief is not an emphasis unique to the Puritans, but if we add the notion of time as something for which God holds his creatures accountable, and additionally an extreme aversion to the fruitless wasting of time, we have a matrix that *is* specifically Puritan. The ideas about time that I have delineated provide depth of field for understanding what all is embodied in the exclamation of surprise and dismay with which Milton begins his poem. The anxiety vision of the octave is a Puritan vision. In line with Edward Reynold's statement in a sermon that "an excellent part of wisdom is to know and to manage time,"[46] the earnest young Puritan Milton accuses himself of not having managed his time acceptably.

43. Watson, *Beatitudes*, 257.
44. Baxter, *Practical Works*, 1:230–46.
45. Hoignman, *Milton's Sonnets*, 98.
46. Reynolds, *True Gain*, 31.

To return for a moment to the criticism that Milton's friend had expressed, even though the argument of the sonnet tends toward a refutation of the friend (as Milton asserts in the letter), Milton does not totally disparage the friend's concern about how he is managing his time. In fact, Milton credits his friend with having raised a valid issue when he writes in his letter, "You are often to me, and were yesterday especially, as a good watch man to admonish that the howres of the night passe on."[47] Milton the Puritan shares his friend's conviction that time must be spent well.

## THE CONFESSIONAL STRAIN IN PURITANISM

As already noted, in the octave Milton not only laments the swift passing of time but also accuses himself of underachievement. He is like an English orchard that even in late spring has no buds on the trees. In physical appearance he does not look like a young adult. He lacks inner maturity, a point on which he compares himself unfavorably to more mature peers. The Puritan context into which I propose to place this self-accusation is the confessional strain that characterizes the Puritan temperament. The Puritans' impulse was to be unflinching in seeing the worst in themselves when they took stock of their spiritual state. In lines 4–8 of Sonnet 7, Milton faces the worst about himself and judges himself accordingly.

While this Puritan strain crops up nearly everywhere in Puritan writings, its most characteristic expression can be found in the Puritan diary, the prose genre that Milton transformed into high art in Sonnet 7. To keep the discussion manageable, I will dip into the diaries of two Puritans who share with Milton the trait of being Cambridge-educated—Richard Rogers and Samuel Ward, whose diaries have been conveniently printed under the title *Two Elizabethan Puritan Diaries*.

Rogers was a leading Puritan minister who wrote his diary two decades after his time at Cambridge. While there were a few good days on which Rogers might feel just a little satisfaction with himself, the prevailing note is self-accusation. Here is a typical entry that epitomizes the content of Rogers's diary: "I purposed to bewail my sin at more leisure, and for that time to proceed in my study, and so did. The next day I had hearty detestation of my sin, and so returned again to my God. . . . It shameth me that I should be trifling out my time thus, whiles the troubles are so great."[48]

But the self-reproach that Rogers expresses is mild compared to what we find in the diary of Samuel Ward that he composed during his twenties

---

47. Milton, *CPW*, 1:319.
48. Rogers, *Two Elizabethan Puritan Diaries*, 78.

when he was a graduate student at Christ's College (also Milton's college). The part that Knappen chose to reprint does not represent the whole tenor of Ward's diary, but it illustrates the self-accusatory strain that we see also in the octave of Milton's sonnet. This part of Ward's diary, unwittingly the funniest Puritan document that I have read, is a litany of things that bothered an earnest young Puritan: "thy wandering mind in the chapel at prayer time";[49] "my negligence in my studies";[50] "my late rising in the morning to sanctify the Sabbath";[51] "my anger at Sir Smith in the hall at dinner, for denying that purgations do purge by attraction";[52] "my too much gluttony at dinner time";[53] "my impatiency when Hobson told me he had no letters for me";[54] "my long sleeping in the morning."[55] Milton's self-accusation is, of course, much more selective, but it shares with Ward's student diary the confessional impulse to record personal failings and render a negative verdict on one's life as a student.

## THE CONSOLATIONS OF PROVIDENCE

Thus far I have looked at the "bad news" aspect of Sonnet 7. In keeping with the problem-solution format of the Petrarchan sonnet, as well as the rhythm of Puritan self-examination, Milton moves from self-laceration to consolation and vindication. Thomas Hooker wrote regarding the twofold purpose of self-examination that it is "powerful and profitable, both for contrition of the heart, and so to bring in consolation to the heart."[56] Two Puritan mainstays make up the consolation in Milton's meditation, the first of which is an empowering sense of God's providence.

With the pivotal word "yet" at the beginning of line 9, Milton's sonnet ceases to view time as a thief and enemy and instead embraces it as a guide. Lines 9–12 employ the rhetorical patterns of parallelism and antithesis that F. T. Prince celebrated in Milton's sonnets and that lend both eloquence and emotional conviction to the utterance:

> Yet be it less or more, or soon or slow,
> It shall be still in strictest measure even

---

49. Ward, *Two Elizabethan Puritan Diaries*, 103.
50. Ward, *Two Elizabethan Puritan Diaries*, 106.
51. Ward, *Two Elizabethan Puritan Diaries*, 106.
52. Ward, *Two Elizabethan Puritan Diaries*, 108.
53. Ward, *Two Elizabethan Puritan Diaries*, 111.
54. Ward, *Two Elizabethan Puritan Diaries*, 112.
55. Ward, *Two Elizabethan Puritan Diaries*, 114.
56. Hooker, *Soules Preparation*, 87.

> To that same lot, however mean or high,
> Toward which Time leads me, and the will of Heaven.[57]

In addition to echoing a statement from Pindar's fourth Nemean ode about time's leading him toward his destiny, Milton adds a specifically Christian reference with his phrase "the will of Heaven." What does this phrase mean? In the Bible, and through centuries of English literature, the word *heaven* was a standard metonymy for God. A customary way to designate providence, in turn, was the word *will*, a practice that Milton adopts in his sonnet. Thomas Manton declared in a sermon on providence that "submitting all things to God's will after the event is patience, and submitting all things to God's will before the event is a notable piece of faith."[58] Richard Sibbes, in a treatise entitled "Of the Providence of God," speaks in his very first point about "resignation to God's will and guidance."[59] Thomas Watson defines providence as "the ordering of things after the counsel of God's will."[60] For William Ames, providence is God's activity "whereby he provides for existing creatures in all things in accordance with the counsel of his will."[61] Milton likewise affirms the leading of "the will of Heaven."

How important was the concept of providence to Puritan experience? It was a mainstay of their daily thinking. When the Puritan emigrant to New England Thomas Johnson came to write his history of the colony, he entitled his account *Wonder-Working Providence*. Providence was a standard Puritan topic for sermons and treatises. John Flavel wrote a 150-page treatise entitled *Divine Conduct or the Mystery of Providence Opened* (1678) in which he examined virtually every aspect of providence like a prism turned in the light. A sentence in the second paragraph of that book highlights how the Puritans felt about providence: "Indeed, it were not worth while to live in a world . . . devoid of God and Providence."[62]

Exactly what was this concept of providence that elicited this degree of enthusiasm among the Puritans? Providence was a very flexible and wide-ranging concept, but for purposes of Milton's Sonnet 7, two dimensions are relevant. Milton's phrase *leads me* in line 12 signals the first meaning of providence. Providence is God's guidance of human events according to his sovereign plan and goal. William Ames, in his discussion of providence, uses the word *government* as a synonym for providence, and he asserts as

57. Prince, *Italian Element in Milton's Verse*.
58. Manton, *Complete Works*, 331.
59. Sibbes, *Complete Works*, 5:35.
60. Watson, *Body of Divinity*, 119.
61. Ames, *Marrow of Theology*, 107.
62. Flavel, *Works*, 4:343.

part of the discussion that "government is the power whereby God directs and leads all his creatures to their proper end."[63] Richard Sibbes says similarly that God "guides our incomings and our outgoings; he disposes of our journeys."[64] Thomas Manton speaks of "the leading of Providence,"[65] and in the most famous definition of all—chapter 5 of *The Westminster Confession of Faith*—we read that "God the great Creator of all things does uphold, direct, dispose, and govern all creatures, actions, and things."[66] All of this lies behind Milton's imagery that time leads him.

But, of course, the concept of God's leading of people to an appointed end would not itself be consoling if it were not for a second aspect of the Puritan doctrine of providence, namely, the conviction that God's appointed goal is benevolent toward those who trust in him. Puritan sermons and treatises on providence are rooted in biblical texts, and the text most frequently referenced in Puritan discussions of providence is Romans 8:28, which in the King James Version reads, "And we know that all things work together for good to them that love God, to them who are the called according to his purpose."

Thomas Watson wrote an entire book on this verse entitled *A Divine Cordial*, and in the preface he stated, "To know that nothing hurts the godly, is a matter of comfort; but to be assured that ALL things which fall out shall co-operate for their good . . . may fill their hearts with joy till they run over."[67] Richard Sibbes also wrote a book on Romans 8:28, and he similarly claimed that the comfort that it affords "is the highest strain of consolation" and "the excellency of the saints' comfort, above all other comforts whatsoever."[68]

## THE PURITAN IDEAL OF STEWARDSHIP

In the last two lines of Milton's poem, the concept of providence branches out to the related doctrine of stewardship, as Milton states aphoristically, "All is, if I have grace to use it so, / As ever in my great Task-Master's eye." These lines are immediately winsome, but there is an elusive element in them as well, and in fact they have been variously interpreted.

---

63. Ames, *Marrow of Theology*, 109.
64. Sibbes, *Complete Works*, 5:35.
65. Manton, *Complete Works*, 332.
66. *Westminster Confession of Faith*, 3:612.
67. Watson, *Divine Cordial*, 6.
68. Sibbes, *Complete Works*, 5:272.

There are elements of ellipsis in the lines, and if we supply the missing words, the meaning is clear. "All is" was a common Renaissance idiom in which the word *all* carried the force "all that matters," or "the ultimately important thing." Thus, late in two of Shakespeare's most famous plays we read the summing-up statements that "the readiness is all" (*Hamlet*) and "the ripeness is all" (*King Lear*). Milton's cryptic assertion "all is" means "all that matters is." With that as a point of departure, here is what Milton's two magical lines say: "All that matters is that I have grace to use my time in such a way that I view myself as being always [*ever*] in my great Task-Master's eye." *Grace* carries the theological meaning of a gift from God.

The Puritan element in these lines is encapsulated in the epithet "my great Task-Master," accompanied by the image of God's "eye." These words refer to the doctrine of stewardship or service to the God who calls people to their tasks. Before I unpack the doctrinal ramifications of the reference to the "great Task-Master's eye," I want to assert the lexical point that this is common Puritan vocabulary by which to refer to God in his role as the one who calls people to their tasks and rewards them for their work. John Howe said that "the faithful servant . . . approves himself, in all that he doth, to the eye of his great Master."[69] "In all Places and in all Companies," wrote William Burkitt, "remember the Presence of God, and walk continually as under the view of his All-seeing and Observing Eye."[70] John Downame said that God gives his creatures talents to "improve them to the glory of our Master."[71] Cotton Mather wrote, "Let every Christian walk with God when he works at his calling . . . as under the eye of God."[72] In a discussion of work, Richard Baxter wrote, "Is it not a delightful thing to serve so great and good a Master, and to do that which God accepteth and promiseth to reward?"[73] We can see immediately the rootedness of Milton's image of "my great Taskmaster's eye" in his Puritan milieu.

The Puritan conception of stewardship viewed work as a personal response to God. Further, this response was viewed as a service to God first of all and to people secondarily. If we are accountable to earthly magistrates, claimed William Perkins, "then much more must every creature become accountable to God his Creator, for the duties of his calling, wherein he doth

---

69. Howe, *Works*, 3:395.
70. Burkitt, *Poor Man's Help*, 12.
71. Downame, *Guide to Godlinesse*, 167.
72. Mather, *Christian at His Calling*, 126.
73. Baxter, *Practical Works*, 1:381.

him homage and service."[74] Richard Sibbes wrote that "we must think our callings to be service of God, who hath appointed us our standing therein."[75]

In Milton's letter to his friend, he asserted that his sonnet, written "some while since," was such a convincing rebuttal of the friend's criticism that the friend "may well repent of having made mention at all of this matter."[76] To understand how this is true, we need to recover what the Puritans believed about stewardship. The effect of Milton's conclusion is to shift the focus away from accountability to people (even oneself) and toward accountability to God. The Puritan context for Milton's maneuver is as follows.

Richard Sibbes wrote, "God is the main object of all our service. Indeed, we serve men . . . , but . . . God is the object that must terminate all our service to men."[77] "One may be too much a pleaser of men," wrote John Howe, "but no man can too much study to please and approve himself to the eye of God. . . . He trusts his master for his final reward, and is content to wait for it."[78] Increase Mather, in a classic sermon entitled *David Serving His Generation*, theorized that "we Serve a better Master than is the Generation whom we Serve, we Serve the Lord Jesus Christ."[79] "We should do nothing but always as in God's presence," claimed Thomas Wilcox.[80] Richard Baxter exhorted his readers to do their work "as in [God's] sight, passing to his judgment, in obedience to his will."[81] Applying this to Milton's situation, he is accountable to God for his actions and not to people.

A common interpretation of Milton's Sonnet 7 is to see it as part of Milton's search for his vocation. I believe that in this sonnet the speaker performs an equally Puritan exercise of *confirming* his calling. This is a poem about the student's life. The problem associated with the student's calling is perennial and consists of a student's *taking in* year after year without adequate scope for *giving out* as an active member of society. Milton, in his letter to his friend, speaks of his life "as yet obscure and unserviceable to mankind."[82]

In the octave of Sonnet 7, Milton defines this problem that besets the student's calling. In the sestet he vindicates his calling as a student by viewing

74. Perkins, *Workes*, 1:777.
75. Sibbes, *Complete Works*, 1:243.
76. Milton, *CPW*, 1:320.
77. Sibbes, *Complete Works*, 6:498.
78. Howe, *Works*, 3:395.
79. Mather, *David Serving His Generation*, 29.
80. Wilcox, *Works*, 28.
81. Baxter, *Practical Works*, 1:97.
82. Milton, *CPW*, 1:319.

it as a life lived in accordance with God's providence and approved as a life of stewardship to God. Milton made good on his resolve as expressed in this poem: upon graduating from college, he moved home and spent the next five years in private study, further preparing for life and equipping himself to be a poet.

## Conclusions and Applications

James Holly Hanford, towering Miltonist of an earlier era, correctly claimed that Sonnet 7 "is perfect Puritanism in its soul-searching and its resignation, equally so in its assumption that God demands of his servants strenuousness as well as worship."[83] In its nuances, too, the poem draws upon Puritan thinking and feeling, including the introspective stance, the confessional strain, and ideas about time, providence, and stewardship.

The backbone of the poem—a quest to find a satisfying solution to a troublesome problem—invites comparison with other Miltonic poems. In his sonnet on his blindness written two decades after Sonnet 7, the newly blind Milton searches for a way to serve God acceptably in his reduced circumstances. Even closer to Sonnet 7 is Milton's elegy *Lycidas*, written some six years after Sonnet 7 when Milton's fellow student from Christ's College, Cambridge, died at sea. In his elegy, Milton searches for consolation in regard to a life prematurely terminated, and he finds refuge in the thought that what matters is not whether a person lived to achieve an expected goal, but rather that a person lived for God. E. M. W. Tillyard's formula is that in Milton's poem God's favor "depends on deeds, not on what those deeds effect."[84] This is a Puritan perspective, as captured by Richard Baxter's claim that "God looketh not . . . principally at the external part of the work, but much more to the heart of him that doth it."[85]

For those who knew Michael Travers well, there is an apparent connection between his life and Sonnet 7. Michael's academic life ended full but incomplete by ordinary expectations. He was a sound scholar, but due to his gracious demeanor and administrative proficiency, he was often redirected from the study and writing that he enjoyed to more mundane matters of budgets, policy, and assessment. His trek through several Christian institutions of higher learning prevented him from ever having a doctoral student to mentor. Michael sought to redeem the time by doing his work well, mentoring those who worked for him, and writing when he had the chance. This

---

83. Hanford, *John Milton*, 44.
84. Tillyard, *Milton*, 72.
85. Baxter, *Practical Works*, 1:111.

resonates, too, with the account of one of Lewis's students who observed: "His writing, apart from his two, big, learned books, was done mostly in the evenings, when he was too tired (as he once said to me) for serious work. He wrote because he could hardly stop himself, running off a few pages on return to his room late at night. . . . His primary energy went into his tutorial teaching."[86] So, too, Michael's best efforts went into the least enjoyable tasks, which he sought to do diligently, for the glory of God. One gets the sense, from Elizabeth Travers Parkers's essay and Michael's own chapter in this volume, what Michael may have accomplished academically given the time.

According to Milton and his fellow Puritans, what matters is Michael's life and actions themselves, even if his career ended prematurely by human standards. "All is" that Michael lived in an awareness of being in his great Task-Master's eye. God's estimate is based on the heart that served him, not a career completed, and this is our consolation in regard to Michael's passing.

## BIBLIOGRAPHY

Ames, William. *The Marrow of Theology*. Edited by John Dykstra Eusden. Grand Rapids: Baker, 1997.

Baxter, Richard. *The Practical Works of Richard Baxter*. 4 vols. Ligonier, PA: Soli Deo Gloria, 1990–91.

Bolton, Robert. *General Directions for a Comfortable Walking with God*. Morgan, PA: Soli Deo Gloria, 1991.

Brewer, Derek. "The Tutor: A Portrait." In *Remembering C. S. Lewis: Recollections of Those Who Knew Him*, edited by James Como, 115–51. San Francisco: Ignatius, 2005.

Burkitt, William. *The Poor Man's Help, and Young Man's Guide*. London: Parkhurst, 1701.

Calvin, John. *Institutes of the Christian Religion*. Edited by John T. McNeill. 2 vols. Philadelphia: Westminster Press, 1960.

Cheek, Macon. "Of Two Sonnets by Milton." In *Milton: Modern Essays in Criticism*, edited by Arthur E. Barker, 125–35. New York: Oxford University Press, 1965.

Cotton, John. *Christ the Fountain of Life*. London: Ibbitson, 1651.

Downame, John. *The Christian Warfare*. London: Cuthbert Burby, 1604.

———. *A Guide to Godlinesse*. London: Stephens and Meredith, 1629.

Eaton, Richard. *A Sermon Preached at the Funeralls of that Worthie and Worshipfull Gentleman, Master Thomas Dutton*. London: Legatt, 1616.

Fish, Stanley. *Surprised by Sin: The Reader in Paradise Lost*. New York: St. Martin's, 1967.

Flavel, John. *The Works of John Flavel*. 6 vols. Edinburgh: Banner of Truth Trust, 1968.

---

86. Brewer, "The Tutor: A Portrait," 117.

Hambrick-Stowe, Charles E. *The Practice of Piety: Puritan Devotional Disciplines in Seventeenth-Century New England*. Chapel Hill: University of North Carolina, 1982.
Hanford, James Holly. *John Milton, Englishman*. New York: Crown, 1949.
Hoignman, E. A. J., ed. *Milton's Sonnets*. New York: St. Martin's, 1966.
Hook, William. *Puritan Sermons 1659-1689*. 6 vols. Wheaton: Roberts, 1981.
Hooker, Thomas. *The Soules Preparation for Christ*. London: Crooke, 1838.
Howe, John. *The Works of John Howe*. 3 vols. Ligonier, PA: Soli Deo Gloria, 1990.
Lewis, C. S. *Christian Reflections*. Grand Rapids: Eerdmans, 1967.
———. *The Collected Letters of C. S. Lewis*. 3 vols. San Francisco: HarperSanFrancisco, 2004.
———. *An Experiment in Criticism*. Cambridge; Cambridge University Press, 1961.
———. *A Preface to Paradise Lost*. New York: Oxford University Press, 1942.
———. *Reflections on the Psalms*. New York: HarperOne, 2017.
Manton, Thomas. *The Complete Works of Thomas Manton*. Edinburgh: Banner of Truth Trust, 1993.
Mather, Cotton. *The Christian at His Calling, in Puritanism and the American Experience*. Edited by Michael McGiffert. Reading, MA: Addison-Wesley, 1969.
Mather, Increase. *David Serving His Generation*. Boston: Green and Allen, 1698.
Milton, John. *The Complete Prose Works of John Milton*. Edited by Don M. Wolfe. 8 vols. Yale University Press, 1953-82.
Perkins, William. *The Workes of the Famous and Worthy Minister of Christ . . . William Perkins*. 3 vols. London: Legatt, 1626.
Prince, F. T. *The Italian Element in Milton's Verse*. Oxford: Oxford University Press, 1954.
Reynolds, Edward. *True Gain, Opened in a Sermon Preached at Pauls*. London: Thomason, 1659.
Rogers, Richard. *Two Elizabethan Puritan Diaries by Richard Rogers and Samuel Ward*. Edited by M. M. Knappen. Gloucester: Smith, 1966.
Sibbes, Richard. *The Complete Works of Richard Sibbes*. 7 vols. Edinburgh: Nichol, 1862-64.
Strong, Augustus. *The Great Poets and Their Theology*. Philadelphia: American Baptist Publication Society, 1897.
Swinnock, George. *The Works of George Swinnock*. 5 vols. Edinburgh: Nichol, 1868.
Tillyard, E. M. W. *Milton*. New York: Collier, 1966.
Watson, Thomas. *The Beatitudes*. Edinburgh: Banner of Truth Trust, 1977.
———. *A Body of Divinity*. Edinburgh: Banner of Truth Trust, 1965.
———. *A Divine Cordial*. Wilmington, DE: Cornerstone, 1975.
"Westminster Confession of Faith." In *The Creeds of Christendom*, edited by Philip Schaff, 3:555-61. Grand Rapids: Baker, 1966.
Whately, William. *Prototypes*. London: Edwards, 1640.
Wilcox, Thomas. *The Works of that Late Reverend and Learned Divine, Mr. Thomas Wilcocks*. London: Haviland, 1624.

# 13

# The Christian Mind of Michael Travers

*Andrew J. Spencer*

I FIRST MET MICHAEL Travers at a C. S. Lewis conference in 2007. It is unlikely he would have remembered me from that meeting, since I was one among dozens of students attending a conference that he coordinated through the L. Russ Bush Center for Faith and Culture at Southeastern Baptist Theological Seminary. I heard him introduce the speakers and interact with conference presenters. The overall impression he gave out was of a kind, courteous man.

My first sustained interaction with Michael was when I joined the staff at Southeastern.[1] He was a senior administrator, and I was an entry-level clerk of sorts. Nevertheless, my initial impression of the man was confirmed and even deepened. I witnessed a man who was consistently thoughtful, careful, and wise. Thus, when he called me to ask me to apply for a more advanced position at Oklahoma Baptist University, I was willing to consider it and eventually accepted the position. By the time I moved to Oklahoma, Michael was already well into his cancer treatments. Despite his fight against cancer, he had accepted a promotion to assistant provost on top of his role as department head and faculty member. Throughout his chemotherapy, Michael did not miss any meetings and only

---

1. I will refer to Michael Travers by his first name when discussing personal anecdotes, since he was a good friend. When I discuss his academic work, I will use his last name as a formal address.

rarely left for a few hours around lunch to take a nap and combat his fatigue. He was, no matter how he was feeling, more concerned with the well-being of others than himself.

That was Michael. In the short time I knew him, and by the testimony of many others, he was a man that largely embodied the Christian mind. That is, no doubt, thanks to his saturation with C. S. Lewis and John Milton. The years spent reading and writing about the Bible as literature and teaching students to carefully read literature as a spiritual discipline no doubt shaped his mind, as well. But all of those were the fruit of the gospel in his life, which he sought to share with others in his administrative and academic work.

This chapter is the conclusion of the volume. It is a tribute to the man whose life was a blessing to the authors of the essays in this book. In this chapter I will outline Michael Travers's biography, work through major themes in his academic work, and conclude by pointing to the hope that Michael had in the gospel.

## BIOGRAPHY

Michael Ernest Travers was born and raised in Niagara Falls, Ontario. He was from a working-class family, and he grew up in an environment that valued work of all kinds. Michael was recognized as an especially bright young man, which pointed toward a promising future, and also set him up for a sense of independence that would shape his early spiritual journey.

His family ensured he was raised under the ministry of the Anglican Church of Canada, the largest mainline Protestant denomination in that country. However, when his father died after a lengthy illness, Michael rebelled against the concepts of God he had been taught as a child. Although he would not have described himself as an atheist, Michael felt that if there was a God of the sort that would let his father die, he was sufficiently intelligent and capable to do without that God.

The death of Michael's father in the spring of his sixteenth year shaped him. His family was left in a precarious position financially, with several boys to feed and too little income. Due to the length of his father's illness, the company balked at paying out on a life insurance policy. This provided a challenge that revealed the character of Michael Travers. Rather than despair or accept the loss, Michael presented the case to the union steward that the company ought to honor the life insurance policy. His argument must have been compelling, because he won the day.

Michael went on to attend McMaster University, where he earned an honors Bachelor of Arts in English in 1970. An extra year of study entailed in the honors degree enabled him to complete his Master of Arts in just one additional year; following that, he earned a diploma in education that allowed him to teach in Canada's public schools from 1972–1979.

It was during his year-long master's program that Michael came to Christ. Each summer while Michael was in high school and university, he worked for the Niagara Parks Commission. A man named Mac Cushing was responsible for hiring summer workers. As a faithful member of the Christian Businessman's Association, Cushing also was active in sharing the gospel. He did so each year with Michael, persistently holding out the hope of the good news in Christ. But Michael, assured of his ability to get by without God, did not respond favorably to Cushing's evangelization. Indeed, by Michael's own testimony, he looked down on his boss for his "foolish" and "simple" belief that he needed a savior.

Despite his assurance of his own independence from God, Michael was miserable, especially under the heavy workload of his master's program. Michael found himself unable to sleep at night during the winter of 1971, so he took up running. Each night he would run until he was exhausted so that he could fall into bed and sleep. One night, he became overwrought with the stress and strain. He found himself kneeling in the snow on one of his runs, weeping and crying to God to reveal himself clearly. At that moment, he had an incredible peace and a sense of hope from the gospel. Most remarkably for those who knew Michael, he instantly went from being a very foul-mouthed, profane young man, to one who never swore. By his account, the transition was not one of his own effort, but an instantaneous blessing from God as a sign of his conversion. So the seeds of the gospel planted by a faithful business man took root and grew.

There are some obvious parallels between Michael's conversion and C. S. Lewis's. This is a point that Michael himself recognized and it is, in part, what drew him to Lewis studies later in his academic career. However, Michael had not yet discovered the power of the Christian mind, in its ability to integrate all areas of life, nor was he aware of the work of C. S. Lewis.

After his conversion and his marriage, Michael remained in Canada, teaching English to high schoolers. Then, in 1979, he and his wife, Barbara, felt called to pursue careers in Christian higher education. Michael subsequently applied to positions at a number of General Association of Regular Baptist (GARB) affiliated colleges. The only one that demonstrated interest was Grand Rapids Baptist College, which is now Cornerstone University, so the Travers family packed up and headed to Michigan.

Although Michael spent only four years in Grand Rapids in that first appointment, this was a vital period in his academic and spiritual development. Through the influence of Jim Greir, who would later rise to be academic dean of Grand Rapids Theological Seminary, and interaction with the neo-Kuyperian ideas from neighboring Calvin College, Michael became both a confirmed Calvinist and an advocate for the integration of faith and learning. During this time Michael completed coursework for a PhD in English at Michigan State University. However, due to his growing family and the financial constraints of his college, Michael and Barbara found themselves struggling and seeking another opportunity to exercise their gifts.

In the fall of 1981, Michael resigned his position effective the end of the academic year. He had been offered a job teaching English at a private Christian school in London, Ontario. However, on a trip through the city to visit family, Barbara and Michael were surprised to find that the institution had changed its mind and had filled the position with another candidate without informing them. Michael found himself looking for another appointment. This time it came from Liberty Baptist College in Lynchburg, Virginia. The Travers drove from Grand Rapids to Lynchburg. They had twenty-five dollars in their pockets and an expectation that God would continue to provide. The offer of employment was a blessing that confirmed God's faithfulness to them.

At Liberty, Michael became acquainted with Richard Patterson, an Old Testament and Hebrew scholar who would be instrumental in Michael's later interest in the Psalms and his careful work on the Bible as literature, with a heavy emphasis on the Old Testament. Within three years, Michael had finished his dissertation on the devotional poetry of John Milton. Michael's interest in Milton is another strong connection with C. S. Lewis, though Michael had not interacted with Lewis since his childhood (at which time he was unimpressed with what he read of *The Chronicles of Narnia*). Though Travers wrote a chapter on *Paradise Lost* in his dissertation, he never considered Lewis's book on the subject.

At some point after he completed his dissertation, in the midst of mind-stretching interdisciplinary conversations among the faculty at Liberty, Michael discovered the wonder of C. S. Lewis. His life would never quite be the same. Even as his intellect flourished, he was troubled by the shifting outlook of his institution. After seven years, the flourishing period the Travers experienced in Lynchburg came to a close, and Michael felt called to serve in another location.

Michael was able to return to Grand Rapids Baptist College as a professor of English in 1989 and rose to the Chair of the Division of Humanities in 1991. During this time as division chair, Michael honed his administrative skills and realized he had a gifting in that area, too. Meanwhile, a large number of students flocked to Michael, growing the English department to record numbers. This was a common theme wherever Michael taught. Students lined up to study with him. (This remained true throughout his life. Even as a white-haired, formal, bow-tie-wearing old man, his classes were always full and his students consistently raved about his teaching on their anonymous feedback forms.[2])

Others began to recognize Michael's administrative gifting, as well, so in 1993, he was recruited by a former colleague to serve as Chair of the English department at Mississippi College in Jackson. Michael continued to explore his passion for the integration of faith and all areas of life as the leader of the English faculty. As he grew the English major in numbers, he also began to write about C. S. Lewis based on the recommendation of a colleague who had heard so much about Lewis from Michael. This was the beginning of a busy period of academic researching and publication by Michael.

In 1997, Michael was named the Humanities Scholar of the Year by the Mississippi Humanities Council. He presented several papers on C. S. Lewis and, in the summer of 1999, spent the summer researching Lewis at the Marion Wade Center in Wheaton, Illinois. He was named a Clyde S. Kilby Research Fellow for his research on a book, which was to be coauthored with Bruce Edwards, but which sadly never came to fruition.

Around the time of this extensive research in Lewis studies, Michael stepped down from his administrative role at Mississippi College to begin writing a book on the Psalms, which would later become *Encountering God in the Psalms*. This volume demonstrates the quality of Michael's scholarship and unmistakably bears the marks of a Christian mind influenced by C. S. Lewis. The work offers the best aspects of a belief in the truthfulness of Scripture and the power of poetry. Travers offers an academically sound discourse on the Psalms that teaches readers to read poetry better and stand in the place of the authors, looking where they are pointing.

In 2002, Michael was recruited to serve on the faculty of the College at Southeastern, a very small institution that originally served as a feeder program for Southeastern Baptist Theological Seminary. Michael was instrumental in helping build the humanities curriculum and growing the tiny college into a vibrant (but still small) undergraduate institution, which has come to be a viable institution apart from its tie to the seminary. The president who hired Michael stated that he was delighted to find a sound scholar of literature so deeply invested in helping others see the truthfulness of Scripture and the beauty of the divine author behind it.

---

2. My positions at Southeastern Seminary and Oklahoma Baptist University gave me access to all of the course evaluations.

Michael's tenure at Southeastern was intellectually fruitful. He was able to work in an interdisciplinary environment again, since the offices of seminary and college faculty were not separated. The college was also too small to divide into isolated cliques by department, thus it better embodied the idea of a university than many modern institutions of higher learning. This was the sort of integration of faith and all knowledge that Michael so richly enjoyed and strove to encourage wherever he worked.

When Danny Akin was appointed president at Southeastern, the institution began to move more significantly toward publicly engaging the culture as salt and light. Thus, the L. Russ Bush Center for Faith and Culture was founded in 2006. In the early days of the center, Michael proposed an academic conference, "C. S. Lewis: The Man and His Works, a 21st Century Legacy." This conference was one of the first major events of the Bush Center, and it was a rousing success for the institution, drawing scholars from diverse backgrounds and disciplines to discuss the work of a man, Lewis, who embodied the Christian mind. It cemented Travers's academic reputation among the faculty, illustrated his administrative skill, and confirmed the decision for choosing him to be a Senior Fellow of the center. It also became a turning point for many students at the seminary and college in their understanding and appreciation of the Christian mind of C. S. Lewis. The volume, *C. S Lewis: Views from Wake Forest*, which Michael edited, was a product of that conference.

By 2008, Michael had begun to miss the opportunities to lead and shape the culture of an institution afforded through administration. Therefore, when Louisiana College sought him out, he accepted the opportunity to serve as Dean of the College and Vice President for Academic Affairs. The decision was good for the faculty of that institution, but a significant strain for Michael and Barbara. Michael was a stabilizing force in a campus culture about to be racked by scandal. There was turmoil at the top of the leadership structure at Louisiana College, which included intrigue and accusations that would later result in court cases and accreditation board inquiries. Working in this situation was a significant test for a man of integrity like Michael. In the summer between Michael's two years at the institution, while in Oxford on a study tour, Michael and Barbara agreed that they needed to move on from the institution.

Despite the trials of his two years at Louisiana College, Michael's time there was not wasted. By the testimony of several faculty, he was the only person in senior leadership who understood the integration of faith and learning, which gave hope to some of the faculty and spurred some on to faithfulness. Despite the significant turmoil on the campus, Michael offered a steadying force. And yet, he felt compelled to leave to preserve his integrity.

On a return visit to Wake Forest, North Carolina, Michael was offered an open door to return to Southeastern. The institution was initially unable to find someone who could fill his shoes. Therefore, once signs of the impending scandal at Louisiana College became public, the College at Southeastern made little effort to fill the position, expecting to get Michael back.

After moving back to work at Southeastern again, it became clear that the return to Wake Forest was providential. The decennial accreditation reaffirmation was looming, and the institution was not prepared—although the school was strong, much of the legwork had not been done to make the best argument for the renewal of their accreditation. Michael's calm, systematic administrative style was a necessary remedy. In the end, Michael's return to Southeastern helped the institution pull the necessary evidence together to show that the school should continue to be accredited. This was no small feat, which made Michael the obvious choice to serve as acting Vice President for Academic Affairs when the incumbent was on sabbatical. Michael had a clear vision and a steady hand.

Michael was, again, a very popular faculty member among the students at Southeastern. In his last episode at Southeastern he taught primarily at the undergraduate level, but also had the opportunity to teach at the graduate level in several courses on C. S. Lewis. Based on student ratings, Travers was given the Excellence in Teaching Award. The award came as a surprise only to Michael.

He did not stay long at Southeastern, though. He taught English and served as Associate Vice President for Institutional Effectiveness until the end of the spring semester in 2013. At that point, Michael stepped down from administration with the intention of writing. He had several book projects on C. S. Lewis he wanted to write.

However, during the following academic year, the administration of Oklahoma Baptist University recruited Michael. Initially, Michael had no intention of moving to Oklahoma. He travelled to Shawnee for an interview with no expectation of taking the job. But while in Shawnee he and Barbara felt a sense of calling to that institution. So, Michael and Barbara again packed up their belongings and moved to start a new adventure. Michael was hired at OBU to be an associate dean of the College of Humanities and Social Sciences, but primarily to serve as the department chair and professor of English. In part, Michael was brought in to help the institution better integrate faith and learning.

The scope of Michael's role would increase within another year, however. He was promoted to Associate Provost after the 2014–15 academic year. The institution was ramping up for an accreditation renewal and needed his administrative skill. Adding to OBU's concern, the Director of Assessment had recently resigned, which left OBU in desperate need of someone with experience in the process of accreditation. It was during this time that Michael contacted me, and I accepted the offer to move my family over a thousand miles from anywhere we had ever lived. In part, my decision was made because of the opportunity to work with Michael.

Simply looking at his *curriculum vitae*, it might not seem surprising that Michael would accept the promotion, since he had previously served in senior leadership at two institutions. However, he was undergoing treatment for an advanced stage of prostate cancer, which had spread into his bones, in the season leading to his promotion. Additionally, there was no reduction in his administrative burden from his role as department chair and associate dean. A man with an uncertain future and ongoing treatment took additional responsibility because he was asked. Such was Michael's character.

During Michael's illness, his first thought was rarely for himself. During the most exhausting portions of his treatment, Michael did not miss meetings and only missed class for necessary appointments. In fact, until the final weeks of his life, outside of his actual treatment times, he rarely missed any work. This was not because Michael found his identity in his work. Rather, it was because he believed the work of educating students in the Christian liberal arts tradition to be worth the sacrifice.

Few, I think, recognized the significance of Michael's endurance. There were a number of times when I would find him in his office, back to the door, gasping as a wave of pain from the cancer in his bones washed over him. About a year before his death, Michael experienced one of these bouts of agony while in a restaurant at a conference. As the tears welled in his eyes, his first thought was to apologize for groaning softly in public and not finishing his sentence. Such a response may seem to be stereotypically Canadian, but for Michael it was a sign of his character. All we could think to do was stop and pray for him. Thankfully, these fits of intense pain were typically short. Yet Michael's response to this excruciating pain was characteristic: he did not want to be a burden to others.

At the end of his life, Michael's loves for the Psalms and for C. S. Lewis were only enhanced. If he was not wrestling with an administrative problem or preparing for class (he taught up until the day he was hospitalized for the last time), I was likely to find him poring over the Psalms or reading from the *Chronicles of Narnia*. Lindsey Panxhi provides some insight from her time working nearby: "Michael told me that one afternoon when he was feeling particularly ill, he spent his time re-reading *The Voyage of the Dawn Treader*, his favorite of the *Chronicles of Narnia*." His focus on the eschaton only increased as he looked toward Aslan's country.

Michael's stamina began fading more significantly during the autumn of 2016. He still taught several courses that semester, but actually requested a load reduction for the spring semester. The reason he gave was to be able to focus on the upcoming accreditation, but I think a contributing factor was the knowledge that the ongoing treatments and continued damage from his cancer were sapping his strength.

In the spring semester of 2017, Michael was scheduled to teach only one course. It was a course on C. S. Lewis. He had told me several times during the fall how much he was looking forward to that Lewis course. As Panxhi aptly notes, "So great was his love of the material that he taught up until he entered hospice care in February, at which point I had the challenge and privilege of teaching the course for the rest of the semester." What she says is perfectly true. When Michael went into the hospital for the last time on the 8th of February, the administration's thought was only that he would need a few weeks off to get some rest. That is exactly what the Travers family was hoping for, too. This turned out not to be the case.

Despite being in the hospital with his body failing, Michael was sending emails from his tablet and doing basic administrative work. During a visit with the Provost, Stan Norman, he made sure to send back word to me with some mundane details that he was afraid we would forget. I have emails from that time, typed by his wife Barbara, about administrative details that seemed important to him.

A week after his hospitalization the doctors were beginning to speak about discharge. However, that was not to be. Michael's condition worsened. The strain on his body had been too much and it became clear that the end of the fight would be sooner, rather than later. Michael entered hospice care on February 24th.

In those last days, I think Michael became even more like Reepicheep, longing for his true and better home. I visited him in his last few days in an austere, joyless hospice facility. His family was gathered by his side, waiting for him to pass. Although he could not speak because of his weakness and the oxygen in his nose, he mouthed the words "Thank you" to me, as if I had done him a favor by coming to say goodbye. A few days later, Michael's coracle crested the great wave, and he headed into Aslan's country on March 2nd, 2017.

## ACADEMIC WORK

Throughout his many years of service in Christian higher education, Travers was also a reasonably productive scholar. His work is not flashy in content or prolific in volume, but it is, like the man himself, steady, faithful, and well-reasoned. Travers's published work falls into three basic categories: Milton studies, the Bible as literature, and C. S. Lewis studies.

## *The Work of John Milton*

The devotional poets became a subject of interest for Travers during his doctoral studies at Michigan State University. He took a course on the subject and, since he was becoming more deeply rooted in the Calvinistic worldview at the same time, took a particular interest in Milton, a late Puritan. The end product was a dissertation, later published by the Edwin Mellen Press as *The Devotional Experience in the Poetry of John Milton*.

Like most dissertations, Travers's first book-length project is significant for the quality of its research rather than the beauty of its prose. It also bears the marks of a research project from the 1980s, with a much smaller number of sources than would be expected today. The book shows all the signs of academic research and publishing during the infancy of word processors and personal computers.

And yet, despite the limitation of *The Devotional Experience in the Poetry of John Milton*, the reader finds a project that is consistent with how Travers lived his own life and helped others to live theirs. In his introduction, he lays out his thesis: "I wish to argue that Milton's own devotion to God is an active expression of his love for God and that he communicates this devotion in his view of poetry and in the experience of the speakers and characters in his poems."[3]

Milton's poetry is not art for art's sake. There is no divide between the spiritual devotion of the blind poet and the literature he created. Instead, Milton's artistic works were designed to point other people toward something worth looking at—the God of the Bible. Helping people to see where he was pointing was the reason he wrote. Travers's dissertation aptly walks through Milton's major works to show how his faith was woven through what he wrote. One reviewer notes, "In reading Travers's effective analysis of Milton's poetic disclosure of true devotional experience, particularly in his character development, I slowly discovered his own 'movement': from analysis to self-knowledge in the knowledge of God. Thus, Travers's scholarly and readable interpretation of Milton actually is an aid toward that which Milton himself desired to progress."[4]

The approach of his dissertation is consistent with how Travers treats Milton in a conference paper dealing with the themes of creation and fall in

---

3. Travers, *Devotional Experience*, 1.
4. Morrison, Review of *The Devotional Experience*, 403–4.

*Paradise Lost*.[5] In this paper, he does the basic work of the scholar well. He deals with Milton's text fairly, in accordance with the approved academic approaches. However, the choice of themes is illustrative of Travers's interests, and more significantly, of his understanding of the real purpose of Milton's writing. Travers looks to where Milton is pointing—the biblical themes and theological paradigms that flow from the Puritanical poet. The epic poem is less important than the greater truths that are interpreted within it.

## The Bible as Literature

The second major interest in Travers's academic career is the Bible as literature. This is where the greatest volume of his work was focused. Much of his work in this vein was coauthored with a peer from Liberty Baptist College, Richard Patterson. Since Patterson was an Old Testament professor, that is where much of their work was focused. The work they did together logically emphasized the literary aspects of Scripture. Thus, "Literary Analysis and the Unity of Nahum" in 1988 and "Nahum: Poet Laureate of the Minor Prophets" in 1990.

Their project was, broadly speaking, to revive interest among evangelicals in the beautiful literary qualities of Scripture. In the last two decades of the twentieth century, conservative biblical scholars were highly invested in careful textual analysis and hedging the orthodox theological traditions off from theological liberalism. However, that emphasis on rigorous truthfulness came at the cost of sometimes missing the soul-stirring wonder of the text of the Bible itself. As Patterson and Travers wrote, "Literary studies are important to Biblical scholarship because, on one level at least, the Bible is a literary book. Unfortunately, however, much traditional Biblical scholarship has ignored the literary features of the Scriptures."[6]

At a basic level, Travers was helping his readers to learn to read again. Much of the value in *Encountering God in the Psalms* is in being taught how to read poetry. He concludes the first chapter, "Reading the Psalms as poems is actually an enjoyable experience. When we read the Psalms the way they were written, we will begin to appreciate the beauty God inspired in the Bible. In fact, reading the Psalms as poetry will give us a fuller appreciation of who God is and what he has done for his people."[7] The reader is encouraged to look carefully at the text, but more significantly, to look where the psalmists were pointing. Thus, Travers both carefully handles the texts of

---

5. Travers, "'Light Out of Darkness' and 'Good Out of Evil.'"
6. Patterson and Travers, "Nahum," 438.
7. Travers, *Encountering God in the Psalms*, 43.

selected psalms in his book and shows how they can be read and enjoyed as literary works. *Encountering God in the Psalms* may be Travers's most significant work. According to one reviewer, "The volume's strength is in Travers's purpose to create an attitude of worship in the reader. Preachers and lay people alike will benefit from this catalyst for a devotional study of Psalms."[8]

Travers also wrote several journal articles and papers on the Psalms and their historical interpretation. All of them focused on rightly reading the text and drawing from it the consistent theological significance. This is well evidenced in the 2010 paper presented to the Evangelical Theological Society's national meeting in 2010, "'Severe Delight': The Paradox of Praise in Confession of Sin." Here Travers traced the sorrow of sin leading to absolute joy in deliverance from its penalty. The paper is faithful to the texts of Scripture, but unquestionably focused on drawing its audience into a deeper devotional relationship with God in Christ. This is scholarship for the glory of God.

Another significant aspect of the work Travers did on the Bible as literature was to trace out symbols in Scripture. Again, this is part of teaching Christians how to read. This shows up in his contribution of a chapter to *Cracking Old Testament Codes*, entitled "Literary Forms and Interpretation."[9] It is also apparent in the five articles he contributed to *A Dictionary of Biblical Imagery* in 1998.

The interest in typology and symbols in the Bible continued even to the end of his career. In 2008, Patterson and Travers again teamed up on a project for Bible.org. Those who knew Travers well will recognize that contributing material to a website falls outside of his typical pattern of behavior, but helping people to read the Bible does not. He contributed a number of articles on figurative language like references to God's eyes, God's ears, and other anthropomorphic symbols. In these articles, Travers does the hard work of tracing through references to images throughout Scripture, helps the reader make sense of them, and most significantly, points people toward the true goodness of God. This paragraph from his article on images of God's ear is representative:

> Who are we that God should hear our prayers? He made the heavens and the earth by the word of his power. He sustains the universe. He is righteous and holy. He is the God of the nations. Why would he listen to any one of us? Because he loves us. We call the love that God lavishes on his people *hesed* love. . . . This

---

8. Barrick, Review of *Encountering God in the Psalms*, 138–39.
9. Travers, "Literary Forms and Interpretation," 29–44.

love saves and forgives us, sanctifies us, and provides for us. This is the love that allows us to call God "our Father," for it places us in God's family. And it is because of this love (and not because of anything good in us) that God hears us when we call upon him.[10]

The purpose of reading Scripture well—that is, reading it for its literary quality—is to more faithfully relate to the God of the universe. Just like John Milton, Travers was not writing articles for their own sake, but with the hope of pointing people toward holiness.

## The Christian Mind of C. S. Lewis

The general theme of Travers's academic work was to point people toward something greater, which is reflected in the third major theme in Travers's academic work: the work of C. S. Lewis. It should not be surprising that a significant portion of Travers's academic work deals with Lewis. As discussed above, Lewis's work became a topic of interest for Travers because of the shared interests in Milton, literature in general, and the influence of Christianity through all of life. There was a consistent effort to point others toward Christ by forming in them the Christian mind.

For Travers, the most interesting aspect of the work of C. S. Lewis was his eschatological vision. Both Travers and Lewis were careful to distance their discussions of eschatology from speculation about the date and exact nature of the end times.[11] Both emphasized the abiding hope offered by a vision of the divinely-initiated new creation. According to Clyde Kilby, "Lewis's apocalyptic vision is perhaps more real than anyone since St. John on Patmos."[12] That reality of the eschatological vision gave great comfort to Travers as he suffered from cancer, and it guided much of his work as a scholar and administrator.

In fact, eschatology was the topic of some of the first academic work Travers did on C. S. Lewis. In a conference paper from his days at Mississippi College, Travers traced the eschatological images in Lewis's fiction. This particular paper emphasized the earthly apocalypse in *That Hideous Strength* and the more fantastical one in *The Last Battle*. The point, however, is clearly not sensationalism, but that eschatology "pricks our longing to be

---

10. Travers, "O God, Listen To My Prayer," 126. There was a limited run of print copies made of this material, but the primary purpose was to populate the Bible.org website.

11. For example, Lewis, "World's Last Night," 42–53.

12. Kilby, *Christian World of C. S. Lewis*, 187.

in God's presence in heaven."[13] He notably follows this poignant comment by quoting one of his favorite passages of C. S. Lewis: "I believe in Christianity as I believe that the Sun has risen, not only because I see it, but because by it I see everything else."[14]

Lewis's vision of Christianity helped Travers to explain hope in Christ to the world around him. In an essay on free will in *Perelandra*, Travers navigates that contentious doctrine of the sovereignty of God, which continues to be a lightning rod in the Southern Baptist Convention, in which Travers worked and taught for decades. In *Perelandra*, readers see the first female, Tindril, choose between sin and obedience. The connections between Lewis's account and that from John Milton's *Paradise Lost* are unmistakable, and Travers does not fail to show the link. However, in reading Travers's article, it is clear that his interest is less in the literary connection between two imaginative works than in the theological point that Lewis and Milton are making—namely, obedience to God is the response to union with him.[15] The purpose of the Christian mind is to be united with God both positionally and cognitively.

There is a clear cognitive element in Lewis's Christianity, particularly through his exploration of the truthfulness of the Christian myth. In a book that never came to fruition, Travers intended to trace out the idea in Lewis that myth became fact in Christ. He wrote, "Lewis believes that all human beings long for heaven, even when most could not admit it, and that the narrative of the human condition can be told in terms of a journey in search of heaven."[16] All of the themes of Travers's work come together in this fragment from 2014: the unity of Scripture, the importance of the devotional experience in all of life, and the hope that can be found only in Christ. He saw "life as a pilgrimage with heaven as its destination."[17]

In one of his last public presentations, Travers read a paper aptly named "Invitation to Glory: C. S. Lewis's Apologetic of Hope." He delivered this paper both as a faculty lecture at Southeastern Baptist Theological Seminary and at a conference memorializing Lewis on the fiftieth anniversary of his death.[18] Travers sums up the nature of the Christian mind and why Lewis remains so popular decades after his death: "C. S. Lewis reminds readers that this longing for God, this hope of heaven, is the proper state for all of

---

13. Travers, "Further Up and Further In."
14. Lewis, "Is Theology Poetry?," 21.
15. Travers, "Free to Fall," 154.
16. Travers, "Myth Became Fact," 1.
17. Travers, "Myth Became Fact," 21.
18. This paper has been published as chapter 2 of this volume.

us in a fallen world. Our culture needs to remember what it means to be human: we are created in the image of God and for the purpose of praising God."

Travers would have never claimed it, but looking back on the themes within his work, he could have been describing his own academic efforts as he described Lewis's: "All of Lewis's writings encourage his readers to long for God and to hope for heaven. And it is fitting that this is so, for the longer we live in communion with Christ, the more we long to see him face to face." Though less prolific than Lewis, Travers's writing embodies the Christian mind, which points people toward Christ and deeper communion with him. That is an accomplishment worthy of significant praise.

## CONCLUSION

For those who knew him, Michael Travers leaves many good memories, but also the sad sense that he had more work to be done. While suffering from cancer, he prayed for another decade to continue his work. He would have been delighted to have partially retired after his last great administrative project (the 2017 accreditation reaffirmation at OBU) to teach part-time and to write on hope and love in C. S. Lewis. Alas, that was not to be. Travers was enough of a Calvinist to recognize that any shortening of his life could not happen apart from the will of God. His hope was always set on the future glory for which all Christians long.

All in all, though he had projects left to complete, these words I wrote to him in an email just a few days before his death capture well my view of his legacy, which I believe to be shared by many others who knew him:

> If there are moments of doubt in these waning hours, know that by the observation of many—including me—your life has been well spent. We can all certainly mourn the hours and days spent in useless worry and selfish ambition. However, as someone coming alongside you rather late in the story and hearing what many others have had to say, I can assure you that your time has been well spent on the whole. That is no little accomplishment for a lifetime. In a few days you will stand before the master in a healed, pain-free body and hear him say, "Well done, good and faithful servant."

When I reach glory, I expect to see him there standing close to C. S. Lewis, nearer to the throne of grace than I will be. Those two men will be talking about joy and love, basking in the fulfillment of the deep longing for

Christ: the longing that led them to him in the first place and shaped their Christian minds while on this earth.

My hope, and the hope of the other authors of this book, is that this volume written in Michael Travers's honor serves as an invitation for readers to acquire the same longing for eternal union with God in Christ that Lewis and Travers shared. That longing is fulfilled only through faith in the perfect life, substitutionary death, and miraculous resurrection of Christ. This is no less than an invitation to put on the Christian mind.

## BIBLIOGRAPHY

Barrick, William D. Review of *Encountering God in the Psalms*, by Michael Travers. *The Master's Seminary Journal* 18.1 (Spring 2007) 138–39.

Kilby, Clyde. *The Christian World of C. S. Lewis*. Grand Rapids: Eerdmans, 1964.

Lewis, C. S. "Is Theology Poetry?" In *C. S. Lewis: Essay Collection and Other Short Pieces*, edited by Lesley Walmsley, 10–21. London: HarperCollins, 2000.

———. "The World's Last Night." In *C. S. Lewis: Essay Collection and Other Short Pieces*, edited by Lesley Walmsley, 42–53. London: HarperCollins, 2000.

Morrison, John. Review of *The Devotional Experience in the Poetry of John Milton*, by Michael Travers. *Journal of the Evangelical Theological Society* 34.3 (September 1991) 403–4.

Patterson, Richard, and Michael Travers. "Nahum: Poet Laureate of the Minor Prophets." *Journal of the Evangelical Theological Society* 33.4 (December 1990) 437–44.

Travers, Michael. *The Devotional Experience in the Poetry of John Milton*. Lewiston: Mellen, 1988.

———. *Encountering God in the Psalms*. Grand Rapids: Kregel, 2003.

———. "Free to Fall: The Moral Ground of Events on Perelandra." In *C. S. Lewis's Perelandra: Reshaping the Image of the Cosmos*, edited by Judith Wolfe and Brendan Wolf, 144–55. Kent: Kent State University Press, 2013.

———. "'Further Up and Further In: Eschatological Images in the Fiction of C. S. Lewis." Unpublished essay from his personal papers, n.d.

———. "'Light Out of Darkness' and 'Good Out of Evil': Creation and Fall in John Milton's Paradise Lost." Paper presented to the Evangelical Theological Society, 2012, Milwaukee, WI.

———. "Literary Forms and Interpretation." In *Cracking the Old Testament Code*, edited by Brent D. Sandy and Ronald Giese, 29–44. Nashville: B&H Academic, 1995.

———. "'Myth Became Fact': C. S. Lewis's Grand Narrative." Unpublished manuscript from his personal papers, n.d.

———. "'O God, Listen To My Prayer' (Ps. 54:2): God's Ear And Our Petition." In *Face to Face with God: Human Images of God in the Bible*, by Richard D. Patterson and Michael E. Travers, 115–35. Richardson, TX: Biblical Studies Press, 2008.

# Subject Index

alienation, 37–43, 48; *see also* exile
allegory, 44, 63, 65, 93, 153
apologetic(s), 2, 11–28, 56–59, 66–68, 82–87, 171; *see also* pre-evangelism
*architecton*, 8, 56–70; *see also* master builder
Augustine, 2–3, 11–12, 16, 35, 41, 60, 62–63, 70, 80–81

Belbury, 16–17, 23, 155, 157–58, 165, 174, 177–78, 181–83; *see also* NICE

collectivism, 183
community, 22–27, 62, 151–66, 183
conversion, 6, 35, 39, 97, 106, 113, 135, 139, 225
Cupid, 91–93, 95, 106

descent, 22, 34–36, 38, 48, 52, 132, 153, 164
desire, 8, 11–13, 16, 18–22, 29–33, 123, 131–50, 154–55, 158–59, 162, 175, 188, 203–4; *see also* longing

disinterested love, 8, 131–50
doubt, 20, 61–62, 64, 69, 133, 142–44, 197, 237

eschatology, *eschaton*, 14, 21, 24–25, 230–31, 235
eternity, 12–13, 35, 51–52, 104, 132, 149
ethics, 8, 120–28, 168–85; *see also* morality
evangelism, 8, 12–13, 29, 86–87, 109–129
exile, 14–20, 23, 27, 38–43, 48, 51–52; *see also* alienation

fair, fairness, 188, 193–94; *see also* justice
fairy story, fairy stories, fairy tale(s), 30–32, 36, 38, 52–54
faith, 4, 8, 12, 14–15, 18, 23–26, 63–64, 72–88, 98, 116, 128, 134–39, 163, 169–72, 188, 197–201, 205, 232, 237–38
fantasy, 30, 38, 40, 53, 110
Filostrato, 181
Fox, the, 92–103, 105–7

freedom, 49, 110–11, 133–35, 140–41, 146, 153, 157, 184
friendship, 56–57, 109, 152, 158–66, 183, 203

gospel, 2, 37, 67, 95, 99–101, 110–29, 132–33, 137–38, 224–25, 238

Hardcastle, Fairy, 158, 161–62, 175–76
harmony, 14, 22–23, 63, 70
heaven, 2, 6, 9, 11–14, 16, 18–28, 33, 40, 43, 46, 54, 57–58, 67, 85, 105, 131–50, 153, 162, 165, 207, 216, 236–38
Hingest, Bill "the Blizzard", 177
hope, 11–28, 43, 45, 53, 57, 61, 67–69, 96, 101, 135, 139, 171, 177, 198–200, 224–25, 235–38

image of God, 11, 110, 121, 237
imagination, 2, 13, 21, 29–41, 56–58, 65, 70, 142–43, 206
incarnation, 5, 25, 29, 32–38, 41–42, 46, 52–54
individualism, 4, 183
Inner Ring, 8, 152–66, 175, 185
integration of faith and learning (or of faith and life), 8, 72–88, 205, 225–30
Ironwood, 152–56, 159, 161, 163–64

joy, 7, 12, 14–23, 33–35, 38, 43–48, 52, 67, 69, 76, 132–34, 136, 142, 145–49, 165–66, 170, 217, 234, 237–38
justice, 77, 91–93, 137, 187–201; see also fair

lament, 9, 73, 187–201
landscape, 31–54, 144–47
language, 22–23, 33–36, 75, 145–47, 182, 234–35
literature, 1–2, 31, 33, 205–6, 224, 227, 232–35
longing, 11, 13–28, 30, 33, 35, 38–40, 43–48, 51–54, 64, 67, 123, 158–59, 231, 235–38; see also desire

MacPhee, 152, 158, 162–64
magic, 32, 47, 51, 180, 185
marriage, 16–17, 23, 96, 178
master builder, 8, 56–70, 150, 153; see also architecton
materialism, 4, 95–99, 101–3, 107; see also scientism, scientific naturalism
metanarrative, 13–15, 24, 27; see also worldview
Milton, John, 9, 91, 203–221, 224, 226, 232–33, 235–36, 238
morality, 123, 127, 170, 179, 188; see also ethics
myth, 2, 7, 10, 33, 54–55, 91–93, 106–7, 117, 168, 179, 182–84, 236

natural theology, 36–37, 78–80, 87–88, 116, 128
NICE, 16–17, 22, 152, 155, 157–66, 173–75, 177–79, 181, 185; see also Belbury

Oklahoma Baptist University (OBU), 227, 229–30, 237
Orual, 48, 60, 92–98, 101–6

parody, 18, 46, 48–53
Pendragon, 152, 155, 157, 161–62, 165, 167; see also Ransom, Elwin
pilgrimage, 13, 15, 19–22, 27, 41, 236
Pole, Jill, 17, 45, 51, 177
prayer, 9, 64, 187–201, 234–35
pre-evangelism, 29, 111–13, 115, 117, 119, 121, 123–29; see also apologetics
progress, progressive, 17, 50–51, 155, 157, 172–86
Psalm, Psalms (book of), Psalter, 8–9, 35–36, 54, 72–81, 83–85, 87–90, 98, 103, 188–202, 206, 222, 226–27, 230, 233–34, 238
Psyche, 91–93, 96–99, 101–8
Puddleglum, 17–18, 60, 176
Ransom, Elwin, 60, 151–53, 160–67; see also Pendragon
realism, 109–129

reality, 4–8, 21, 24, 33, 37, 43–46, 57, 59, 62, 64, 85–87, 93–99, 106, 109–129, 140, 146, 153, 157, 162, 168–70, 173–74, 176, 179–82, 185, 198, 235
Reepicheep, 20–21, 25, 44, 46, 231
relativism, 115, 119
rest, 12, 14–15, 22, 47, 65, 231
revelation (general and special), 36–43, 67, 72–81, 122, 172
rhetoric, rhetorical, 8, 56–70, 215
romance, 32, 46, 63

sacrifice, 14, 33, 36, 93–97, 99–101, 103–7, 176, 193
science, 4, 86, 110–11, 115, 121, 168–85
scientism, scientific naturalism, 8, 115, 119–20, 169–74, 176–77, 179–80, 182, 185–186Screwtape, 8, 16, 28, 132–39, 141, 143, 145, 147, 149–50
Scrubb, Eustace Clarence, 17, 20, 45, 51, 177
self-righteous, 188–89, 191–96, 199–200
sin, 12, 14, 16–17, 19, 23, 27, 69, 74, 76–79, 84, 93, 104, 123–24, 134, 137, 145, 148, 188, 193, 195, 210, 214, 221, 234, 236
sola scriptura, 80–84, 88–89
Southeastern Baptist Theological Seminary (SEBTS), 11, 88, 109–110, 223, 227–29, 236
St. Anne's, 22–23, 151–66, 184
stewardship, 217–20
Studdock, Jane, 16–17, 22–23, 152, 155–64, 166, 177, 184

Studdock, Mark, 16–17, 22–23, 36, 96, 139, 154–55, 157–60, 163–64, 166, 173–79, 184–85
suffering, 9, 64, 67, 146, 164, 187, 197, 237

terror, 23, 45–48, 52, 93, 141, 144
transposition, 32–38, 51–52, 138, 143, 146

Ungit, 94–96, 98, 100–103
unity, 3, 22–23, 62–65, 73, 86, 88, 93, 112, 115, 128, 156, 165, 236

vocation, 61, 212–20

wisdom, 5, 8, 11–13, 58, 74, 76, 78, 84–88, 91–107, 132–33, 141, 161, 185, 210, 213
Worldview
    Creation, 8, 14–16, 24–25, 27, 36, 38, 49, 72–80, 87–88, 111–12, 116, 123–24, 232, 235
    Fall, 8, 14–16, 19, 21, 23–24, 27, 50, 64, 77, 79, 86, 108, 117, 123–24, 138, 217, 225–26, 231–32, 236, 238
    Re-creation, 8, 15, 21, 27; *see also* eschatology
    Redemption, 8, 13–15, 25–27, 100, 137
Wormwood, 16, 133–36, 139
worship, 14, 26–27, 74, 94–95, 101, 220, 234

# Index of Works by C. S. Lewis

*Abolition of Man, The,* 6, 16, 94, 144, 169, 172, 174, 178–82, 184–85
*Allegory of Love, The,* 65
"Apologist's Evening Prayer, The," 59
"As the Ruin Falls," 59

"Bulverism," 125–26, 129

"Christian Apologetics," 87, 106, 114
*Christian Reflections,* 186, 222
"Christianity and Literature," 113, 205
"Christmas and Cricket," 125
*Chronicles of Narnia, The* 8, 15, 17, 29–31, 39, 122, 226, 230
*Collected Letters,* 20, 111, 116, 123, 125, 152–53, 204

"De Descriptione Temporum" 67, 184
"Discarded Image, The" 58
"Dogma and the Universe," 180

*English Literature in the Sixteenth Century,* 58–59, 206

*Experiment in Criticism, An,* 59, 67–69, 205–6

"Fern-seed and Elephants", 113
*Four Loves, The,* 79, 131–32, 139, 150, 162

*God in the Dock,* 186, 191
"Good Work and Good Works," 87–88
*Great Divorce, The,* 6, 8–9, 18, 24, 28, 46, 52, 116–17, 131–50
*Grief Observed, A,* 202

"Inner Ring, The," 8, 151–67, 175, 185
"Is Progress Possible?", 175, 179, 182–83
"Is Theology Poetry?", 7, 170, 236

"Language of Religion, The", 205
*Last Battle, The,* 15, 18, 25–28, 45–46, 48–53, 122, 235
*Letters to Children,* 28
*Letters to Malcolm,* 9, 67, 188, 200–202

*Lion, the Witch, and the Wardrobe, The,* 26, 31–32, 45, 48, 50, 168, 177, 183

*Magician's Nephew, The,* 15, 25, 40, 45, 49–50
"Meditations on a Toolshed," 7
"Membership," 183
*Mere Christianity,* 13, 16, 18–19, 44, 67, 110, 113, 123, 127, 149, 181, 184, 188
*Miracles,* 33, 66
"Modern Man and His Categories," 114
"Myth Became Fact", 2, 106, 236

"On Stories", 31, 37
"On the Reading of Old Books," 185
"On Three Ways of Writing for Children", 30–32, 47

*Perelandra,* 57, 68, 151, 162, 236
*Personal Heresy, The,* 3
"Petitionary Prayer," 200
*Pilgrim's Regress, The* 19, 115, 118, 123–24, 126, 144
"Poison of Subjectivism, The," 180
*Preface to Paradise Lost, A,* 58, 203–5, 207

*Prince Caspian,* 39–43, 45, 48, 52–53
*Problem of Pain, The,* 16–17, 19, 42, 54, 67

*Reflections on the Psalms,* 9, 35–36, 72, 78, 188–201, 206
"Religion without Dogma?", 194

*Screwtape Letters, The,* 8, 16, 131–50
"Seeing Eye, The," 66
*Silver Chair, The,* 17–18, 45, 51, 176–77
"Sometimes Fairy Stories May Say Best What's to be Said," 30
*Space Trilogy, The,* 22, 33, 68, 152, 154
*Surprised by Joy,* 19, 21, 28, 38, 41, 43–44, 54, 118, 126, 129

*That Hideous Strength,* 8–9, 16, 22–24, 110, 151–67, 168–86, 235
*Till We Have Faces,* 8, 16, 48, 63, 91–107
"Transposition," 32–36, 64, 143, 146

*Voyage of the Dawn Treader, The,* 20, 22, 26, 45–48, 51–54, 177, 230

*Weight of Glory, The,* 16, 18–19, 33–35, 44, 64, 66, 68
*World's Last Night, The,* 235

www.ingramcontent.com/pod-product-compliance
Lightning Source LLC
Chambersburg PA
CBHW050851230426
43667CB00012B/2247